The

People, Place and Ministry: A Theological and Practical Exploration

Edited by

Malcolm Torry

CANTERBURY
PRESS

Norwich

© Malcolm Torry

First published in 2004 by the Canterbury Press Norwich
(a publishing imprint of Hymns Ancient & Modern Limited,
a registered charity)
St Mary's Works, St Mary's Plain,
Norwich, Norfolk, NR3 3BH

www.scm-canterburypress.co.uk

British Library Cataloguing in Publication data

A catalogue record for this book is available
from the British Library

ISBN 1-85311-586-X

Typeset by Regent Typesetting, London
Printed and bound by
Biddles Ltd, www.biddles.co.uk

Contents

Acknowledgements

I would like to thank David Atkinson, now Bishop of Thetford. When he was Archdeacon of Lewisham he established the Woolwich Area Theology Group, and it is from that group that this book has emerged. I would also like to thank Jeffrey Heskins and Christine Bainbridge, who helped to plan this volume; Jeffrey John, for his support and encouragement; Christine Hardman, the current Archdeacon of Lewisham, for help with the glossary; and Christine Smith of SCM-Canterbury Press for her enthusiasm for the project. Above all I must thank the contributors, who have given much time and trouble to writing drafts, hearing criticism of them, and then revising them. And we would all like to thank those many people who have commented on our draft chapters. The final responsibility for what we have written, of course, remains ours.

Malcolm Torry

Dedicated to the parishes of the Church of England: to their territory, their communities, their congregations, their clergy, and their church buildings.

Foreword

There are right and wrong ways of defending the parish system. The fact that the whole territory of England and Wales is divided into units administered by the Anglican Church can be a buttress for an unthinking and unreal triumphalism; and it can divert us from facing the unwelcome question of why the parish unit these days often seems unsuccessful in planting and nurturing faith among those not yet touched by it. Frustration and exasperation about this have led to a pretty widespread assumption that the parochial system is intrinsically the enemy of progress, the brake on any advance towards a creative, flexible, evangelistically effective Church.

But before we run into a new set of prejudices – and thus a new set of unreflective fictions – we need to look harder at what it is that the parish structure makes possible. That is to say, we need to think less about the questions the system wasn't designed to answer and more about what it uniquely and actually does. The essays in this book address this with vigour and subtlety and passion.

If their theme had to be summed up in a few words, it might be that the parish system provides a model of the Church's life as essentially, not just occasionally and accidentally, hospitable. The Church exists so that there may be a place where certain human things can find a home, things that will not be accommodated in other places and in other ways. That isn't all the Church is for, but it could be said that unless it is *at least* this, whatever else it says and does will lack credibility: it will risk appearing as a community that requires you to define, for yourself and others, who you are and what you believe before you can properly encounter the welcome of God. And that sits very badly with the mission of Jesus as we read of it in the Gospels.

So this is a book which helps us to see the parish vision as profoundly evangelical; as and where it is also *evangelistic*, it is because of this deep awareness of God's initiative of welcome. The Church of England is working hard and creatively at 'new expressions' of church life, and that is one of the best things currently happening. But instead of making that an occasion for sidelining the experience of parish ministry and mission, we should be taking the opportunity of thinking with greater clarity about why, if parishes didn't exist, we might have to invent them. And here we have a fine resource for such thinking, distilled from the distinctive experience of South London – a rapidly changing, ethnically varied, economically complex area, with plenty of creativity alongside disturbing levels of deprivation. It deserves close reading – and much gratitude for so searching a contribution to our reflection at this crucial moment in the Church of England's life.

Rowan Williams
Archbishop of Canterbury
2004

Introduction

About five years ago, David Atkinson (now Bishop of Thetford, but then Archdeacon of Lewisham) invited the clergy of the Woolwich Episcopal Area of the Diocese of Southwark to study theology together. Since then, three times a year, clergy have gathered at noon. There have always been two speakers. The first has addressed us, and then answered questions and led discussion on their topic; at 12.50 p.m. we have consumed our packed lunches (tea and coffee courtesy of St Michael's, Blackheath Park, our regular venue); and at 1.10 p.m. or thereabouts the second speaker has spoken, and answered questions and led discussion.

Sometimes the address has gone on longer (James Bogle once took the whole 50 minutes without noticing, and it was sufficiently interesting that no one wanted to stop him). Sometimes we have tried a different method. One Advent everyone present offered three minutes on 'the destiny of the cosmos'.

All of the contributions have come from within the Woolwich Episcopal Area, and everyone who has led a session has at some time held a parochial post.

In April 2003 a planning meeting, looking back on so much good theology, thought it was about time to ask some of the clergy of the area to go into print. The obvious topic was 'the parish'. The last substantial study of the Anglican parish was Giles Ecclestone's *The Parish Church?*,[1] and while there have been books since then on various aspects of the parish, and particularly on its ministry, there has been nothing which explores the nature of the parish itself.

We also had in front of us the newly published *Anglicanism*, edited by Duncan Dormor, Jack McDonald and Jeremy Caddick, three Cambridge college deans.[2] This collection of essays explores some important aspects of modern Anglican thought, but the parish hardly gets a mention. Believing as we do that the Church of England *is* its parishes, we thought we ought to try to remedy the deficit.

We therefore asked a number of parochial clergy in the area to write about those aspects of the life of the parish in which they were particularly interested, about which they had experience, and about which they felt passionately, hoping that by outlining those aspects and by illustrating them from the parishes of South-East London we would encourage our readers to draw their own comparisons and contrasts, and thus encourage yet more new thought and writing on the nature of the parish.

We are conscious that there are a number of ways in which we might be criticized. First, this is an entirely clerical exercise, and a stipendiary clerical exercise too. This is because the Woolwich Area Theology Group was designed to enable the clergy to do theology together and it met during the middle of the day to enable as many stipendiary clergy as possible to attend. We look forward to a group of laity, and also to a group of non-stipendiary clergy, whether in South-East London or elsewhere, taking this publication as a challenge to write out of their own perspectives on the Anglican parish.

Second, every author is writing about particular places which they have known, even though some of the contributions look beyond the contributors' own parishes. All we can say is that there is no such thing as a typical parish, that any essay about 'the parish' will actually be about a particular parish or parishes, and that we hope that what we have written will encourage our readers to do their own thinking about *their* parishes.

Third, every author tackles their subject from within their own experience. This is not an academic treatise. Maybe this publication will encourage a more in-depth and objective study of the Church of England's parishes; but, in the meantime, we offer sketches of particular aspects of particular parishes: for, in the end, that is all there is, even in apparently objective studies: snapshots, from particular angles, of particularities.

Fourth, every subject has its own jargon, and we are conscious that the Church of England, and particularly the clergy, have their own jargon. We have tried to minimize the jargon-level, and just in case we have not managed that sufficiently we have provided a glossary of terms we use.

We are conscious that there are questions that need to be asked about any exercise such as this. For instance: Have we written a book, with a coherent theme, or is what we have written a series of essays? We have attempted to write a book, and one way in which we have tried to do this is by reading each others' first drafts and then meeting for a day to discuss them. We enjoyed that day enormously, and we hope that our readers will receive as much pleasure from reading what emerged as we have experienced from writing and discussing our contributions.

A related question is this: Have we provided an argument *for* the parish? We are all aware how much the world has changed. Fifty years ago most people lived and worked in the same or nearby communities (and this was as true of South-East London as it was of the rural world, for people often lived very locally to the heavy and light industry in which they worked along the south bank of the Thames). Today people will often live in one community (or in one community during the week and another at weekends), they will work in another community, and they will seek their leisure activities in yet another. Is the territorial parish relevant to this new reality?

We shall take up these questions again in the conclusion.

Notes

1 Ecclestone, Giles (ed.), *The Parish Church? Explorations in the Relationship of the Church and the World*, Mowbray, London and Oxford, 1988.

2 Dormor, Duncan, Jack McDonald and Jeremy Caddick (eds.), *Anglicanism: The Answer to Modernity*, Continuum, London and New York, 2003.

The Contributors

James Bogle was ordained in 1961 as a member of the Bermondsey Group Ministry. After four years there he moved to York as Church of England Chaplain in the new university. He moved to be Vicar and Team Rector of Brayton, near Selby, North Yorkshire, before returning to the Diocese of Southwark as Vicar of St Augustine, Forest Hill in 1976. He has ministered in South-East London since that time. He has written *South Bank Religion* (Hatcham Press, 2002).

Nicholas Cranfield is Vicar of All Saints, Blackheath and a member of the Diocesan Advisory Committee. Before coming to South London he was a curate at Ascot Heath in Oxford Diocese, Principal of the Berkshire Christian Training Scheme, and Chaplain and Fellow of Selwyn College Cambridge. Since 1995 he has written on art for the *Church Times*, and he is a reviewer for the quarterly journal *ACE*. He is currently writing a book on European perspectives in Christian art and an illustrated gazette of Christian art in the Woolwich Area 1901–2000.

Bruce Saunders is Canon Pastor at Southwark Cathedral, which includes pastoral responsibility for St Hugh's, Bermondsey (Charterhouse-in-Southwark). He has been a curate in Bristol Diocese, an assistant chaplain at Bristol University, Team Vicar at Holy Trinity, Fareham, Team Rector of the Mortlake with East Sheen Team Ministry, and Canon Missioner for Church in Society at Southwark Cathedral.

Michael Marshall is Vicar of St John's, Blackheath Park. He was curate at St Mark's, Kennington and Vicar of St Alban's, Streatham Park before coming to Blackheath.

Barry Thorley is Team Rector of Thamesmead. He was curate at St Mary's, Moseley, in the Diocese of Birmingham, Vicar of Birchfield, and Vicar of St Matthew's, Brixton before coming to South-East London.

Alyson Peberdy is Vicar of St Saviour's, Brockley Hill, and, concurrently, has also been Priest-in-charge of St George's, Perry Hill, and of St Augustine's, Honor Oak. Before this she was curate in the New Windsor Team Ministry in the Diocese of Oxford. She is presently chair of the Christendom Trust, which aims to develop Christian social thought and its application. Immediately before ordination she worked for the Open University. She was Vice-moderator of the Movement for the Ordination of Women. Her most recent publication is *Promoting Health: Knowledge and Practice* (with J. Katz) (Open University Press, 1997). She was a contributor to *Voices of this Calling* (ed. C. Rees) (Canterbury Press, 2002).

Richard Bainbridge is Vicar of The Good Shepherd with St Peter's, Lee. Before that he was Curate of St James's, Bermondsey. Before ordination he worked for the Diocese of Southwark's Lay Training Team.

Dianna Gwilliams is Vicar of St Barnabas's, Dulwich. Her first degree was in physics and chemistry, and she worked for many years as a sound engineer. Following ordination she served her curacy at Copleston Centre Church in Peckham, in South-East London, before becoming curate at St Barnabas's, Dulwich, and subsequently Vicar in the same parish.

Michael Harrison is Vicar of Holy Trinity, Eltham. Before that he was curate at St Anne and All Saints, South Lambeth, and then chaplain at Bradford University.

John Paxton has been in the parochial ministry for thirty years. He was Rector of Christ Church, Southwark, and Senior Chaplain of the South London Industrial Mission when he wrote his chapter for this book. Before that he was an industrial chaplain and parish priest in Manchester, Winchester and Southwark Dioceses, as well as a priest in the Middle East. He has recently moved to be Social Responsibility Officer in the Diocese of Worcester.

Grahame Shaw is Vicar of St Paul's, Newington, in Walworth. Before that he was a curate at St Andrew's, Grange, in the Diocese of Chester, then Team Vicar at East Runcorn with Halton, and then a Team Vicar in the Thamesmead Team Ministry.

Christine Bainbridge is Priest-in-Charge of St John's, Deptford. Before that she was curate at St Matthew's, Newington, at the Elephant and Castle in South London, and then Priest in charge of St Peter's, Lee. Before ordination she worked for the Diocese of Southwark's Lay Training Team.

Jeffrey Heskins is Rector of St Luke's and St Thomas's, Charlton. Before that he was curate of St Mary's, Primrose Hill, curate of St Mary's, Enfield Chase and Enfield Deanery Youth Officer, and Team Vicar in the Kidbrooke Team Ministry. He is the author of *Unheard Voices* (Darton, Longman & Todd, 2001).

Malcolm Torry is Team Rector in the East Greenwich Team Ministry. Before ordination he worked for the Department of Health and Social Security. Following ordination he was curate at St Matthew's, Newington, at the Elephant and Castle, then curate at Christ Church, Southwark, and industrial chaplain with the South London Industrial Mission, and then Vicar of St Catherine's, Hatcham, at New Cross.

Colin Buchanan is Bishop of Woolwich. Before that he was curate at Cheadle in Chester Diocese, on the staff and eventually Principal at St John's College, Nottingham, Suffragan Bishop of Aston in the Diocese of Birmingham, and Vicar of St Mark's, Gillingham.

1. An Interim Measure:

The Parish in Its Context

MALCOLM TORRY

> Greet Prisca and Aquila, who work with me in Christ Jesus, and who risked their necks for my life, to whom not only I give thanks, but also all the churches of the Gentiles. Greet also the church in their house. (Rom. 16.3, 4)

Churches are particular churches, and this book is about many different parishes and about their incorrigible diversity; but having said that, I want in this first chapter to raise an issue that relates to *every* parish: the ambiguity of the term 'parish'. Among the definitions of 'parish' in *Chambers' Twentieth Century Dictionary* are 'a district having its own church and minister or priest of the Established Church', 'the people of a parish', and 'a congregation'. Thus I have in my filing cabinet a map showing recent changes to the boundaries of the parish of East Greenwich, a list of streets in the parish, a list of people on the parish's Electoral Roll (the nearest thing the Church of England has got to a list of its active members), and a paper on the Diocese's (excellent) 'Fairer Shares' scheme which explains how each parish is expected to contribute to Diocesan funds in relation to its 'congregational count'.

Ambiguity is, of course, a common feature of all religious language. The 'fulfilling' of the law that Jesus promises in Matthew 5.17–20 could be either a fulfilment that regards the law as having a continuing validity (as the sayings in Matthew 5 suggest) or a fulfilment that leaves the law behind (as much of the rest of the Gospel suggests); Rudolf Bultmann's 'Jesus' can mean either the Jesus of history or an event which happens today; and 'myth' in the book-title *The Myth of God Incarnate*[1] can mean either the expression of the other-worldly in terms of the this-worldly or a commonly held belief which is untrue.[2]

Ambiguity is particularly common in language about religious institutions, and the ambiguity of 'church' begins in the New Testament. In Colossians 1.24, the whole universal Church is meant. In Romans 16.5 it is a particular gathering of people in a particular house. Today, 'church' can mean the mystical body of all believers throughout Christian history and beyond; it can mean a congregation, or its building, or both; and it can mean a particular denomination.[3] And when we study particular denominations or congregations, we find even such basic concepts as 'member' ambiguous. A recent seminar at the University of Surrey was set the task of studying documents relating to the Church of England as an institution: the Canons (the Church's fundamental rules), the Church Representation Rules (which govern how Parochial Church Councils and various other representative structures are chosen and run), and the Electoral Roll form. It was asked to come up with criteria for membership of the Church of England. A number of possible definitions emerged, and they were found to be incompatible. Is someone who is baptized but is an atheist and never attends a member? Is a believer brought up in the Salvation Army and never baptized but who attends every week a member? Is a Roman Catholic who attends and who receives Holy Communion but doesn't want to undergo a welcome by the bishop a member?

Similar ambiguities are found with the words 'laity' ('people') and 'congregation'. Does the definition of 'laity' include the clergy? Do the clergy belong to the congregation? Is the congregation those who are present or those who come at least once a month (which is the definition implied by the term 'congregational count' in the Church of England)?

Most importantly for our purpose, is the parish (understood either as territory or as congregation and building) the fundamental unit of the Church of England (implying that the diocese is an umbrella organization serving a federation of parishes); or is the diocese the fundamental unit (implying that the parish is a local branch subject to a head office)? In my experience, attitudes in the parish suggest the former; and greater reliance on congregational giving is slowly bringing the diocese's officers to the same view.

Whilst in this study we leave most of these ambiguities as ambiguous as we find them, we presuppose that the Church of England is fundamentally its parishes – for without the parishes there would be no Church of England, and without the parishes there would be no world-wide Anglicanism (and the same goes for every other denomination). Yes, the Church of England is defined by its Christian faith 'uniquely revealed in the Holy Scriptures and set forth in the catholic creeds, which faith the Church is called upon to proclaim afresh in each generation',[4] and it is defined by its view that 'from the apostles' time there have been these orders in Christ's Church: bishops, priests, and deacons';[5] but without its parishes there would be no Church of England.

Other institutions are, of course, useful and important. General

Synod performs an important legislative function, and Church House, Westminster fulfils a useful co-ordinating and administrative role. But these remain subsidiary functions. It might therefore be better for literature produced by Church House Publishing to describe itself as *'for* the Church of England' rather than as *'from* the Church of England'. The telephone at Church House is answered with an enthusiastic 'The Church of England'. The enthusiasm is welcome: the statement that Church House *is* the Church of England is not.

What we do is as real as what we are,[6] so we can legitimately say that a parish *is* its activity – and so it is the diverse activity that the contributors to this volume describe which defines the parish and thus the church. So in relation to the parish of East Greenwich, and in particular to St George's, Westcombe Park (the congregation, the building, and the district where my licence says I am the vicar), the parish is its Sunday morning Eucharist, its study groups, its Children's Church, its young people's group, its sharing of its building with various groups, its social events, its Christian Aid collecting, and its community drama.

And the same goes for every Church of England parish. When I was a rural dean and conducted inspections on behalf of the archdeacon, it was the *diversity* that constantly amazed: diversity of activity, of style, of congregation, of language, of building . . . It is this which gives the Church of England its strength and its ability to evolve successfully as the world changes. No top-down organization could ever have achieved such a diverse Anglicanism, and no top-down approach will do it now. It is therefore a pleasure to be able to include in this volume an account of our bishop's survey of the mission activity of the parishes in his Episcopal Area. He came to us to discover what we were doing, and he found diverse and creative activity, generated by each congregation in its own context.

It is not only diversity to which this situation gives birth. It also generates innovation. What are called 'Anglican mission societies' were started by groups of individuals, as was industrial mission, and as were the various passion plays that occurred throughout South London during the year 2000. It is out of local initiative, not out of central decision-making, that new responses to new situations emerge. It is always, of course, helpful if central structures are supportive, are constructively critical, and provide channels of communication from one initiative to another: but it is not from the umbrella organization that the ideas come. Thus admission of children to communion (and now the giving of consecrated bread to infants), the marriage of divorcees in church, lay training, women's ministry, church-planting, the Alpha Course, and the blessing of same-sex relationships – these all started as local initiatives and either have been accepted as national policy or are under consideration. There is always, of course, a tendency for the umbrella organization to take control, as when at General Synod recently the House of Bishops tried to stop children receiving communion, and when they tried to give themselves the power to sack locally-elected churchwardens. In the first case, General Synod (largely through its Southwark representatives) came to our aid; in the second, sadly, it had to be the Parliamentary Ecclesiastical Committee. But on the whole, and eventually, what emerges in the parishes is what happens.

And this is as it should be, for the parishes are the heart of the Church of England: the parishes which are their territory, their buildings, their people, and their congregations. And it is here that the ambiguity of the term 'parish' is so important. If ever the congregation, its building, its patch of ground, and the people living and working on that patch, are taken apart, then that will be the death of the Church of England, for it is the territorial parish that locates and shapes the congregation's mission, it is the building that the parish's people identify as the congregation's home and as theirs, and it is the congregation that conducts the Church's mission on behalf of the parish as a whole.

The deans who wrote the book *Anglicanism*[7] regarded Anglicanism as 'the answer to modernity'. There is some justice to their claim. But, even more importantly, the Anglicanism that is the parishes is an answer to secularization.

There are many definitions of secularization, and many suggestions as to its causes, but my research in the history of the South London Industrial Mission suggests that a central part of any definition must be the distancing of ecclesiastical institutions and their representative persons from other social realities. If this is correct, then the parish, understood as a patch of ground, as the people who live and work on it, and as the congregation and its building, has been and still is a bulwark against secularization in ways that other styles of religious organization cannot be. The Roman Catholic Church, while retaining a territorial system, in practice regards its parish as those Roman Catholics living within a particular territory, rather than as *everyone* living within it. The Church of England often regards even those who actively dissociate themselves from the Church of England by belonging to some other Christian denomination or some other religion as somehow still belonging to the Church of England, and is sometimes regarded by those members of other religious organizations as somehow their parish church.

After the Second World War industrial mission in Sheffield and elsewhere was conducted by teams of full-time chaplains (because large steel-works took little notice of parish boundaries), but industrial mission in South London was, and still is, mainly the parochial clergy visiting local industry. When I visit the food refinery on the

Greenwich Peninsula, I am regarded as a representative of an ecumenical industrial mission (which I am), and also as the local incumbent – and it is the latter which seems to be more easily comprehended and seems to create the most bridges across the widening gulf of secularization. The same goes for the more recent multi-faith relationship with the company appointed to develop the peninsula: I am both a representative of the faith communities in Greenwich and the local Anglican vicar. It will be interesting to watch the different effects generated by each of those roles and by the combination of the two.

This bridge-building character of the Church of England parish should never be regarded as a mark of privilege: it is merely an accident of history, and it has little to do with the shape of the Church in its first century. But whatever its origin, the parish is an opportunity, a responsibility, and a possible snare. It is a snare because it can distance us from the catacombs, the martyrdoms, and the proper marginalization of the Church of the crucified Jesus; but in a world rapidly secularizing, the bridge-building function of the parish remains a serious responsibility, for the parish is one of the few means of building bridges between the gospel committed to us and a society whose members and institutions now have only tenuous connections with that gospel. These connections are even more tenuous because they are post-Christian and not pre-Christian, and it is this new and serious situation which the parish helps to address by locating a congregation of Christians in a locality and defining their area of responsibility. The parish boundaries positively speak to a congregation of a clear responsibility to carry out God's mission within that locality. The parish boundaries also limit that responsibility and thus make it bearable.

But it is not merely as an instrument of mission and evangelism that the parish should be valued. It should be valued as a *theological* reality. The theological order is God – created order – Church – ministry: God has created a world, has redeemed it, and by the Spirit has given birth to the Church to be a servant of the gospel of the Kingdom of God. To that Church God has given gifts of ministry. So the order is: territory – community – congregation – minister. The Church of England's parish system reflects this theological reality. This is not to say that other patterns are not helpful in other situations. It is important for universities to be treated as universities, hospitals as hospitals, and industrial premises as industrial premises, and so chaplaincies attached to such institutions, where the theological order is God – created order – servant church, are an important extension of the parochial system. But they are an extension of it, and to a large extent rely upon it, and they, as much as the parishes, need the parish's theological order to remain intact.

Unfortunately, some recent developments have not helped. Team ministries start with the clergy, organize congregations around the clergy, and often abolish parish boundaries, thus not only relegating the territory to a subordinate position but in effect marginalizing it completely. The order has become ministry – congregation – community – territory. While some team ministry schemes retain parish boundaries or operate appropriately within a single natural community, and while many clergy in team ministries would subscribe to the theological sequence territory – community – congregation – minister, the very name 'team ministry' of a parish or parishes rather suggests the opposite.

Some recent developments have been helpful, and particularly the ordained local ministry. For some time to come we shall have a deployable ministry, both paid and unpaid, and we should try to keep it as long as we can, for it helps to keep parishes alive to ideas and styles from elsewhere. The ordained local ministry, for which candidates are selected and trained locally in order to serve locally, reflects well the theological order of territory – community – congregation – minister, and will contribute to the bridges between gospel, Church and society which we shall need to build if we are to continue to tackle a growing secularization.

In the midst of diversity we have found two related constants: the ambiguity of the term 'parish', and the vital connection between territory, people, congregation and building. Underlying it all is the constant of the action which is the Eucharist: the taking of bread and wine, the giving thanks, the breaking of the bread, and the sharing. The style could not be more different from place to place, but in every parish this action is done for and by the parish. Both the theological primacy of the grace of God and the logic of this introduction suggest that there should be *no* barriers to participation, and in practice in many parishes there are no barriers (another aspect in which parochial innovation might one day lead to national change). In principle this set of actions, which expresses and constitutes the heart of the Christian faith, is done by and for the parish, and we might say constitutes the parish. For without this action, done in each place by the people of each place, there is no parish, just as without the parish there is no Church of England.

> The Lord Jesus, on the night when he was betrayed took a loaf of bread, and when he had given thanks, he broke it and said, 'This is my body that is for you. Do this in remembrance of me.' In the same way he took the cup also, after supper, saying, 'This cup is the new covenant in my blood. Do this, as often as you drink it, in remembrance of me.' For as often as you eat this bread and drink this cup, you proclaim the Lord's death until he comes. (1 Cor. 11.23–26)

Yes, this is an interim measure. It is in awaiting a final consummation of the Kingdom of God that we take bread and wine, give thanks, break the bread, and share the bread and the cup. And the parish too is an interim measure. There is nothing ultimate about it. But it is a particular gift which the Church of England offers to the world, and I would even go so far as to say that, given its theological meaning, it is a sacramental gift. It is this gift that this book is about.

Further reading

Congregations

Ammerman, Nancy Tatom, et al., *Congregation and Community*, Rutgers University Press, New Brunswick, New Jersey, 1997.

Becker, Penny Edgell, *Congregations in Conflict: Cultural Models of Local Religious Life*, Cambridge University Press, Cambridge, 1999.

Harris, Margaret, *Organizing God's Work: Challenges for Churches and Synagogues*, Macmillan, London, 1999.

Heskins, Jeffrey, *Unheard Voices*, Darton, Longman & Todd, London, 2001.

Hopewell, James F., *Congregation: Stories and Structures*, SCM Press, London, 1987.

Wind, James P. and James W. Lewis (eds.), *American Congregations*, University of Chicago Press, Chicago and London, 1994.

Secularization

Brown, Callum G., *The Death of Christian Britain*, Routledge, London, 2001.

Bruce, Stephen (ed.), *Religion and Modernization: Sociologists and Historians Debate the Secularization Thesis*, Clarendon Press, Oxford, 1992.

Bruce, Stephen, *Religion in Modern Britain*, Oxford University Press, Oxford, 1995.

Chadwick, Owen, *The Secularisation of the European Mind in the Nineteenth Century*, Cambridge University Press, Cambridge, 1975.

Davie, Grace, *Religion in Britain since 1945: Believing without Belonging*, Blackwell, Oxford, 1994.

Davie, Grace, *Europe: The Exceptional Case: Parameters of Faith in the Modern World*, Darton, Longman & Todd, London, 2002.

MacIntyre, Alasdair, *Secularization and Moral Change*, Oxford University Press, Oxford, 1967.

McLeod, Hugh, *Class and Religion in the Late Victorian City*, Croom Helm, London, 1974.

McLeod, Hugh, *Religion and the People of Western Europe, 1789–1970*, Oxford University Press, Oxford, 1981.

Martin, David, *The Religious and the Secular*, Routledge & Kegan Paul, London, 1969.

Martin, David, *A General Theory of Secularization*, Blackwell, Oxford, 1978.

Norman, Edward, *Secularisation*, Continuum, London, 2002.

Torry, Malcolm, 'The Practice and Theology of the South London Industrial Mission', unpublished PhD thesis, University of London, 1990.

Wilson, Bryan, *Religion in Secular Society*, C. A. Watts, London, 1966.

Yeo, Stephen, *Religion and Voluntary Organisations in Crisis*, Croom Helm, London, 1976.

The Clergy

Ramsey, Michael, *The Christian Priest Today*, SPCK, London, 1972.

Russell, Anthony, *The Clerical Profession*, SPCK, London, 1980.

Towler, Robert and A. P. M. Coxon, *The Fate of the Anglican Clergy*, Macmillan, London and Basingstoke, 1979.

Warren, Yvonne, *The Cracked Pot: The State of Today's Anglican Parish Clergy*, Kevin Mayhew, Stowmarket, 2002.

Notes

1 Hick, John (ed.), *The Myth of God Incarnate*, SCM Press, London, 1977.

2 Torry, Malcolm, 'Two Kinds of Ambiguity', *King's Theological Review*, Vol. 3, No. 1 (Spring 1980), pp. 24–8.

3 Dulles, Avery, *Models of the Church*, 2nd edn, Gill & Macmillan, Dublin, 1988.

4 Canons of the Church of England, Canon C15.

5 Canon C1.

6 Torry, Malcolm, 'On Completing the Apologetic Spectrum', *Theology*, Vol. CIII, No. 812 (March/April 2000), pp. 108–15; Torry, Malcolm, 'Action, Patterns and Religious Pluralism', *Theology*, Vol. CVI, No. 830 (March/April 2003), pp. 107–18.

7 Dormor, Duncan, Jack Donald and Jeremy Caddick (eds.), *Anglicanism: The Answer to Modernity*, Continuum, London and New York, 2003.

2. What We Do in Church

Liturgy in the Parish

DIANNA GWILLIAMS

For most people, whether they attend church regularly, irregularly or never, 'church' means what happens in a building. It is in buildings or places that people meet to do things, whether it is worship or fellowship and friendship. Theologically we believe that the church is the people, but even within this understanding there is a well-developed sense of place and space. The primary purpose of our church buildings is to provide space for the worship of God. The worship of God is never an afterthought when new buildings are designed nor when old buildings are re-ordered. So the worship offered to God in the church buildings of each parish is what comes to both define and shape the people who worship, with whatever frequency and degree of commitment.

Worship is that which enables humanity to come close to that inner celebration that is at the heart of the Godhead. In worship the character of God and the nature of God's relationship with creation are revealed and it thus provides both a framework and a foundation for all human relationships. Worship is primarily something that God initiates. It is a mistake to think of worship exclusively as something addressed by human beings to God: it is, as J. G. Davies observes, first and foremost God's approach to us, and this approach then elicits our response.[1]

So, too, with mission. Worship and mission are not two distinct activities, the one theocentric and the other anthropocentric. Both are aspects of a single divine activity in which, through Christ, we are included. What Christians do in their response to God, Christ has already done in his earthly ministry, and so the true worship of God has been disclosed in Christ's action. This enables us, the Church, to understand our worship in the context of our total life in the world.

Worship is both inward and outward. The outward aspect of worship is perceived when the elements within worship direct hearts, minds and actions towards others and to the society within which Christians live and within which the action of Christ is discerned. The inward aspect of worship is what enables and encourages emotional and intellectual growth in faith for individuals.

Individuals live together in communities and in order for a community to experience and express corporate worship there must be corporate identity. People need to know who they are and how they are related to others, to their environment, and ultimately, to their creator. These corporate and collective identities are life-giving and affirming when they celebrate the diversity of the human community at the same time as declaring the equal place of all people as God's children and as sisters and brothers in Christ. It is within worship that these identities are discerned.

> Worship is the practising of our history by a people who remember, and this master story (of which we declare some parts each week [during worship]) gives us, over time, a frame of reference in which to understand ourselves and to know more profoundly the splendour of God's presence in our worship and lives.[2]

The vehicle for this worship of God's people is liturgy.

Liturgy is 'the work of the people' in worship. It is what is done and said in church. Although this happens mainly on Sunday, it also takes place at other times in the form of daily prayer and the occasional offices, especially funerals and weddings. For the Eucharist and for Services of the Word each place develops regular and well-understood liturgy to provide a corporate and collective framework for the expression of the people in worship. This framework provides for awe and wonder, declaration and question, movement, story and fellowship. Within our liturgies space is created to enable praise and thanksgiving, petition and supplication, memorial and recollection. The liturgy we use is communal and shared, shaped and determined by both people and cultures.

For most people everything that is included in the liturgical drama from entry to church to leaving it is experienced as 'church', and there is a marked degree of repetitiveness. For example, many regular attenders sit in the same places each week, even in churches where the seating moves around. People become used to what is expected of them and what is 'normal' or 'usual' in their church or churches.

All churches use liturgy. Some liturgy is written down and available to all who can read, some is only known by habitués. The norm varies from church to church, or congregation to congregation, but there is always a norm. Just as 'Good Morning!' in some settings elicits a response, and in others is heard as a statement, so in some churches 'Let us pray' really means 'Please kneel'. In some churches the music modulating up a semi-tone means 'let's have a time of open praise or singing in tongues'. Upon hearing the priest say 'In the name of the Father, and the Son, and the Holy Spirit', many Christians will sign themselves with the cross. All these, and more besides, are liturgical instructions and responses. Very few are taught, most are caught or imitated.

Part of what our liturgies teach us is how God can be known. Through the elements of movement, recollection, re-enactment, narrative and discourse we learn both about the character of God and the nature of relationship within the Godhead. In all we do in our worship, whether it is active or passive, we are responding to concepts of God, and regardless of anything we may *say* we believe about God, it is largely in our non-verbal communication that we truly *tell* how we experience God. Through authentic liturgy we learn that the worship of God is a continuum and that our present worship is but the latest in a series which links the past with the future.

In a Service of the Word, we recall the story which has shaped and is shaping the people of God. We are enabled to place ourselves within the historical context of a people on a pilgrimage as well as to discern ourselves as part of that 'peculiar people' called to be salt and light in our contemporary setting. We bring praise and supplication to God, we receive forgiveness and we intercede on behalf of others. We remember the story of our faith and Lord together as we hear the gospel proclaimed.

In the Eucharist we hear again and again the story of Jesus giving himself for us. We hear about his one oblation of himself, once offered, we hear that as tenderly as a mother gathers her children God embraced a people as his own. We hear, and learn, that we are all baptized into one body and we hear the priest pray on our behalf that all who share in the communion of the bread and wine may be gathered into God's kingdom.

Liturgies are multi-dimensional. They are dependent on both the past and the present while at the same time pointing towards the future. The worship they facilitate and provoke is directed towards the Almighty and, both consciously and subconsciously, forges connections between people. These connections all contribute to the shaping and moulding of the individual's response to, and concepts of, God. Liturgy communicates something about the character of God that is dependent upon and at the same time distinct from the words used. When there is consonance between the words and what is communicated, authentic notions of God, church, community and the individual can be apprehended. Where there is dissonance the integrity of both the conscious and subconscious messages are called into question.

So then, what makes worship authentic? What do our liturgies communicate about the God who initiates worship in human beings? How are people changed and shaped by the way they worship so as best to serve God's mission in their parish?

Some answers, and inevitably more questions, emerge if we look at the liturgies in two different churches. Although of different traditions both use *Common Worship, Order One* (contemporary language). They share a parish boundary and are in the same deanery, both in the London Borough of Southwark, and in the same parliamentary constituency. In both churches the main Sunday service is one of Holy Communion.

Similarities between the Copleston Centre Church in Peckham and the neighbouring parish, St Barnabas, Dulwich, are that they are both known for their engagement with their local community, that both churches have a high number of young people who remain throughout the 14–19 transition, and that both have schools in the parish and provision for children and young people outside school hours. In other ways they are very different, because they serve very different communities. Although both churches use *Common Worship, Order One*, the ways they use the liturgy provide different lenses through which to view their engagement with their community and through which to glimpse God.

At the northern end of Dulwich Deanery is the parish of St Saviour, Peckham, which is known as the Copleston Centre Church. According to the last census the parish is among the ten most socially deprived in the diocese. The church at the heart of the parish is an Anglican/United Reformed Church Local Ecumenical Partnership (LEP) which was formed in 1978. This amalgamation happened following ten years of the people from Hanover United Reformed Church (URC) and from St Saviour's working and studying together. In order to have the right space for all they wanted to do their assets were pooled, some buildings were sold, and the present church centre was created in the shell of the Victorian Anglican church building.[3]

The parish which is their neighbour to the south also has a building that is purpose built in order to meet various needs of the church and community, although this wasn't built entirely through choice. On 6 December 1992, a year short of its centenary, the landmark Victorian red-brick church was destroyed by arson. Over four years the people of St Barnabas met for worship in the Parish Hall. Part of what sustained the people through this 'pilgrimage' was a particular tradition of worship and liturgy.[4]

St Barnabas is the only parish in the deanery not to be designated an Urban Priority Area. The parish itself is almost completely contained within the 400-year-old Edward Alleyn Estate, and as well as St Barnabas the parish has a second place of worship, Christ's Chapel, consecrated in 1616. At Christ's Chapel we use the Book of Common Prayer for the regular Sunday services (Holy Communion, Morning Prayer and Evensong) and the schools of the Foundation also have regular worship there. But because the majority of worshipping members of St Barnabas attend the 10 a.m. Parish Communion in the parish church, it is this liturgy which I shall examine.

Both church congregations reflect the ethnic mix of their parish, and in both churches about half of the members on the electoral roll live outside the parish. At Copleston youth work has had a high profile for decades, historically via the URC congregation's Boys' Brigade Company, then latterly via local authority provision, as well as through church youth clubs. The presence of a community nursery at the church centre and three primary schools within easy walking distance makes it an area full of children.

At St Barnabas, certainly since the 1980s, youth work has also had a high profile, and young people are involved in many aspects of the church's life together. Education is a priority for the people in the parish and within ten miles of the parish church 10,000 children and young people are in school each day. In the parish itself there are eight schools, one of which is a Church of England Infants' School and six others are part of the Foundation of Edward Alleyn's. Since 1957 the Vicar of St Barnabas has also been the Foundation Chaplain.

Groups for children which meet during Sunday worship are different only in the number of children involved, and in both churches adults and children worship together on the first Sunday of the month. Both churches admit children to communion before confirmation, following a time of preparation, and almost all go on to be confirmed, usually at about age 15. Other similarities include social outreach in different ways. At Copleston this has taken the form of an Advice Centre, groups for refugees and asylum seekers, groups for people with mental health difficulties, and adult education. People from St Barnabas were instrumental in founding the Dulwich Helpline, the Dulwich Volunteer Bureau and the 'Advent Appeal', now the domain of 12 churches in the area which provides year-round support for 14 projects involved in support for homeless people.

At both churches entry is easy and informal. At Copleston the worship area is reached through the sports hall, created from the nave of the old church. A team of welcomers greets people and see that they have the necessary service books, a Bible, hymn book and pew sheet. At St Barnabas people enter to find themselves in a busy narthex with much activity. A team of welcomers and stewards hand out books and direct children to their own groups, which begin as the worship begins. People receive a service book, with musical setting, a hymn book and a pew sheet which has the readings printed out. If children are present for the whole service they have their own copies of the service books. The preaching style is intellectually robust and didactic. Preachers know to expect response at the church door. A regular feature is 'focus' Sundays when the readings, intercessions and sermon (or sometimes discussion group) will concentrate on an area of social justice.

Due to the intimate size of the congregation and the informal structure of the worship at Copleston, visitors are easily recognized and welcomed. People don't rely greatly on printed material and so instructions are given verbally in a conversational style, which is also a mark of the preaching style. At the distribution of communion the whole congregation gathers in a circle in the sanctuary around the altar table. They remain there until the blessing and dismissal. Being in the round is a powerful symbol of the inclusive nature of the gospel, and of the shared nature of the mission of God through the Church.

At St Barnabas, people are also in the round, but this is because of the design of the building. There are no pillars, and the altar table is in the middle of the circle. This is a striking sight, particularly for those who are used to a cruciform design, with a hidden choir and organ. At St Barnabas the robed choir of adults and children complete the circle with the organ behind, but completely visible.

The structure of leadership at Copleston is flatter than at St Barnabas. When the project was conceived there were to be both an Anglican vicar and a URC minister, but since the retirement of the full-time URC minister in the late 1980s the vicar has provided the only ordained leadership. There is a well-developed eldership, in line with URC practice, two lay preachers and currently a part-time Anglican curate. Decisions are made by the Elders and by all members at Church Meeting. Worship is planned by the clergy and lay preachers. Interestingly, the rite used alternates weekly between the URC and the Anglican rite, but according to the constitution all festivals use the Anglican rite. Clergy don't robe for URC Sundays but wear alb and stole for Anglican ones.

At St Barnabas, the staff team of vicar, assistant clergy, Readers, Southwark Pastoral Auxiliaries, Youth Minister and Director of Music meet termly to look forward, including broad planning of the worship. The parish was one of the parishes testing Common Worship and much discussion has taken place at PCC meetings. The vicar and PCC agreed upon which eucharistic prayers to use and on what shape of rite would form the core service booklet. Choices about eucharistic prayer are taken by the president with reference to readings and theme.

At Copleston an Elder begins the service, at St Barnabas it is the President. At Copleston there is no procession, and if it is a Sunday for the URC rite, there are no robes. If mistakes or omissions occur, they are easily rectified with little embarrassment on the part of the clergy or congregation. The worship appears informal and spontaneous. There is an opportunity for anyone to give a notice during the service, and the sermon will sometimes be punctuated by responses from the congregation.

At St Barnabas, partly due to the size of congregation and to the fact that everyone is visible to everyone else, it is difficult for the clergy either to make or to fix mistakes without causing unease to the congregation. The worship begins with a processional hymn and the procession is led by the crucifer, with choir and clergy following. Lay people read the lessons, which are printed on the pew sheet. Intercessions are also led by lay people. As well as clergy and readers, lay people in training for authorized ministry also preach. Much of the liturgy is sung by choir and congregation together.

As worship begins there are also differences. At Copleston there is a feeling of relaxed informality. The preaching style is conversational and familiar, and is based on the gospel for the day. There is often a specific few minutes for young children before they go to their groups. Intercessions are idiosyncratic and personal. Due to the small scale of the congregation and the character of the clergy, people feel at home very quickly. Each Elder has responsibility for a 'pastoral list' of people they bear especially in mind. This mirrors the shared nature of the work that happens in other areas of the life of the community.

When we worship at St Barnabas there is a formal structure, but this doesn't lead to formalism as there is also a marked degree of spontaneity and responsiveness. The worship is professionally led, particularly the music. The sermons are well-prepared and intellectually robust and there is a high degree of engagement with the congregation. The service books contain instructions and explanations about the rite and tradition, and the worship itself proceeds almost unannounced. The return of the children for the breaking of the bread is viewed by some as disruptive, but by others as a wonderful representation of all God's people.

At both churches music is shaped by the worshippers. Music at Copleston is led by a roster of pianists and consists of traditional hymns both Anglican and URC and worship songs. The music is both accessible and easily led by those without professional qualifications. At St Barnabas the full-time Director of Music is able to rely on a dedicated choir and orchestral players as well as an organ scholar and conductor. The music is professionally planned and led and we use a sung setting written by a one-time honorary curate. The high standard of musical understanding and literacy within the congregation is both nurtured and shaped by the music we use as we worship. It is, for us, accessible.

The liturgical drama which constitutes going to church communicates that God is accessible and that there are a good many people who would say that they know God and that they respond to the call of God on their lives. They would also believe that when they come to church they meet with God in the worship and also in the fellowship with others. A warm welcome, and ease of use of the material required for worship, says much about the God who goes out. Those who come regularly take responsibility for the comfort, welcome and instruction of visitors and new members. Being together in a circle where all can be seen speaks of the incarnation and of the importance of the human condition, and is a reminder of our common inheritance as children of God, equally valued and equally valuable to God.

At the end of worship both congregations have a time for coffee and meeting up, and at both churches about half the number of people remain behind for coffee.

Looking in from outside these two churches look very different. What works well in St Barnabas would not work at all at Copleston, and what works well at Copleston would not work at St Barnabas, yet each is offering to God worship that is pleasing and acceptable, and each is nourishing its members for their part in God's mission in their own parish, household and work-place.

The worship in both our churches is authentic, not because it slavishly follows a text or pattern, but because it derives from the life of the community in which it is placed. At Copleston the informal nature of people gathering, the coming together of people from imme-diately apparent different backgrounds, the shared leadership and the physically small space in which the worship happens resonate with the rest of their lives. The gathering together in a circle for the breaking and sharing of the bread and wine of the Eucharist enables everyone to see each other. The nature of God, uniquely revealed in Jesus, is reflected in the faces and lives of real people whose lives have been changed by being members of this community. God is under-stood to be both transcendent and immanent, and Jesus is perceived as a co-worker, a brother and a friend. The birth and early years of Jesus with his refugee parents is relived and real for many who are members of the church, or who use the building.

Each week worship is different. It is difficult to predict exactly what might take place, because it is very dependent on who is present, on who is leading, and on what people have brought with them from their week. The rites used provide a flexibility necessary to people whose lives are generally very flexible and often driven by circum-stances over which they have little control. The congregation is small enough for this to happen without it provoking uncertainty or con-fusion and without it interrupting the flow of the worship, from God to the people and back to God.

At St Barnabas, too, the worship is authentic because the lives of the mostly professional and highly educated members are reflected in the professional leadership, in the theologically challenging approach to the scriptures and tradition, and in the importance attributed to social action. During worship we learn that the revelation of God in Jesus is relevant today, and that the gospel gives Christian people an imperative to live lives in the service of others. We have an opportunity to engage in thought and prayer about major political and business issues, and many members of the congregation are in positions to make a real difference through their working lives to the life of nation and world.

In both churches the emphasis on care for the community and an awareness of social justice initiatives locally, nationally and internationally is found in the worship, during prayers and preaching and in the use to which the members put their buildings. Certainly the members of Copleston Centre Church know that their buildings are also considered as belonging to other members of the community, only some of whom would be part of the worshipping community on a Sunday.

Regardless of how liturgy is used it must be a vehicle for authentic worship. Worship is authentic when it does what it is meant to do, and that is to connect human beings with each other and to communicate something of the God who initiates worship. So the language, both verbal and non-verbal, needs to be accessible. Accessibility doesn't mean simple or simplistic. The language of worship should invoke something of the character of God who is both immanent and transcendent. What happens during worship on Sunday must also be congruous and contiguous with the lives of people from Monday to Saturday. Language or concepts that are never encountered outside the church building can make God and the gospel seem far off, and unconnected with the bread-and-butter concerns of worshipping Christians; but if the language and language-systems in use during worship, along with the setting and the human contact, connect with the rest of life then they will contribute to an atmosphere that is life-giving.

In both of our churches *Common Worship, Order One* (contemporary language) is used. A choice of eucharistic prayer is made that reflects the needs and concerns of the congregation. The prayers of penitence are said at the beginning, thus clearing the way for hearts and minds to engage fully with the liturgy of word and sacrament. In Copleston Centre Church no explanation is offered as to why certain choices have been made. To do so would imply to the congregation that the vicar and Elders were looking for advice. In St Barnabas, short explanations are given along the way in the service books, which, for this congregation, communicate the fact that the vicar and PCC have really looked into it and have made decisions about the rite for considered reasons. This helps people feel comfortable.

In both churches the initial welcome is quite similar. Recognizing that newcomers can be overwhelmed by what is happening, a warm and human approach, treating all the same, says much about God's unconditional welcome to all people. It is easily spotted if there is only lip-service paid to welcoming newcomers, or to welcoming those who live in the parish but only worship very occasionally. 'Nice to see you again!' sounds very different from 'We haven't seen you for a while!' The corporate and collective identity of people who worship together can be life-giving both to members and to visitors, and what it communicates about God is that God is relationship. As Christians participate in the action of the God-who-goes-out, so they too are enabled to grow in relationship with others. This can produce funda-mental corporate and collective identities, if only subconsciously. It is within our worship that these identities are discerned. If worship is about giving worth to God then it follows that there will be some locus of the being of God identified. This happens at an individual and at the corporate level. In identifying the action of God within worship the worshippers are able to discover that they are part of a history of grace. The church's corporate identity is formed through its worship. Individuals are then freed to find their identity within the identity of the whole worshipping people.

So in our churches the worship must be Christ-centred. God's revelation in Christ is learned through the scriptures, the hymns and the proclamation of the gospel, and it is perceived in the telling and re-telling in the Eucharist of the story of Jesus' self-giving. In both churches, and in very different ways, the weaving together of word and sacrament complement each other in a dynamic of love and response. In the informal sermon the preacher and the response locate Christ in each other and in the lives of many. In the more formal sermon, the cognitive processing is in parallel with an appeal to the heart, and this cognitive processing has to do both with what is 'true' and with 'what works'.

In both churches, in one due to worshipping in the round, thus all being visible, and in the other due to receiving communion in the round, the sense of being in community with each other is reinforced and encouraged. All are welcome at the point of remembering Jesus and are drawn into the company of the faithful.

As the end of the liturgical drama comes in sight, we are in a spirit of thanksgiving. We have received God's blessing and the sacrament of the bread and wine. We are preparing to be sent out to be part of God's mission in our parish, our households and our places of work, education or leisure. If our liturgies enable and invigorate us for that task which is the mission of God, then we have engaged in the worship of God, in both spirit and truth, and the lives of all those who participate in the worship of God will be changed, as will their communities. Jürgen Moltmann writes:

It seems to me that the Christian community is singular in that it discovers Jesus in the people, and the people as the people of the kingdom. Before this community initiates programs and concludes historical alliances with other groups, it eats and drinks with the people and breaks the bread of poverty in the common hope. And when the persons of this community sit together in a circle and eat a common meal they can express their concrete needs and discuss the possibilities of common action and the strategies of self-liberation. Collective identity is practiced before it is promoted and mobilized.[5]

God is a missionary God. Moltmann reminds us that it is not the Church's mission to bring salvation to the world, but the mission of the Son and the Spirit through the Father, and this mission includes the Church.[6] So there is Church because there is mission, not the other way around. Therefore, to participate in mission is to participate in the movement of God's love towards people. In other words, the mission of God is not something the Church does but it is part of who God is.

Through participating in the liturgy of our churches we hear and re-hear, tell and re-tell the story of our salvation. God is not far off, but God meets us in his Son in order to bring us home. Home is represented by a community, an alternative community of trust and embodied faithfulness to our story and its God. This home is both a place and space, and we call it 'Church'. This Church has authentic Christ-centred worship at its core and like Copleston and St Barnabas, and hundreds of others besides, it is deliberately engaging with others in ways that will communicate something about engagement with God.

The Church participates in the mission of the God who goes out, and it responds to the call of God primarily through worship. The vehicle of that worship is liturgy. Liturgy that is truly 'the work of the people at worship' is adaptable and accessible. It reflects the language and the cultures represented among the community. It puts into word and action the deep yearnings of the human heart and mind for wholeness. It enables a recollection of the history of God's people and of God's people as they have engaged with God. It provides an opportunity to experience a fusion of the past, present and eschatological future. It enables the people of God, week in and week out, to remember their story, their community and themselves.

The only adequate test of the liturgies we use in our churches is that applied over time. Do the liturgies we use derive from the experience and language of those who use them, or are they simply taken off a shelf and delivered? Do they reflect the needs, fears and concerns people bring with them as they gather for worship? Are they Christ-centred, using the scriptures to bring both challenge and comfort?

And do our liturgies tell and show others that God's love and welcome is unconditional, or are they inaccessible except to initiates, thus communicating something very different? The final test, of course is that of changed lives and changed communities.

Further reading

Worship

Dawn, Marva J., *A Royal 'Waste' of Time, The Splendor of Worshipping God and Being Church for the World*, Eerdmans, Cambridge, 1999.

Fiddes, Paul S., *Participating in God*, Darton, Longman & Todd, London, 2000.

Harrison, D. E. W. and Michael C. Sansom, *Worship in the Church of England*, SPCK, London, 1982.

Torrance, James B., *Worship, Community and the Triune God of Grace*, Paternoster Press, Carlisle, 1994.

Wainwright, Geoffrey, *Doxology, The Praise of God in Worship, Doctrine and Life*, Epworth Press, London, 1980.

Mission

Bosch, David J., *Transforming Mission*, Orbis Books, Maryknoll, 1999.

Bowen, Roger, *So I Send You*, SPCK, London, 1996.

Moltmann, Jürgen, *The Open Church: Invitation to a Messianic Lifestyle*, SCM Press, London, 1979.

Zizioulas, John D., *Being as Communion*, St Vladimir's Seminary Press, Cresswood, New York, 1997.

Liturgy

Bell, Catherine, *Ritual, Perspectives and Dimensions*, Oxford University Press, Oxford, 1997.

Page, Ruth, *Synergy in the Church*, SCM Press, London, 2000.

Ramshaw, Gail, *Christ in Sacred Speech*, Fortress Press, Philadelphia, 1986.

Notes

1 Davies, J. G., *Worship and Mission*, SCM Press, London, 1966, p. 71.

2 Dawn, Marva J., *A Royal 'Waste' of Time, The Splendor of Worshipping God and Being Church for the World*, Eerdmans, Cambridge, 1999, p. 27.

3 Bowie, Jackie, *The Copleston Story: A Celebration of the Copleston Centre 1978–2001*, The Copleston Centre, London, 2001.

4 Stevens, Clare, *Building for the Future*, St Barnabas Church, London, 1997.

5 Moltmann, Jürgen, *The Open Church: Invitation to a Messianic Lifestyle*, SCM Press, London, 1979, p. 111.

6 Moltmann, *Open Church*, p. 111.

3. Not Merely Reacting

Pastoral Care in the Parish

ALYSON PEBERDY

Whenever I am asked why I am Anglican rather than, say, Methodist or Roman Catholic, I find myself explaining that it has much to do with the Church of England's commitment to care for anyone and everyone in a parish, not simply those who come to church. Yet increasingly very many people have no idea that the parish and priest exist *for* them, and can see no potential connection between themselves and their parish church. In a plural and often secular context is it really possible for the Church to maintain a broad vision of pastoral care? If so, how can this best be done? These are the main questions addressed in this chapter. I am learning on the job and what follows is simply what I have discovered so far.

Parishes vary enormously in the extent to which the church is seen as central to the local community. The first parish in which I served, in Windsor, was a place in which many of those who were not active church members saw the parishes and their priests as a clear link with the local community, the Queen (who lived on the hill), and, possibly, also with God. Churches were very much part of the social fabric: their clergy's comings, goings and opinions were a matter of public interest. The licensing of new clergy was attended by civic dignitaries and reported in the local press, and even the curate's letter in the parish magazine would often find its way into one of the local newspapers. Though the sight of a woman in a dog-collar was a surprise for some, the dog-collar itself was readily recognized and welcomed whether in the park, the pub, or the patisserie. In many ways people felt they knew me even before we had met and this was often helpful in establishing pastoral relationships with those who were not members of the congregation.

In my present South London parish it is all rather different and more typical of many urban and suburban contexts. Here the parish church and clergy have no privileged links with other institutions and no widely recognized public role and purpose. There is little or no sense that a priest might be interested in local issues such as the closing down of a community facility. If I want to be part of a local consultation arranged by a housing association or the Borough Council I have to argue the case on the grounds of being a local resident and not by virtue of my role as parish priest.

Although just over 60 per cent of my parishioners in the 2001 census described themselves as Christian, probably only 6 per cent of parishioners are in any sense active members of their parish church. Some parishioners attend neighbouring Anglican churches, and some attend one or other of a wide range of Christian, often Pentecostal, churches in the area and beyond. About 6 per cent identified themselves as Muslim, Hindu, Buddhist or Sikh. Almost a quarter of parishioners described themselves as having no religious affiliation and an additional 10 per cent gave no response at all. As in much of surrounding Lewisham there is also considerable ethnic diversity. Twenty per cent describe themselves as Black or Black British, 10 per cent as mixed, Asian or 'other', and 70 per cent as white.

This plural and sometimes secular nature of the parish has implications for pastoral care. It makes things more difficult in many respects, and has prompted me to look for ways of making pastoral care more accessible and in some sense proactive. Before ordination I worked for the Open University, an institution designed to open the doors of university-level study to those who had been either unable or unwilling to go to university earlier in their lives. It has been enormously successful in so doing. Perhaps we too can find ways of providing more flexible and imaginative points of contact for those who see the Church as having nothing to offer them.

As a way into this discussion I want to begin with my own experience as a lay person because it is precisely from such a lay perspective that most people receive and view pastoral care. I grew up in the 1950s and 60s in a largely industrial, and entirely white, parish on the edge of Leicester. There I was baptized, confirmed and married. Looking back on my experience of pastoral care in that parish I recall one home visit by the vicar, telling my parents (not me) that I was the right age to be confirmed, and then some ten years later a visit to the vicarage for a rather simplistic marriage preparation session. That is all I can remember, though it may not be all that was offered or received. Much later when my parents died I made contact again and this time the care was kind, imaginative and good. In these brief and rare pastoral encounters the quality of care, or lack of it, was evident, and made a major difference both to the immediate experience and to my understanding of the nature of God.

I now occupy a different role, in a very different parish, and have a broader understanding of pastoral care. Yet I want to hold on to those early experiences which remind me that even the briefest of pastoral encounters has the potential to communicate something of God's love, or not. A later chapter on evangelism will speak of the way in which the company and care of Christians enables others to discover and respond to God's love for them. Lay people are the key players in this central task. But what of those people living in my parish who happen not to have an actively Christian neighbour, friend or work colleague? This is surely where the particular calling and responsibility of the Anglican parish and priest to care and minister to all who live within the parish comes into its own.

I believe passionately that the parish and priest exist for all because such is the nature of God. The only necessary qualification for access to infant baptism, marriage and funerals in the church is residence in the parish, and as everyone belongs to one parish or another no one is excluded. Such deliberate and radical inclusivity may easily be disregarded and trampled underfoot, yet it provides an enormously powerful sign of God reaching out in love to all irrespective of their believing or consciously belonging. We all belong even though we do not all believe.

As a lay person my only understanding of pastoral care was in the context of 'rites of passage' but, of course, much more is possible and required. One enormously ambitious definition of pastoral care describes it as 'that activity, undertaken especially by representative Christian persons, directed towards the elimination and relief of sin and sorrow and the presentation of all people perfect in Christ to God'.[1] I like this definition because it reminds us of the breadth and purpose of pastoral care. Such care cannot be reduced to counselling or to any other secular model of care (though it may draw on any or all of them); it is corporate as well as individual; it is about both relief and development. It is an integral part of mission because, as Paul Avis puts it, 'people cannot respond to God's loving purpose for them unless they have basic identity, basic dignity . . . By building salutary forms of community the Church is creating the climate of moral values . . . within which people find it possible to believe the essential Christian message.'[2]

As a priest I have had to learn that almost anything may be required of those offering pastoral care. The work is never purely 'spiritual'. If, for instance, bad housing makes life especially difficult for some of my parishioners, my pastoral concern for them will lead me to challenge those responsible for the state of their housing. If isolation causes suffering for lone parents, my pastoral care of them may require me to introduce them to a local group, or to help put such a group in place. In pastoral care it is necessary to really listen to those who do come to us asking for help and to learn from them what different approaches and wider initiatives may be called for in this particular parish.

Learning on the job

So what kinds of needs and situations do people bring to a parish priest? How have I responded? What more might be required? There have been the expected encounters focusing on birth, marriage and death. In addition I have found myself trying to help people in the midst of an enormous variety of difficulties and crises including mental illness, disability, life-threatening or terminal illnesses, infertility, miscarriage, abortion and still birth, unemployment, separation and divorce, domestic violence, and sexual abuse. Thankfully there have also been the more obviously joyful events of births, marriages, and renewal of marriage vows.

As well as listening and guiding, encouraging and sometimes challenging people, there have been times when it has felt helpful to use or fashion an appropriate liturgy enabling those concerned to place their suffering, grieving or guilt into the hands of God. One example was a woman who many years earlier had chosen to have an abortion for health reasons. She had never regarded the foetus as a person until her daughter became pregnant and proudly showed her a scan of her own child in the womb. The flood of awareness was devastating. I turned to my books: in them are liturgies for use after a miscarriage or still birth but nothing that corresponded to her particular situation, so together we wrote a simple service enabling her to acknowledge the sorrow and guilt, receive absolution, and commend her unborn child to God. The candle we lit that day remains in church for her to re-light whenever she wishes. As she is a member of my congregation it was relatively easy to find common ground. I wonder how I would have responded if there had been less I could have taken for granted?

Pastoral care is not always as individualistic and short-term as the pattern I experienced as a layperson. Take for instance marriage. In the Berkshire and South London parishes in which I have served most marriage preparation has been conducted in the context of couples meeting for several sessions with other couples in a relaxed, informal atmosphere. A glass of wine and a few carefully planned activities have encouraged people to take time to think about what marriage means: what aspects of their relationship have not, so far, been open to discussion? Why do they want to get married in church? What might God be wanting to give them? Attendance at these sessions is simply requested, not required, but almost everyone accepts the invitation. Such groups are surprisingly popular, with couples often asking for extra or follow-up sessions. Baptism preparation can follow a similar pattern and be almost as welcome, well-attended and enjoyable. Both kinds of groups have benefited from clergy and lay people sharing the pastoral care and teaching. Working with me in the parish is an ordained local minister and two lay pastoral assistants.

Although such groups work well, it is important to be aware that they do not necessarily result in people joining the church that provides them. Frequently, newly married couples and young families move home to other areas soon after the marriage or baptism. It is difficult to know whether the relationship that has developed between them and the parish is strong and deep enough to enable them to begin to relate to a new and different parish. In the short term I suspect that often it is not, but because the experience has been positive people may well feel more confident in their approach when they next want to make contact with a parish church. (The question of whether the measure of good pastoral care is a growth in faith and commitment is a question to which I shall return below.)

The needs of people in the midst of dying, death or bereavement feature prominently in parish ministry. As with birth and marriage, requests come from parishioners who were previously unknown, as well as from members of the congregation. Caring for a member of the congregation can often be shared with lay people, but accompanying the dying of a person who was previously unknown to the parish falls mainly to the clergy. This is an enormous privilege and a new experience each time. There are no rules to be followed. Several times the request has come from someone with a Christian background, often Roman Catholic, who has rejected the Church, and yet feels able to call for help as death approaches. There have been people with no faith asking to be accompanied by someone with faith. There have also been those who have carved out their own path but who welcome someone who will respect their integrity and be content to find points of contact and resonance. One example was a young man who had decided to die in a Buddhist manner and yet also wanted a church funeral with lots of very good music and song. It is important to keep in mind this diversity of background and lack of familiarity with church culture when responding to requests from people unfamiliar with or alienated from the church. Imagination and flexibility are vital.

In my present parish there are on average three funerals a month. In addition to home visiting after the funeral it is increasingly the case that parishes provide bereaved people with an opportunity to join with others each year (or more frequently) for some kind of service of remembrance. Invitations are sent out to all bereaved families known to the parish, usually for an All Souls Day service. The response is high and growing. Many people who accept the invitation are not church members so it is important to be as inclusive as possible, inviting people to light candles and sing the most familiar hymns rather than providing a Requiem Mass which might leave many people feeling bewildered and alone.

As well as such visible and structured pastoral provision in which lay people and assistant clergy can play an active part, there are the very many unexpected knocks on the vicarage door. In my former parish there had been no curate's house and so the diocese paid the rent of a small house in the middle of a residential area equidistant from the various churches in the team. There was no distinguishing sign on the door. Only church members knew where I lived and so most visitors were people I already knew.

I now live in a clearly signed vicarage across the road from the church and life is very different. There are frequent surprise visits, usually not from members of the church. For the first year or so they were almost entirely from people asking for short-term loans of money which they promised to repay within days. Stories of family breakdown, imprisonment, and homelessness have been told and retold in my study. To begin with I chose to act as though I was being told the truth, although typically I sensed I was not. The final straw was a young woman calling late at night telling me she needed money for food and disposable nappies for her baby. Together we went to buy them and I promised to call round the next morning to see her. The story had been long, detailed and convincing but the next day I found the address she had given me did not exist. The food and nappies had presumably been resold for a small amount of cash. A tougher response has reduced the number of people turning up on the doorstep looking only for a source of money.

Unexpected callers continue to come to the vicarage but now with rather different requests. Two very recent callers illustrate well the tentative and confused longings that 'unchurched' members of the parish may direct towards those of us who dare to represent the Church.

The first caller was a youngish man urgently knocking on the door at 8.00 a.m. on my day off. He was holding a Bible and asking why he couldn't get into the church to talk to someone: he had been phoning churches all night without success. Why weren't we active in the ways and at times that suit younger people, he asked. I invited him in. He explained he lived in my parish and wanted to know why the Church is so inaccessible and out of touch and why it doesn't communicate in ways familiar to him. He also asked how he could find out how God wanted him to live when the Bible is so obviously written for another place and time. At one point he initiated a debate about the Prodigal Son and whether this story could possibly have any relevance in a non-agricultural society. His questions, suggestions and words tumbled out and were very difficult to follow. I tried to focus on his feelings. There was certainly something in him that felt lost and also something not wanting easy or familiar answers. There were also lots of judgements and assumptions about the Church being run by authoritarian elderly men. By the end he had run out of energy and acknowledged having lost the thread which had eluded me much earlier. I invited him to dip his toe into a church that isn't led by an elderly authoritarian man. I have no idea whether he has done so.

The second surprise visitor was more organized. She phoned first asking to come round, telling me we had met at a funeral a year ago. She wasn't a Christian, as neither was her friend whose dying I accompanied, but she said she had a problem she felt might have a spiritual dimension. Before talking to me she wanted to know whether I was like a counsellor and whether I observed professional codes of confidentiality. Having reassured her on the matter of confidentiality we agreed to meet. She was very articulate and reflective and there was little I could do other than sit quietly in my dog collar and visibly represent something she felt she lacked. This time biblical imagery played no part in the conversation. Casting around for something that might help I suggested the development of the pearl in the oyster. Her face lit up and she offered to return in a few months to show me the pearl.

I spend quite a lot of time on such encounters, aware that neither of these people is likely to become part of any statistics of annual church attendance. But no discussion of pastoral care in the parish can ignore them. They are but the tip of an iceberg which is frequently invisible to the Church but massively real. Having a clearly signed vicarage within easy reach of the church is enormously helpful. It means people know where to go for help. (Here I have a distinct advantage over Methodist, Baptist and Pentecostal neighbouring clergy who live several miles away from their churches.) But increasingly I have come to feel that this isn't enough.

It is also important to spend time walking through the parish, not simply to be seen but also in order to see beyond the surface. What from the car window looked like a large house owned by a professional family at closer range turns out to be subdivided into small units of social housing, or unmarked bed-and-breakfast accommodation. Using local shops means having to see how many times the glass on the shop front gets broken. Getting to know the area and the kinds of difficulties people face as well as the hidden signs of hope is essential. This will be true for all parishes and especially for those in which the church does not have well-established links with the very many different kinds of people living or working locally. But after a great deal of walking I sensed that much more was needed.

In 2001, with the help of a small Church Urban Fund grant and a research consultant, nine local Christian churches worked together with my own parish on a social audit of the area. The resulting report began with these words:

For Jesus, good news was never locked inside buildings or restricted to liturgical expressions of worship, whether old or new. It was to be earthed in the experience of the poor, the blind, the oppressed and the captive. It was both freeing and life transforming. As Churches Together in Forest Hill we want to be good news to our community, taking concrete action to respond to the needs of people in this area. As part of that process we need to know the facts, figures and feelings of our community, so that we can make an active response to them.[3]

Information was gathered from a variety of sources including census data, written reports, individual interviews and focus groups. Visits were made to reminiscence groups, youth clubs, parents waiting at school gates, health centres, residential establishments, health visitors, social workers, local councillors and many more. We discovered that Forest Hill lies within the top 10 per cent of deprived wards when it comes to housing and that deregulation of the private sector has made things particularly difficult for those on low pay or on benefits to find secure housing. In this parish numbers of people in hostel-type accommodation are higher than average for the Woolwich area and the local primary school has a far higher number of casual admissions directly from outside the UK, and a higher number of children qualifying for free school meals, than neighbouring schools. A lack of recreational and leisure facilities for young people, especially those in poorer families, stood out as a major cause for concern. So too did a sense that all sorts of people on the margins often feel unheard.

Action aiming to reduce social isolation across the board, and to improve recreational facilities for young people, was clearly called for. In response it has been possible to begin to initiate pastoral programmes in partnership with other churches and secular groups who share our concerns. Such partnerships involve developing the kinds of connections and networks that make the church more known and accessible.

The first initiative was a secular youth group. The local police officer, the head teacher of the primary school, youth workers, local residents and the church joined forces to provide a youth group based in the church hall and open to all. The police and youth workers first consulted with young people hanging around the area before the group was set up and their views have been taken into account. The youth group has been very well attended.

In the light of this success, the parish church invited other churches to help plan an open Christian youth group that might enable young people who have had little or no contact with the church to explore questions of faith in an exciting way through drama, music, dance and so on. The aim is to attract the kind of young people who attend the secular youth group. Again the Church Urban Fund has agreed to provide financial support and other funding is being sought. Working with other churches on a project like this has the advantage of providing a wider range of talent and skills, but the disadvantage of having to spend quite a lot of time debating widely different approaches, expectations and understandings of youth work. After a long incubation we expect to be in action in 2004, three years after the audit report was completed.

A second initiative arising from the social audit recommendations aims to help address the problem of isolation. This is a proposal by the church to work with secular local organizations such as the community centre, a housing association, local mental-health workers, an elderly persons project and local councillors to set up a 'time bank'. A time bank is a way for people to come together and help each other. Participants 'deposit' their time in the bank by providing practical help and support to others, and are able to withdraw their time when they need something done themselves. Everyone's time is worth the same whatever the nature of the task and an organizer or 'broker' links people up and keeps records. A comprehensive evaluation of time banks found that they have successfully attracted participants from socially excluded groups such as people who are disabled, unemployed, housebound or from ethnic minorities. The evaluation also found the main motivations for joining a time bank were to help other people, and to make friends and meet people.[4] So, we hope our time bank will connect all kinds of people who feel isolated, uninvolved or unnoticed and that it will do so in a way that builds confidence, skills and mutual trust.

In all these projects partnership is crucial. At a practical level this is because the parish church is too small to proceed alone, but more importantly because the process of co-operative planning will help to strengthen the local community and be more likely to have a fruitful and durable result. Partnership is risky and it is always possible that the final project might make no mention of the church. If this happens then it will be crucial to remember that, whatever its name, the enterprise will still express the pastoral concern of the church for the people in this parish.

Some conclusions

Reflecting on what I have learnt, I became aware of some general issues and questions. The first lesson was one I learnt as a lay person and could easily be lost. It is that when people turn to the Church, especially at critical points in their lives, we must never underesti-

mate the difference the quality of our care and attention can make –
for good or ill.

This links with a question raised earlier in this chapter about
whether the measure of good pastoral care is growth in commitment
and faith. This is a difficult question to answer. It can well be argued,
as it is by Paul Avis,[5] that in late modernity the Church's mission
needs to be fundamentally pastoral. I tend to agree. But this does not
mean that good pastoral care necessarily results in something that is
immediate or in any way visible to us. Much of the time we simply do
not know.

None of this touches on the question of how people in the parish
can get to know about and trust us in the first place. Visibility,
accessibility and active concern about community issues are, of
course, essential in this process. A well-signed and central vicarage is
a definite asset (though if I had a young family I might well see this
kind of vicarage as a mixed blessing). Getting out and about, *in the
dog-collar*, is also important. I stress the dog-collar because it gives a
sign of a public role not reducible to the person wearing it.

Beyond this, working in partnership with other local groups, both
secular and faith groups, helps to establish links with others in the
parish. Such activity might be mistakenly regarded as secondary to,
or even a distraction from, the need to put the Church first. Yet it is
precisely through serious engagement with the diversity of our
context that the Church discovers itself and its calling. The kind of
engagement required of the Church involves being

> . . . contemplatively alert to human personal and cultural diversity,
> tirelessly seeking new horizons in its own experience and under-
> standing by engaging with this diversity, searching to see how
> the gospel is to be lived and confessed in new and unfamiliar
> situations; and doing this because of its conviction that each fresh
> situation is already within the ambience of Jesus' cross and resur-
> rection, open to his agency, under his kingship.[6]

This conviction – that each fresh situation is already open to the
agency of Christ and under his kingship – means that we are free to
reach out to people and situations very different from those we know
well, without trying to force them into a more familiar pattern. We
really can risk pastoral generosity. Such generosity and humility
might well be what is most needed by those responsible for pastoral
care in the parish.

Further reading

Moody, C., *Eccentric Ministry: Pastoral Care and Leadership in the Church*, Darton, Longman & Todd, London, 1992.

Avis, Paul, *Church Drawing Near: Spirituality and Mission in a Post-Christian Culture*, T. & T. Clark, Edinburgh, 2003.

Pattison, S., *A Critique of Pastoral Care*, 3rd edn, SCM Press, London, 2000.

Notes

1 Pattison, S., *A Critique of Pastoral Care*, 3rd edn, SCM Press, London, 2000, p. 13.

2 Avis, Paul, *A Church Drawing Near: Spirituality and Mission in a Post-Christian Culture*, T. & T. Clark, Edinburgh, 2003, pp. 184, 185.

3 Robertson, C., *Social Audit*, Churches Together in Forest Hill, London, 2001, p. 7.

4 Sayfang, G. and K. Smith, *The Time of our Lives*, New Economics Foundation, London, 2002.

5 Avis, *A Church Drawing Near*, p. 180.

6 Williams, R., *The Resurrection*, 2nd edn, Darton, Longman & Todd, London, 2002, p. 57.

4. Place, People, Building, Priest – and People

Some Parochial History

JAMES BOGLE

What *is* the parish? This chapter, by exploring the history of the parish system and the histories of a number of South London parishes, concludes that the parish is its territory, its population, its church building, its priest, and its congregation. While others might prefer a different order, this seems to me to be the order of priority that the historical survey offers to us.

The English parish system is generally attributed to Theodore, the able monk from Asia Minor who was sent by Pope Vitalian to be Archbishop of Canterbury in the seventh century. Theodore was a determined and wise decentralizer, and he saw the need for smaller units than the diocese, which was often very large. It seems that he built on pagan practice, including a form of patronage in the relation of landlord and pagan priests in pre-Christian times when the owner of land was bound to provide facilities for worship for his dependants, appointing a priest as his agent for the purpose. By the high Middle Ages the parochial norm was that the landowner was patron of the parish and he appointed the priest. That the priest was instituted by the bishop gave him considerable protection. The priest was given sufficient land by the patron to support himself. The essence of this rural system remained the same until the industrialization of the late eighteenth and early nineteenth century. Patronage remained.

The territory

There are a number of determining factors that go to make up a parish. First there is its territory. The ancient parishes of South London were relatively large, having been formed when they were rural. In 1750 there were only two urban parishes in South London – what is now the Cathedral parish and the parish of St George the Martyr. There are over two hundred urban parishes today. A measure of urbanization is given by the figures for population in the parish of Camberwell. Already in 1841 Camberwell was a populous middle-class suburb, with a population of 39,868. But by the end of the century it was a metropolitan borough with a population of 259,339 – a vast increase. Urbanization was variable and some of it relatively recent. I once heard a parishioner say he could remember sheep being grazed on Forest Hill. The ancient parishes gradually reduced in size as daughter churches were formed. Some twentieth-century parishes cover a considerable area, but they have been broken down by having several churches built in them. There has been an unofficial goal in an urban context of always having a church within easy walking distance.

Parish boundaries are sometime natural, for example, rivers. The spreading network of railways has formed effective boundaries. A main road will form a well-marked boundary. But there is much force in the contention that urban parish boundaries have little meaning and fail to mark off one community from another. They merely serve to determine the area for which a particular parish priest is responsible. There are some curiously shaped parishes. A parish in New Cross Gate is crescent shaped, straddling a main road to serve three churches in that form.

At one time, civil and ecclesiastical parishes were coterminous. In an urban situation this has not been the case for a long time.

The population

Within the territory of particular parishes there is the widest variety of population. There may be a solidly prosperous middle-class population. A parish may consist uniformly of white-collar workers. There are large and uniform council estates. There are parishes that centre on Peabody Buildings built during the nineteenth century to house the urban working poor. There are parishes with run down tower blocks. And it is also a characteristic of London that there may be different types of housing in close proximity.

With any parish community there may be a strong or a weak sense of belonging to a community, and generally in an urban context the sense is rather weak. Bermondsey, however, was a special case. In 1900 it was the worst slum in Europe, with a population of well over 100,000 in quite a limited area. The Borough Council did everything it could to encourage migration out of the borough and to discourage migration in, so that by 1960 the population was about 50,000. The result of this pressure was a very tightly knit community, in which the church played its part. There was a similar community sense in Deptford. The South London villages, Blackheath, Dulwich and Charlton represent local identities, but are scarcely now villages in the traditional sense. On the other hand the parish of Holy Trinity, Rotherhithe, cut off by the docks as it used to be, was a true village community where mutual knowledge and a sense of belonging was strong.

The church building

Each parish must have a church. When the great development of Thamesmead was beginning, the Bishop, Mervyn Stockwood, protested

> Think for a moment of the absurdity of the housing estate at Abbey Wood in the borough of Greenwich. In order to get the stipend of a clergyman to work in the area I have had to build the William Temple Church. Nothing could be more irrelevant; nothing could be further removed from the spirit and teaching of William Temple. What I need on the estate is a building like the one in Wimbledon with flats for specialist clergy and laity. By all means have a small place of worship in the building, but what is more important is the wherewithal with which to engage a team of competent men.[1]

He was right in what he affirmed, but wrong in what he denied, for each parish must have a church building.

The growth of population in the nineteenth century led to much division of parishes and much church building. The Victorians were prosperous and munificent but over a century later they have left a legacy of building problems. Some churches were far too big and never finished, as the cathedral-like St Mary le Park in Battersea. Stockwood protested at the overprovision of churches and took Deptford as an example. There were eight parish churches, three daughter churches and a mission hall served by twenty-two clergy and other workers. The Roman Catholics had just one church and it was estimated that their Sunday congregations were double the combined attendance at Anglican places of worship. 'Instead of using our resources sensibly to spread the gospel and run the church efficiently, we are squandering our energies and money upon preserving the fabric.'[2] Was he right?

There are few parish churches in South London of the calibre of St Paul, Deptford or St John the Divine, Kennington. But there are many where it is possible to join readily enough in worship with the local community.

It matters what the building is like, but as Bishop John Robinson warned:

We are now being reminded that the church people go to has an immensely powerful psychological effect on their vision of the Church they are meant to be. The church building is a prime aid or a prime hindrance, to the building up of the Body of Christ. And what the building says so often shouts something completely contrary to all that we are seeking to express through the liturgy. And the building will always win – unless and until we can make it say something else.[3]

The priest

Every parish must also have a priest, whether it be a rector, a vicar, a priest in charge or some other designation. Within a parish and in the life of a church a priest is exceptionally influential. Almost all the decisions in the life of the congregation are channelled through him or her. In most matters of worship the priest has sole responsibility. And people come to the priest not merely for christenings, marriages and funerals, but with their spiritual and other problems. It is a sad fact that a congregation is unlikely to progress spiritually much beyond the level of its priest. Conversely, a good priest can have a considerable influence on a congregation and a community, and South London has had some notable priests.

Arthur Tooth was educated at Trinity College, Cambridge and travelled extensively to Australia, Japan and China before he was ordained. He served three short curacies before he was inducted as Vicar of St James, Hatcham in 1868. He found the church in poor condition and over the following years refurbished it, creating a baptistery in the north transept where he also put a confessional. He abolished pew rents and other fees, which endeared him to his parishioners who were mostly poor. He set up schools, a convent and an orphanage. On Sunday evenings there were large-scale musical performances. And he greatly increased the congregation, which came to number hundreds.

In 1874 the Public Worship Regulation Act was passed by Parliament with the intention of regulating Anglo-Catholic worship. Cases were to be tried in a secular court (which did not enhance its authority among the Anglo-Catholic clergy). St James, Hatcham was early targeted and Tooth was the first person to be tried under the Act. He was accused of six prohibited practices: presiding facing East, mixing water with wine in the chalice, the use of unleavened bread, candles as altar lights, vestments, and incense. Tooth was imprisoned, a fairly comfortable imprisonment admittedly, with his own furniture and nuns cooking his meals. He was even given a brace of pheasants. Nevertheless it was imprisonment. He was suspended from performing divine service for three months. He resigned and was never offered a further position in the Church but devoted himself to educational work.

The effect of the persecution of the Anglo-Catholic clergy was to move public opinion right round to the ritualists. The Public Worship Regulation Act was greatly discredited and it virtually became a dead letter. Tooth himself was an able, devoted, earnest and honest priest, but uncompromising. Everything he stood for is now accepted in the Church. Perhaps his imprisonment was the price paid for that.

Nicolas Stacey was appointed Rector of Woolwich in 1959, one of Mervyn Stockwood's first appointments. As an undergraduate he had been an Olympic runner. He had served a conventional curacy at Portsea before becoming Chaplain to the Bishop of Birmingham, where his talent for journalism flourished, as did his ideas for the reform of the Church. He showed himself to be a dynamic and caring priest. At Woolwich he quickly assembled a team of very able curates; a genuine team where decisions were made by all, not just by the rector. Soon the great church of St Mary Magdalene was transformed with a crèche for babies, a lunch-time snack bar, an all-day coffee bar, and the galleries turned into a variety of rooms for meetings and exhibitions. It immediately became a centre of much social and pastoral life. Later a discotheque was opened in the crypt with a licensed bar.

Baptisms were quarterly and became grand occasions. A highlight was a procession of mothers with their babies from the first floor lounge at the back of the church into the nave. At the pews where the families were sitting the priest conducting the service asked 'What do you in the name of these children ask of the Church of God?' And received the reply 'We ask for baptism'. The priest then asked, 'Why do you ask for baptism?' and received the answer 'That our children may be made Christians'. Stacey commented, 'I think the parents who had their children christened at St Mary's felt something important and solemn had happened to their babies.' Marriage preparation was also careful, with three sessions for each couple. Care was also taken over sermon preparation, with the preacher going over the sermon with a colleague before delivery, and questions after the service over coffee.

Stacey was a convinced ecumenist and played a big part in the formation of a new Woolwich and District Council of Churches. The St Mary's team came to include a Methodist minister, a Presbyterian minister, a Baptist minister and even (with the qualified permission of the Archbishop of Southwark) a Roman Catholic priest. Even more remarkable was the sharing of St Mary's with the local Presbyterian congregation, which required fresh legislation.

Without losing hold of the spiritual, Stacey was practical. So a branch of the Samaritans was set up in Woolwich. In the local hostel for the homeless a family planning clinic was set up. Stacey wrote, 'If there is any connection between increasing human happiness and building the Kingdom of God, the work of God was being done in that clinic.' Together with City friends he also set up an exceptionally effective housing association, Quadrant.

In spite of dedicated pastoral work the numbers coming to church increased from 50 only to about 100, and Stacey was moved to write an article for the *Observer Colour Supplement* under the title 'A Mission's Failure':

> For 4 1/2 years in Thames-side Woolwich I have been head of one of the largest and ablest teams of clergy in any parish in England. We have had a remarkable opportunity of making a breakthrough in getting people to come to church . . . But we have achieved not one of the modest things we hoped for. We have quite obviously failed.[4]

The article caused a furore. By then anything at all controversial from Southwark elicited a strong reaction, but even more tellingly secularism was plainly beginning to bite. Stacey was not the only one to feel a failure. Bishop Mervyn Stockwood warned Stacey that he would not be offered another post in the Church of England and indeed he was not. Stacey commented, 'This may be an exaggeration, but I sense that since my article nobody any longer expects a working class parish to come alive in the traditional way.'

The members of the clergy team mostly ended up in secular employment, which they considered the right pattern for the future. Stacey himself left Woolwich to become deputy director of Oxfam and continued a priest in secular employment until his retirement. As he left Stacey said, 'What I do care about desperately is having the opportunity to build God's kingdom of love in a sad, sick and suffering world.' There can be little doubt that he and his team seized the opportunity to fulfil that purpose in Woolwich.

David Diamond was inducted as Rector of Deptford in May 1969. He had had a particularly successful curacy at Tuebrook, in Liverpool, running a huge youth club. He found St Paul's a good deal run down. There were those who advised that the church should be pulled down and something smaller built, but Diamond saw the merits of a grand building at the heart of the Deptford community.

His faith and practice centred on the incarnation, maintaining God's presence in the community, and he treated those who did not come to church as lapsed Christians, still with a feeling for God. He would not make a barrier between Church and community. Flowing from the incarnation were the sacraments, especially the Mass, which lay at the heart of church life. On special days the Mass would be celebrated with full ceremonial, processions, vestments, candles, incense and music. Diamond never forgot that he was a priest, nor did he let others forget it. He would wear a black suit with a clerical collar or a cassock with a biretta. And he was 'Father Diamond' or 'Father' or even 'Farv', but not Father David. But he was not a gloomy man; infectious enthusiasm was more characteristic of him. His heroes were the Anglo-Catholic priests who worked in the slums in the nineteenth century: Mackonochie, Stanton, Lowther and Dolling.

A great innovation was the Deptford Festival. On the first day coach loads of the elderly were driven to the seaside, seen off by all the children lining the route. There were street parties and estate parties followed by games. A celebrity or even royalty would come to the Festival's beginning, which was marked by the firing of a cannon. Though he shunned church administration, a congenial task like the Festival Fr Diamond saw through with panache. The Festival concluded with a Mass as splendid as he could make it, and the church was packed.

Diamond's ministry would be unrepeatable. Working-class communities such as Deptford used to be no longer exist. The assumption that people in a particular community are lapsed Christians has become impossible. Nevertheless he brought God to the community of Deptford and the community close to God. Only David Diamond at Deptford could give the lie to Nicolas Stacey's judgement that 'nobody any longer expects a working class parish to come alive in the traditional way'. He was a great priest.

Nicholas Rivett-Carnac had to follow a long trail before he came to his priestly maturity. For a time he served as an army officer. Next he was a shipbroker. Then he acted as a probation officer, which provided him with an insight into the seamy side of life and gave him a sympathy with those whom life had treated badly. He was ordained and served in the parish of Holy Trinity, Rotherhithe, the 'island village' parish, as it was in those days. But he was still not at ease spiritually. He made contact with the Orange Street Congregational Church, of which the minister was Vic Ramsey, and through him received baptism in the Spirit.

Such an experience was not for its own sake; it led him to further avenues of ministry. For a time he assisted at Holy Trinity, Brompton and then he was invited to act as Priest in Charge of St Mark's, Kennington. He was able to share his charismatic experience with others and build up a large congregation. Giving rose from £2,000 in 1972 to £150,000 in 1988. Rivett-Carnac was a bachelor when he first came to Kennington. He wanted to live in community and provide a home in the vicarage for the homeless and unstable. A group of friends from the church supported him. Incomes were pooled and possessions held in common. Though the arrangement broke down after 18 months, further enterprises of a similar kind were later tried, with only one needy resident per household. For a time the church was left open day and night, with a single member of the congregation present, as a witness to the parish's commitment to the deprived and homeless. Eventually it was felt that the dangers were too great and the demands on the cleaners unacceptable.

In charismatic worship the devotion is almost tangible. Rivett-Carnac's long personal pilgrimage led him to be able to share this devotion with many others and build up a church with that as its foundation.

It is priests such as these who have shaped the diversity of the parishes of South London. Will there be such priests in the future?

The congregation

However important the priest might be to the character of the parish, the congregation and its officers can have a considerable influence.

The congregation of St James, Hatcham was urban poor. It was necessary to begin schools and an orphanage. The churchmanship was meticulously ritualist. The congregation was large, in the hundreds, and, we may expect, rather formal in its relationships. Arthur Tooth attracted both large support and large opposition. The opposition to ritualism centred on William Sanders, a wealthy, single-minded and uncompromising man, who managed to get himself elected as churchwarden. He thought nothing of stopping a service on the grounds there were less than three communicants and took it upon himself to make sure that wafers were not being used. The division was so serious that there was the danger of rioting and the police were called in to close the church. St James was not the happiest of congregations and perhaps the only slight consolation is that even his Protestant opponents recognized that Tooth did good work with the poor and in the schools.

St Mary Magdalen's, Woolwich, was also run down when Nicolas Stacey took over as Rector. The parish was solidly working class and almost wholly unchurched. Not long after he came, a delegation of sorrowful ladies came to offer their resignations from their posts so that the Rector's wife and the curates' wives could take over. Stacey refused to accept the resignations, which was both tactful and wise. However after two years in the parish he wrote to his bishop, John Robinson, and was not flattering about the congregation, 'We found very little indigenous lay leadership . . . inevitably it was for the clergy to lead'. On the other hand a lay person wrote, 'It was not surprising that, despite Mr Stacey's assurances that their help was needed, many hung back, feeling perhaps that better qualified people were now at hand to do the jobs that they had previously done.'

Valerie Pitt, a sharp observer, noted that the Woolwich ethos was '*de haut en bas*'. And a member of staff commented 'it was not *of* the people, it was *at* the people and *to* the people'. Nevertheless personal relationships were good and there was real affection between lay people and the clergy. It may well be that the failure of the clergy team to carry the laity with them accounted in part for the lack of carry-over when the team broke up. And this weakness by no means vitiates the vast amount of good in a wide variety of fields which emanated from this church.

The congregation at St Paul's, Deptford was also run down when David Diamond took over, besides which there was much to do on the building and with furnishings and decoration. It is difficult to write of the congregation, for Diamond was firmly of the opinion that there should be no demarcation between the congregation and the Deptford community at large. The congregation did grow markedly and for the annual Festival the capacious church would be entirely full. Diamond came to stand for Deptford. In the name of the Deptford community he fought a great battle, which he eventually lost, to retain a branch of Marks and Spencers in Deptford High Street. Despite a certain personal reserve he was very widely trusted. Children and young people were drawn to him and he to them. Lads would come and serve at Mass for him. In 1981 a disastrous fire broke out at a house in New Cross Road filled with young black people. Thirteen young people lost their lives. There were suspicions of racist arson and feelings were running very high. Diamond was the only white person that the surviving youngsters would talk to. Deptford had a culture of petty crime to which he turned a Nelsonian eye. He regarded anything said in confidence to him as equivalent to the confessional. It led to great difficulty when two young men were accused of murder. Latterly Diamond gave considerable time to prisons, where he tended to find men he knew. He would invite church members to accompany him, which they willingly did, and together they established a substantial prison-visiting programme.

It is impossible to write of the congregation at St Paul's without writing of Diamond himself and the community at large. Young and old, men and women, white and black, criminals and straight, sick and well were drawn through him to the Church. He did not spare himself (it was too much for one man) and when he died he left a devoted congregation. One member of it was typical, Sid Blackman, who daily served the Mass for over 30 years.

At St Mark's, Kennington, Nicholas Rivett-Carnac did not outwardly greatly differentiate himself from the members of the congregation. Church members were heavily involved in what was undertaken. Nevertheless the leadership and the guidance of Rivett-Carnac were always there. Members of the congregation were greatly involved in the ministry of healing through prayer and the laying on of hands; one person was completely healed of lung cancer, without medical explanation.

As a congregation they were exceptionally generous in giving to the church and one tenth of the parish's income was in turn given away. Experiments in community living all involved members of the congregation. If there was a weakness it was that acts of spontaneous generosity were made without being sustainable in the longer term. But that was a fault of generosity much greater than could be found in other inner-city parishes.

Conclusion

A parish consists of a territory, a population, a church, a priest and a congregation. These are the bare bones and one might hope to find in a parish church:

1. worship conducted with reverence and care;

2. the Word of God declared with intelligence and conviction;

3. sufficient mutual knowledge and affection in the congregation to create a caring community;

4. the disabled, the unstable and the isolated made welcome in the congregation;

5. some sort of social action from the church for the good of the community.

'Parochialism' is usually a pejorative term expressing a concern with the petty and the trivial. These, though, are not the limits of most parish churches. The parish church has been and still is for many a springboard for the work of God both in the parish itself and in the wider world. South London's church history makes that plain.

Further reading

Bogle, James, *South Bank Religion*, Hatcham Press, London, 2003.
Bomford, Rodney and Potter, Harry, *Father Diamond of Deptford*, Ditchling Press, Burgess Hill, 1994.
Coombs, Joyce, *Judgement on Hatcham*, Faith Press, London, 1969.

Notes

1 Letter to the Bishop of London, 8 November 1966.

2 Southwark Diocesan Review, May 1966.

3 Cope, Gilbert (ed.), *Making the Building Serve the Liturgy: Studies in the Re-ordering of Churches*, Mowbray, London, 1962, p. 5.

4 *Observer*, December 1964.

5. Growing a Black Church

The Multicultural Parish

BARRY THORLEY

Surveying the landscape

It is a commonplace that there have been black people in Britain since Roman times and the first and great Elizabeth of England was 'discontented' that 'great numbers of negars and Blackamoores which [as she is informed] are crept into this realm'. Certainly, there were black people in some numbers in the seventeenth- and eighteenth-century slave-ports of London, Liverpool and Bristol. Sir Joshua Reynolds (famously) painted a black servant holding the Marquis of Granby's horse, for instance. It was not until the middle of the last century, however, that larger numbers of black people migrated from the Caribbean and the Indian subcontinent, followed by a second wave of people from West Africa, which began in the early 1990s – the new African diaspora.

Currently, the wider black community in the United Kingdom, despite a periodic high profile, usually for negative reasons, is nevertheless numerically small in relation to the population as a whole. This is certainly true in comparison to the African-American community in the United States, which has serious economic clout. The tendency here has been to lump together British-born black people with Africans, people from the Caribbean, the Indian subcontinent, China, everyone, into a collective salad bowl of 'minority ethnic communities', irrespective of their many and diverse differences.

This tendency is also prevalent in the Church. At major events, such as the enthronement of an archbishop, for example, when the Church of England in particular seeks to honour black Christians, it turns to the black-led Pentecostal churches. Otherwise, it imports foreign dignitaries, buys in a gospel choir or show-cases 'secular' dancers and drummers. This presence and profile are welcome, but nevertheless disguise and underline the poverty of the black constituency at its heart. The Church of England is in the kindergarten when it comes to matters of race.

Growing black Anglican churches at the grass roots, in the parishes, is therefore of the essence. It is a cliché that the Church of England's roots are in its branches, the parishes. The parochial system, among other things, provides an important and protective 'safety-net' of accountability, which many other churches might envy.

The glory of the Church of England is that the parish church is established to serve the entire community. Its parishes, with clearly defined boundaries, patchwork the land. Particularly in the inner cities, these communities are pluriform, containing a wide variety of people from across the country and all over the world. Nevertheless, many of our inner-city churches survive simply because of a loyal but often marginalized black presence, historically (as we have indicated) from the Caribbean or Africa. It may not be a desired aim to grow a black church, but it might be considered a God-given duty and joy to nurture what is a given. In fact, the future of the Church, for reasons to be explored further in this chapter, especially in the inner city, may well hang on it.

This perspective invites comparison with one of the most intense theological debates in the New Testament, when the Early Church wrestled with a similar issue over the challenge of an increasing number of Gentile Christians in an essentially Jewish religion. It concluded that if it were to survive then Christianity had to be embedded in the heart of human cultures, if it is to be true to its incarnate God. This is certainly the challenge, now and forever, for the Church of England and its parishes.

The soil

In the mid-1970s, Lascelles Anderson was stabbed and killed on the steps of the Parish Hall at St Giles' in Camberwell. At the police station, his mother screamed, stamping her feet on the concrete in the rhythms of high Greek drama, but she wasn't (of course) play-acting. Like Roland Adams, Stephen Lawrence and Damilola Taylor, her boy was dead. The funeral was a magnificent affair, humbling in its dignity. The community takes its licks, bears its pain, with dignity, but the community also remembers. The licks and pain are burned into a collective memory, often buried, but which, nevertheless, defines an important aspect of our collective experience of life in England.

One of the problems with the Church of England and its parishes is that we characteristically want things to be 'nice'. The tragic sense of life is not natural to a typical English sensibility. Sunday by Sunday, therefore, we contemplate a crucified God, then obscure him in the trappings of our notoriously 'formal' religion. We blanket him, like a child's comforter, in sonorous words and solemn ritual. This peculiar cultural phenomenon leads to a kind of institutionalized repression, which breaks out from time to time, as it did over the matter of women's ordination in the 1980s and, more recently, over the proposed consecration of Canon Jeffrey John as Bishop of Reading.

A common defence of this peculiar pattern of church life is that we seek to live by faith, in the light of the resurrection. We are civilized and balanced because we believe. In our view, the collective memory of hurt and pain is best buried. Certainly, the Stigmata are nowhere to be seen as the Risen Christ wipes all tears from Anglican eyes. There is little reference to pain or sorrow, because the Lord makes all things new. It is a kind of gospel: a smile, please, not bitterness; a handshake: not anger, never anger.

Black people, however, not exclusively, but day to day, know and celebrate that it is Christ crucified, Christ on the cross, who is so high you can't get over him, so low you can't get under him, and so wide you can't get around of him. Our tears are washed in his tears, and our blood is cleansed in his blood, the Blood of the Lamb, the Lamb of God, who takes away the sin and torment of the world, authentic and (in fact) universal 'good news'.

Meanwhile, in the mid-1970s at St Giles', Camberwell, without malice or forethought, black people sat in the aisles, behind the pillars, while the traditional, excellent, cultured and Catholic show rolled on. The preaching on matters of social justice was passionate and sincere, the prayers deep, the teaching second to none. There was first-rate fellowship and much love, but while the church had many loyal black members nothing of black culture was evident in the liturgy. There were, however, some 'international' evenings when food from various parts of the world was happily shared.

Later in the decade, at St Mary, Moseley, in Birmingham, there was a developed out-reach programme at Centre 13. Nevertheless, the core life of the church, the liturgy, was unremittingly derived from a similar, but rather more middle-of-the-road, cultivated Anglicanism. It did not begin to address or answer the need of the Jamaican husband of one parishioner, a seemingly sane and balanced professional, who sometimes felt the urge to go into the centre of town with a machete to lop off white heads. He buried his pain, and probably still does, deep within his heart, but the Church of England failed to engage with him where it hurt. It almost certainly wasn't aware of the depth of suffering he carried. Other churches can bury similar pain in compulsory 'joy' or 'salvation' confidence. Whichever way, the black community, by and large, is far too polite to let the pain show, except when it spills out in periodic, rank and inevitable riot and protest.

At the end of the 70s, again in Birmingham, Bishop Hugh Montefiore described the file on Holy Trinity, Birchfield, as 'thin'. He meant the church was dead on its feet. There were rarely more than twenty at the weekly Mass and these were genuinely kind, but older white folk, who had simply loved the church to death. With one notable exception, they had failed to engage with the growing, dominant, black constituency that colours the demography of Handsworth, the deanery in which the church is set. The vibrant Rastafarian community might well have been on Mars. The church had no inkling of the young black man who had been unceremoniously thrown out of his children's home months before sitting his A-levels.

In the early-1980s, police gunmen shot and paralysed Cherry Groce at her home in Brixton. It came in the context of a heavy 'stop-and-search' programme, swamping the community in a crack-down on drugs. In the rioting that followed, a car burned at the bottom of the vicarage garden and one young man fled into St Matthew's Road. He flung a package over the garden wall just as a police transit van turned the corner and pulled to a stop about fifty yards in front of him. A line of policemen, keeping contact with the van, poured out, surrounding him. With no questions asked, he was beaten and left to find his way home. The community in which the church lived, moved and had its being, at that time, in that place, was a community in turmoil.

Nevertheless, St Matthew's, Brixton, the parish in which the rioting mainly happened, is famous for its engagement with that same community. The distinguished previous incumbent, Bob Nind, turned the listed 'Waterloo church' radically upside down to make space for a wide variety of community activities. In fact, Bob sought to place the church at the disposal of the community, in so far as canon law and Bishop Mervyn Stockwood allowed. Bob had the stature to hold together a lively, diverse church in an honourable drive for relevance, based on a profound understanding of the kenotic principle, in which the Second Person of the Trinity pours out his glory to share our human condition, warts and all. However, after a long interregnum, without the glue of Bob's love and the strength of his guiding principles, the church was split, at war with itself. It boiled down to a battle royal between radical black and equally radical feminist factions. You could cut the atmosphere with a knife. It was unhealthy.

In the mid-90s, St Alfege, Greenwich, had an eye on the Millennium. Nicholas Hawksmoor's first parish church does traditional Anglican liturgy as well as anyone, with a notable choir which offers a wide repertoire of excellent church music from Tallis (buried in the crypt) to the present day. The present incumbent, Giles Harcourt, honours that tradition and has done so for well over ten years. But Giles is painfully aware that this polished liturgy may not attract and hold the diverse communities from the housing estates in his patch. Jefferson Goddard, a key black member of the church, has stuck it out over many years, in an unsung but heroic counter-cultural statement, from his back pew. Jefferson is not alone. Another black family, equally faithful and loyal, came consistently without husband and father. Tunde, let us call him, had gone back to Nigeria to bury his dad, but for eleven years had been refused permission to return. The judge who eventually reversed this decision lamented the injustice of his exile. The church held a great party for his eventual return, 'buying in' (of course) the services of an excellent drummer, who filled that august space with the rhythms of Africa. It was a triumph.

The soil in which the Church of England, in many of its inner-city parishes, seeks to grow its churches is shot through with tragedy. Mostly simmering beneath the surface, there are great wells of blood and pain, incipient madness and riot, rejection and injustice of all kinds. Anger and bitterness are a given, part of the matrix of the struggle.

Digging away

It should be clear by now that 'the black experience' of Anglican parish life was or is on the margin of a marginalized community. The show rolls on or grinds down, taking its black members for granted, with the exception of St Matthew's, Brixton, which was locked in an unseemly power struggle. What this gloomy analysis fails to recognize, however, is that black people come to our churches already deeply imbued with the Anglican spirit. English is the lingua franca in many of our countries of origin and the various Anglican traditions have been deeply rooted in many home soils. For example, they probably sing Tallis (at the very least, Handel) at St Alban's, Dar-es-Salaam!

Settling in this country in some numbers since the middle of the last century our hearts thrum and thrill as much as any to the strains of Jerusalem, Mozart's '*Ave Verum Corpus*' and the 'Hallelujah Chorus'. We are elegaic about country churchyards, awed at Westminster and Salisbury. Our relatives are archdeacons and bishops at home. Great-uncle Akinwale is a diocesan secretary and many of us have been on Parish Church Councils. We understand the preaching of salvation by faith alone and appreciate the 'burning glass' at the heart of the Mass. We certainly know about giving, since the tendency to tithe is a natural instinct in home congregations with no established wealth.

At the same time, we bring precious new gifts.

Father Alexio Chaparika is the incumbent at St Michael and All Angels, Nyanga, in Zimbabwe. From that base, he leads 15 congregations in a district the size of the Woolwich Episcopal Area in London. Alexio is a spirit-filled Anglican Catholic, working in a supremely effective team with his wife, Blessing. In 2001, a mixed group of 20 people from the Woolwich Area were welcomed to the Diocese of Mutare by Bishop Sebastian Bakare and one member of the group was sent up to Nyanga for ten days.

Alexio was prepared. With his own hands, he had cut a series of chapels in the forest. From the back of the church, he took his machete to the bush, clearing a wide aisle to a tree. He cleared a circle around the tree, then at an angle continued the aisle. He made another clearing around a second tree, and then angled off to a third, in which he hung a plastic rosary, in fact a Trinity of chapels. Chaparika had had a vision from God that the man from Woolwich was interested in the contemplative life. 'I thought,' he said, 'you might want to get close to nature and be with God.'

One of the precious things that black people bring into the life of the Church of England, and its parishes, is a continuing and visceral connection with nature, which feeds the contemplative spirit. Where we come from, the pace of life remains slower. Stars spread the heavens like a curtain. Space and silence abound. It is all still within the living memory of people in Camberwell and Moseley, Birchfield and Brixton, Greenwich and Thamesmead. Of course, there are great and noisy African and West Indian cities, where the silence is lost and space is often at a premium. It would be wrong and insulting to be naively romantic. Nevertheless, for a little while longer, perhaps for another ten years, if we are very lucky, people remain fundamentally in touch with this precious contemplative vibe.

Over twenty years ago, two hundred black Anglicans descended from around the world on Sam Lord's Castle in Barbados. We met to discover what might hold us together, exploring our common heritage for the distinctive food we might bring to the world-wide Anglican table. Two things still stand out.

There was agreement that African spirituality maintains close contact with the unborn and ancestors. This has deep resonance with the universal doctrine of the communion of saints and could give it fresh life. It is certainly the case that when this profound spiritual experience is exposed to the cataclysmic outpouring of the Holy Spirit, the Spirit of Jesus, the Resurrected One, then phenomenal energy is potentially unleashed. Victor Atta-Baffoe, recently reading for his doctorate in London, is now Principal of the Anglican Theological Seminary at Cape Coast in Ghana. Victor attests to the way in which this energy vibrates through Anglican parishes in Ghana. It is a deep sadness that this energy is so often suppressed in our inner-city churches.

The Barbados Conference also found common cause in our universal experience of poverty. The poverty we experience, live among, minister in, is different in different parts of the world. The shanty towns of Accra are different from the tenements of South-side Chicago. It is all, nevertheless, poverty. Theologies of liberation, therefore, resonate. But many of our communities remain in bondage to poverty. They are pre-Exodus communities, longing for the freedom to breathe fresh air, the air of the Promised Land. In the direst of circumstances, we have delayed hope of earthly gratification, transposing our dreams to 'the sweet by-and-by' beyond the grave. Many of us, however, cling on to a thirst for justice in the here-and-now, nurturing a Kingdom theology that rests on the present proclamation of good news to the poor. It is a thirst soon slaked by prosperity and almost entirely foreign to the wealthier African elites, who regard their often copious riches (simply) as 'a gift from God', a sort of Prosperity Gospel!

Digging away at who we are, at what 'the black experience' brings to Anglican parish life, a deeply internalized understanding of 'English' Anglicanism, a residual contemplative attitude, suppressed wells of spiritual energy and a thirst for justice, are significant. They are not inexhaustible, and won't last forever, unless we are very careful indeed. We need to be careful to nurture strong and confident black people, especially black young people, in our churches.

Growth

St Paul's, Thamesmead, in the Diocese of Southwark, with the Church of the Cross, William Temple Church, and a new church plant in West Thamesmead, is an Anglican Team Ministry in a set of convoluted ecumenical relationships. The ecumenical enterprise, as is indeed the case with evangelism, taps into the same dynamic involved in growing a black church: inclusion. Each seeks commonality in difference. In the 1970s, Thamesmead 'ancestors', our very own communion of saints, John Robinson, Jim Thompson, and then later Keith Pound, with their ecumenical colleagues, caught a moon-beam, visible unity for the whole of Christendom by the end of the millennium. It was a grand dream in the virgin, unchurched territory of a new town, to be built on what amounts to a water-meadow in the upper Thames Estuary. The 'ancestors' moved on, but the dream caught the imagination of those who remained and they held onto it for dear life. The legacy of the 'ancestors' was, in fact, written in stone, to the point where it became an act of ecumenical sacrilege to begin to question the structures they had laid down to carry that dream into its hoped for realisation. By the turn of the century, when the dream had faded, the then Archdeacon of Lewisham, when asked to explain the way in which Thamesmead church life was structured, remarked that he would need a diagram in four dimensions.

Meanwhile, the fault-lines in these structures and the complexities had taken their savage toll on successive pastors, who lived with high degrees of stress and frustration. (The joke is of a Thamesmead 'survivors' support group.) This is not to say that good things hadn't happened. Chris Byers, for example, the then Anglican Team Rector, established a series of distinguished Rainbow Days, in memory of Roland Adams, the black teenager killed in his parish. Hundreds gathered from local schools to celebrate the rich diversity of cultures by that stage pouring into the town. But there were no clear lines of authority, too many chiefs and too few Indians. The Church of the Cross attracted numbers in the teens,

William Temple Church in the twenties, and the United Congregation at St Paul's (Anglican, Methodist and URC) in the thirties and forties. It is hard to say, but (especially at St Paul's, where the complexities were sharpest) there was an ingrained spirit of back-biting and bitterness, frequently spilling over into anger. The United Congregation at St Paul's was pulled apart by the rival demands of simultaneous Eucharists with the Catholics and the need to make room for a Methodist liturgy, both on a monthly basis. It lacked focus and direction. The ecumenical dream had become a logistical and pastoral nightmare.

What has now happened is that some of the structural complexities have been painfully unravelled. The guiding principle has been that each congregation should have its own integrity: its own council, its own money, and its own acknowledged pastor. What is lost are simultaneous Eucharists. These amounted to (usually) the Anglican priest, with his RC colleague, 'mouthing' the Catholic liturgy, at twin communion tables, at one and the same time. It might be argued that these Eucharists merely sharpened the debate between Roman and Reformed theologies of the Eucharist. The shared Mass is to be the fruit of unity realized, whilst the Lord's Supper can be a means towards that noble end. This is especially the case in a climate where the Roman Catholic Church is rather more reticent in these matters than it was thirty years ago. New arrangements, avoiding disruption to the monthly rhythm, are in place to care for Methodist and URC members of St Paul's. It took three hard years to achieve. There is blood on the carpet, but one way and another everyone appears to have found their niche.

All this was necessary to release the energy locked up in wrangling. In a small, parochial imitation of the great Pope John XXIII, it was necessary to open a window and let in some fresh air. It was necessary to make space for new growth. The demography of the town is once again radically changing. In a post-recessional flurry of activity, new houses are being built by the day. Many are bought by young black professional families, who happen to come to church, more than doubling the size of the congregation at St Paul's. There has been no design to grow a black church, but that is in essence what is now given, and it brings its own duties and joys.

It was David Jenkins, a former Bishop of Durham, who famously remarked that the resurrection wasn't just 'a conjuring trick with bones'. Nevertheless, in the resurrection of Jesus there is a radical continuity with what had gone before. He ate fish, and he invited Thomas to touch him (Luke 24.43; John 20.27). At one and the same time, there is an equally radical discontinuity. In His resurrection body, he materialized through locked doors (John 20.26). The Early Church, as we have indicated, struggled to make sense of its Jewish heritage, whilst feeling swamped by hordes of Gentile Christians. In the world-wide Anglican Communion, parent churches are often struggling for survival, while the vast majority of the Church's members are black. We live, if we live at all, with ambiguity.

It is like the child who comes into her parents' bed early in the morning saying, 'make space-room for me'. Growth, even survival, in many of our inner-city parishes hinges on our ability to make space-room for the gifted stranger, who is (in fact) no stranger, but bone of our bone and flesh of our flesh. It is normal to have children and should be normal to welcome people of colour into our church life in the homelands. We are all fearfully and wonderfully made in the likeness and image of the same God, sharing a common baptism, meeting at a common table, settling before the same hearth. The child, precisely, doesn't want to remove her parents from the bed. She simply wants them to make room for her, to create space for her, in the warmth of the bed, or, alternatively, at the fireside or table. The process of welcome, however, rests on a willingness to change, and in that process there lies a critical ambiguity.

In the arrival of a baby, the young couple experiences a radical continuity with what has gone before, but the new arrival radically changes their way of life. So it is when our inner-city parishes welcome the now not-so-new black presence. Change is inevitable and should be counted as normal, but change often brings fear as well as joy. Many young parents fear an inevitable loss of freedom, but still look forward to the birth of their child with inexpressible joy. Babies, unceremoniously dumped into a harsh environment, breathing sharp air, scream. This is the stuff of life and shouldn't cause surprise. Homeland congregations fear loss of identity, and deep within the heart of the black presence in our parishes there is often a silent scream. It is the scream of Lascelles Andersen's mum and Edvard Munch's painting *The Scream*.

What we are actually looking for, however, is the resolution to be found in contemplation of the great Benin bronzes. These bronzes, for those who haven't seen them, have the quality of the *Mona Lisa*, an enigmatic smile, knowing, experienced, at peace. Similarly, in our parishes, through all the changing scenes of life, in trouble and in joy, we seek peace, resolution of conflict, maturity. This is the journey we share, black and white, a journey into the Kingdom of God, lion and lamb at peace, led by the Bethlehem babe.

Each congregation is a cell in the Body of Christ with its own nucleus, substance and boundaries. What follows is a far from exhaustive attempt to highlight some of the essential elements in growing a black church. First and foremost, it is necessary to honour those who have carried the dream thus far. They will often be tired. They will feel threatened. They will resist change. Nevertheless, they will carry a story, the history of that congregation's journey, and it will be shot through with both triumph and tragedy. It has infinite value. At St Boris's in Ardvaark, at one point in their journey, there was a white congregation, an African congregation, and a congregation made up of people from the Caribbean.

This arrangement has its own short-term rationale, but in the end makes no sense. White people should feel welcome at the same banquet as those from Africa and the Caribbean. Africans should examine their prejudices against people from the West Indies, and this cuts both ways. The guiding principle is our essential unity in Christ, the Church's one foundation.

The nucleus of a congregation, however, should 'mirror' its substance. At St Paul's, Thamesmead, the parish priest is a mixed-race, British-born black person. Sunday by Sunday, he is joined at the altar by a sharp, white lawyer, training for ordination, a Nigerian 'professional', offering for ordination, and a Caribbean musician and teacher, training as a lay reader. Black and white women join them at the administration, and children from all races have a high profile at the Peace. In an unstated, visceral kind of way, powerfully, this allows everyone to feel 'at home'. Every person (what they bring of a particular history, origin and culture) is legitimized, without a word being spoken. The Brit-black, white, African and Caribbean nucleus, however, is not simply passive. Eating together, praying together, they are a dynamo, energizing the substance of this particular cell, enabling growth, through their teaching, preaching and prayer, which come from the centre of 'who we are'. Race is rarely mentioned, but 'who we are as a church' is given routine articulation, as a matter of course, in the style of worship, in the concerns that engage attention, and in the very persons of those who form the church's nucleus.

At Holy Trinity, Birchfield, the exceptional person mentioned earlier was Carlton Porter, from Porter's Mountain in Jamaica. Every Friday night, Carlton took his then incumbent to what amounted to a shebeen in Handsworth, teaching him to drink beer and cane rum chasers. They became friends. In growing a black church, it is necessary to recognize and win the trust of seminal individuals. It was Carlton, in fact, who grew the church at Birchfield. He simply told his friends, 'You can trust him. You'll be welcome.' At St Paul's in Thamesmead, there are a number of such seminal individuals: Jedidah Enoch-Onchere, who first suggested the title of this chapter, Akin Sodipo, Milly Rowe, Ralf Sanyalu, and Gertrude Bruce spring to mind. Others are seminal in maintaining a strong white presence. Jeanette Cryer stands out. The point is to recognize and win the trust of those who will grow the church.

At St Paul's, our most precious inherited treasure is to be found in the centrality of the Mass, which gives shape and focus to our liturgical life. The shape of the liturgy, however, is flexible. It can contain all our hopes and dreams, challenges and hurts. It should also contain more dynamic preaching, where we are weak. People long to be fed with the good news that in the blood of Jesus we are saved from the slings and arrows of outrageous fortune. It should be a place in which the charismatic Spirit of Pentecost is unleashed. Visiting a black church in Chicago, there were several hundred doctors and lawyers, a general, teachers, regular folk from the South-side. At one point in the service, they all prayed, collectively, in tongues. Reflecting on this phenomenal experience, the pastor said there was a kind of group therapy going on. People were exorcising the hurts of a week in mainstream America. Certainly, at St Paul's, the Mass is flexible enough to welcome half-an-hour's 'praise worship' before the service begins, with more at the Peace. We are also experimenting with African drums. At Keur Moussa, the French Benedictine House in Senegal, the original, white brothers, including some of the best musicians from their Mother House at Solesmes, taped Wolof and Mandinka village music. They found that some of the modes were exactly the same as those of their historic Gregorian chant. They have now developed a fusion in which the psalms are chanted over the sound of kora, tam-tam, and balafon. At St Paul's, we drum the European rhythms of *Hymns Ancient and Modern*, but these are over-laid and under-girded with a genuine African beat. It will be interesting to see what emerges.

Oak-stroke-mahogany

What is happening is that African mahogany, with its Caribbean and Black British derivatives, is being grafted into the mighty oak of English church life, especially in the parishes. Space does not allow a proper exploration of the implications of this grafting for the wider Church. The Committee on Minority Ethnic Anglican Concerns in the General Synod of the Church of England, various diocesan instruments, targeted training for clergy, the established theological work at The Queen's College in Birmingham, are all important. Useful conduits into the Doctrine Commission, the Liturgical Commission and the Ministry Division of the General Synod might be opened. The Association of Black Clergy soldiers on. Inroads are made into deanery and diocesan synods. What is needed is a determined, focused strategy for the inclusion of 'the black experience' at all levels in the Church's life.

Black people also need to be about our own business. Ivor Smith-Cameron, the spiritual father of the Association of Black Clergy, says that we are against no one but for each other, and that only in specific, domestic ways, designed ultimately to enrich the whole. We need our own hearth and home, a meeting place, a place of fellowship, a thinking, worshipping space, where we can kick off our shoes and get down to being 'us', without expectation of immediate 'results'. Such a desire is not an act of disloyalty. It is based on the hope that our costly, fundamental loyalty to the Church of England is trusted, that 'space-room' to explore and develop our own agendas might be found in the shade of its mighty oakness. Sentamu House might do well as a name, a place to grow our very own English and Anglican Janani Luwum or Martin Luther King.

Blossom

Let us be quite clear where we are. At one level, of course, growing a black church is a contradiction in terms. It is a literary conceit, a polemical device, to gain attention. The Church of Christ the King is universal. It is the Church of Jew and Greek, slave and free, male and female. Some would (and do) argue that it is also the Church of gay and straight people, equally made in the likeness and image of the living God. Certainly, it is the Church of black and white.

At the end of time, there is promised a great Eschatological Banquet, a party in heaven to celebrate God's reign on earth. It will be a grand turn-out. There will be shalwar kamis and cheongsam, Geives and Hawkes' and little Chanel suits, agbada and kanzu, Church's and Jimmy Choo shoes, pink t-shirts, much bling bling and chic South Sea Island grass. We shan't all have been assimilated down into brown uniforms. It won't be a 1930s Nuremburg Rally. It will be a celebration of diversity. The tables will be decorated with roses and hyacinths, orchids and petunias, rhododendron will float in vast crystal goblets, all included, tout compris. French, Urdu, Ga and Mandarin will be spoken, but all will hear in their own tongue the mighty work that God will have accomplished. The universal Church of Christ the King will include it all, and then some.

The point is that we are not quite there yet. There is still much work of redemption to be done. In fact, down to earth, in one small corner of the vineyard, at this precise moment in time, it has been suggested that the very survival of the Church of England, in many of its inner-city parishes, is dependent upon positively welcoming an ineluctable 'black presence', on growing 'black' churches. At the same time, we are faced with the enormous challenge of our young black men and women deserting us in droves, sometimes into Pentecostal churches and sometimes (merely) for money. There is a yawning gap opening between the generations when it comes to matters of faith, worship and values. It is for young black people's sake, as much as any, we need to take the 'black presence' in the Church of England infinitely seriously. It is for their sake we seek to grow black churches, so that their voices might still be heard in the land, blossom (even) in the mighty oak of the Church of England, when we are long dead and gone.

However, the question we must sooner or later face is this: Is the Church of England actually a safe place for black people? Is there an authentic space within its branches, the parishes, for strong and confident black people, or will it only and forever receive the other as a victim, a client or a token, and therefore, in many places, rightly and inevitably die?

It seems a pity to end on such an obviously commonplace question, although we began with another such commonplace. Nevertheless, it serves to illustrate the inescapable dynamic implicit in this chapter.

Assimilation sucks. Inclusion is all, all are in fact to be included, but all must find their own unique voice, if the end is to be healthy. Getting it right once means getting it right, for young people, for black people, for women, for men, for the whole darn shebang.

Further reading

Fryer, Peter, *Staying Power*, Pluto Press, London, 1984.
Fanon, Frantz, *Black Skin, White Masks*, Pluto Press, London, 1986.
Fanon, Frantz, *The Wretched of the Earth*, Penguin, Harmondsworth, 1967.

6. The Classic Car

Ecumenism in the Parish

CHRISTINE BAINBRIDGE

What kind of vehicle are you? This is a question which I have often asked as Archdeaconry Ecumenical Advisor when faced with a Local Ecumenical Partnership (LEP) which I have been asked to help to review. The answer is often enlightening. What often emerges is the view that the LEP is like a classic car: a cherished inheritance, difficult to maintain, and not necessarily appropriate to the roads on which it now has to run.

In this chapter I draw on some of my experience in the advisor role, and also on my experience as a parish priest, to review the kinds of ecumenical activity that have emerged during the past forty years, to ask what is emerging now, and to ask in what direction we might now be travelling.

One of my first assignments in 1999 as a new ecumenical adviser was to visit Thamesmead: a new town started in the late 1960s and still expanding. The Thamesmead LEP (the Thamesmead Christian Community: TCC) was established in 1977 between the Church of England, the United Reformed Church (URC), the Roman Catholic Church and the Methodist Church. The Anglicans and Roman Catholics own one building each, and there are two buildings under legal Sharing Agreements; one shared between the Anglicans, Methodists and URC (the Church of the Cross) and the other (St Paul's) shared by all four. A significant feature of worship in the latter was the regular simultaneous celebration of the Eucharist by the Roman Catholics and Anglicans.

The TCC was a pioneering initiative at a time when there were high hopes for closer institutional links between the main denominations. It seemed particularly appropriate to establish an ecumenical church from the outset in areas of new housing like Thamesmead, where the LEP was regarded as something of an ecumenical beacon and people establishing LEPs in other new housing areas came to look at what Thamesmead Christians were doing and were excited by what they saw. People in Thamesmead still treasure the excitement generated during those early years as different denominations did together things which they had never done together before.

Since the 1960s, change has been by slow evolution: for instance, the 'Team' at the heart of the partnership became wider than the clergy representing the formally constituted LEP as more churches arrived and wanted to work together. But still the simultaneous Eucharists, the different denominational liturgies on different Sundays of the month, and the complex management arrangements survived: arrangements which forty years before had been intended as interim arrangements pending the greater unity of the Church for which many Christians then hoped. Increasingly, the individual denominations were making their own demands, a group of Thamesmead Christians who had been there at the beginning of the partnership were frustrated by the apparent lack of understanding and support from their respective denominations for their ecumenical project, and the emotional energy required to manage the complex management arrangements was becoming unsustainable. The classic car was experiencing some difficulty in getting over new terrain.

A recent period of rather faster evolution has led to a very different situation. At St Paul's, the Sunday simultaneous Eucharists have ceased, and there is a single pastor (an Anglican) for the Anglican, Methodist and URC congregation; and for that congregation Sunday worship is Anglican rite, with a Methodist preacher once a month. At the Church of the Cross, the pastor of the Anglican, Methodist and URC congregation is a Methodist minister, and Methodist liturgy is used. In West Thamesmead, where large amounts of new housing are being built, a new church-plant initiative is taking place. Management structures have been simplified; congregations are growing; and the areas of significant ecumenical growth are a 'Churches Together' with a very broad membership, a partnership of churches at work in the Thamesmead and Abbey Wood community, and new relationships between black-led churches and traditional denominations. Some in Thamesmead believe that these new relationships between the traditional denominations and the new black-led Pentecostal churches are the most significant and the most exciting ecumenical relationships of our time, and they might be right. In structural terms, the end result in Thamesmead is likely to be separate single congregation LEPs, a united initiative in West Thamesmead, possibly two covenanted groups of churches, and a Churches Together in Thamesmead which will include as many different churches as want to participate.

The evolution of the Thamesmead LEP over the years has not taken place in a vacuum. Developments there reflect changes in the wider church and on the ecumenical scene nationally and internationally. As with most projects involving buildings, the original vision for an ecumenical church in Thamesmead predates bricks and mortar by some years. The vision emerged from the real possibility of visible organic unity between denominations. The Anglicans and Methodists seemed to be moving towards a joint church. The Presbyterians and Congregationalists were already uniting to form the URC. The Second Vatican Council breathed a new spirit of openness into the Roman Catholic Church. The time seemed ripe for pioneering experiments. The Thamesmead project was seen as a trail-blazer, a sign to the Church of the way forward. Unfortunately, organic unity between the Methodists and Anglicans did not materialize and the Roman Catholic Church did little more than nibble occasionally in more ecumenical pastures. Each denomination struggled to relate structurally to the Thamesmead ecumenical experiment, causing the LEP to become more protective about its organization than it might otherwise have been.

In South-East London as a whole there are many parishes where significant regeneration is taking place. New town-houses and whole-lifestyle blocks of flats designed for single professionals are going up in areas traditionally seen as deprived. The Church finds itself ministering to a different context. It is faced with change. There are a number of ways in which organizations may react to change. One is to be protective about their way of operating and keep going in the same way. Another is for individuals to launch pre-emptive, innovative strikes into the new territory whilst base-camp remains the same. A third is to acknowledge the difficulties represented by the changes and to talk with others both within and outside the organization about how best to respond. All these approaches can be seen in Thamesmead and it is to the Thamesmead Christian Community's credit that they have undertaken the challenging task of working with others to address the situation. The original reason for an ecumenical church in Thamesmead was to enable mission to be carried out more effectively. With the new structures in place the church there is able to continue its faithfulness to that vision.

Another major change facing all churches is a context that may be loosely described as post-Christendom. There is no longer any clarity about the place and function of churches in society. They are often seen as a somewhat puzzling relic from the past. Government and local authorities group them together with followers of other religions as 'faith communities'. There seem to be fewer people wanting to give long-term, loyal service to the institutional Church. The numbers of those attending church weekly has declined. Outsiders make no distinction between different denominations. They simply see 'Church'.

One pragmatic denominational response to fewer people in church is to rationalize church buildings. It can be a waste of resources to run two half-empty buildings near each other if one will suffice. In the 1980s a joint Methodist/URC congregation and Christ Church

Anglican church in East Greenwich decided to join together in the Anglican building. They entered a formal Sharing Agreement and in partnership with others transformed the premises into a centre for people with disabilities as well as a place of worship. Christchurch Forum sent out powerful signals about how the Church understands its mission. In this case the transformed building conveyed a commitment to a particular group of people, an openness to change and a willingness to work in partnership. This church is a flagship of a different kind. It is often held up by Greenwich Council as a creative example of local authority and church co-operation. The council is probably unaware that there is also a partnership here between different denominations.

This particular ecumenical venture has encountered many problems. When the main founder of the enterprise moved on the structures he had set up proved difficult to work with. He had been the one holding together all the different threads, many of them in his head, rather than in a place accessible to others. The community project developed in numbers and management capacity, giving it more power than the two small congregations. The Anglican congregation found itself in disagreement with the centre management committee over the use of its worship area by groups outside the church. The two congregations discovered that they had different understandings of Church. For the URC/Methodist group the nature of the worship space was relatively unimportant. 'Church' was the group of people who gathered in the space. For the Anglicans the worship area represented sacred space and was to be treated accordingly. The hallowed feel of the space enabled 'Church' to happen. The relationship between the two congregations deteriorated as did that between the Anglican congregation and the management committee of the whole centre.

Without realising it the two congregations were engaged in the challenge facing the whole Church. How do we define ourselves in a post-Christian society where our meaning and purpose may no longer make sense? The Methodist/URC congregational response was to draw little or no distinction between themselves and other groups in the centre and to play an active role in its management. The Anglican congregation, meanwhile, drew an ever sharper line and gradually directed its mission focus to those in the immediate neighbourhood outside the building. The two groups were unable to draw on the insights of each other.

A reassertion by the Diocese of Southwark of its ownership of the building has now altered the balance of power in favour of the Anglicans, an approach that was not favourably viewed by the URC which had invested a considerable sum in the initial conversion of the building. However, with the Anglicans feeling more comfortable in their building they may be able to develop fresh ways of working with both the Forum management committee and their ecumenical partners. New staff will soon be entering the situation and they too may be a catalyst for change.

Meanwhile, in another corner of the parish, on the Greenwich Peninsula, the largest single development since World War Two is beginning to take shape. What is being adopted here is a multi-faith approach, with the faith communities providing a single chaplaincy service, but one where people can receive help from the tradition of their choice. The different faith groups are in dialogue with each other, but they worship separately. The Peninsula represents a new phase in ecumenical ways of working, moving beyond denominational barriers to co-operation with those of other faiths. By taking pluralism seriously the Church has been able to work with secular partners. It has, however, managed to retain its own identity and define a clear role for the Church in a new context. It may well be setting the pattern for Church involvement in similar situations elsewhere.

The traditional ecumenical model of enabling several churches of different denominations to converge in an LEP seems to result in too much energy being absorbed internally. Perhaps local groupings of churches together work better. My last parish was part of Churches Together in Lee which includes Methodist, URC and Roman Catholic churches. They take part in traditional ecumenical activities such as a Good Friday procession of witness and exchange of pulpits during the week of prayer for Christian unity. On the whole such events are supported by the same group of people and it is a struggle to sustain the committee that organizes them. However, they also run Lee Oasis, a flourishing project that helps homeless people and asylum seekers with furniture and clothes. They are able to raise funds for this project from the Council as well as member churches. The furniture project is an effective means of involving some men in a church activity. On the whole those running Lee Oasis are a group of older people and there are strong bonds of friendship between them. It has to be said that there is more energy for Lee Oasis than for the other activities of the Churches Together. The difference is between doing ecumenical things (such as worshipping in member churches during the Week of Prayer for Christian Unity) and working ecumenically for a specific reason, as with Lee Oasis. A local survey had uncovered a lack of provision for homeless people and the only way for churches to meet it was to work together. This kind of ecumenism does not involve any structural changes to the participating churches and its purpose is easily understood by those outside. However, perhaps it is not an either/or situation, because this initiative might not have taken place without the solid foundation of good relationships built up over many years of doing ecumenical things.

Where Churches Together have been going for a number of years they too face the question of how to adapt to changes in context. The biggest challenge for many in inner London during the last 30 years is the growth of independent churches and so called 'new churches'. There are now large numbers of predominantly African churches in South-East London. They are a vital part of the ecumenical scene but are not able as yet to participate in existing ways of doing things. They do not belong to traditional ecumenical groupings. Churches Together and clergy fraternals regularly talk about how to include black-led churches without much actually happening. In Lee a West African church that worships in the local URC now attends meetings after being encouraged by the URC minister. The house church, Ichthus, approached CT in Lee itself and has become a member. Gradually the membership of Churches Together may change, but more through circumstance than by design.

In fact the most likely way in which newer, independent churches may be able to engage with the main denominations is through a phenomenon well known to churches with space to share. It can be something of a surprise to Anglican churches to discover that their biggest ecumenical challenge lies within their building. Like the URC in Lee, many Anglican churches let out space in their church building to another congregation, often one that is predominantly African. This situation is so common that Churches Together in England has produced guidelines on how to handle the relationship between the host and guest church.[1] The most usual role for the host church to adopt is that of landlord and the Churches Together in England (CTE) paper responds to some of the difficulties inherent in this kind of unequal relationship. However, it also makes a plea for trying to get alongside a congregation that may be from a different tradition and often from a different part of the world. Here is a unique opportunity for mutual learning. At St Peter's church in Lee an Afro-Caribbean church worships in the building. Both congregations are small and the two women ministers occasionally meet for prayer and mutual support. When the Anglican church joined with others to run a children's summer holiday club the guest church took part as well by providing one of the leaders. Children associated with both churches attended the club. At the Copleston Church in Peckham (joint Anglican/URC) the New Testament Church of God uses the building. Over a number of years the two churches have developed a pattern of leading worship together on Maundy Thursday when they take part in foot washing and on New Year's Eve for a Watchnight service. In Blackheath the Vicar of St John's meets regularly with the pastor in charge of the New Wine Church. This congregation worships not in his church but in a former cinema. New Wine is one of the biggest, black-led independent churches in the area. From time to time groups from both churches meet for prayer. The two ministers have also spoken together at an annual lecture held at St John's.

At a recent meeting of Churches Together in South London, the Revd Jacky Bowers, ecumenical officer for the Methodist Church, entitled her talk 'Let's get rid of ecumenism!' In the year that the Anglican and Methodist churches agreed to a covenant as part of a process leading to full union in the future, she expressed concern that the traditional way of doing ecumenism does not sit well with a post-modern context where relationships, networking, experience and belonging are valued more highly than tradition and denominational allegiance; and flexible, time-limited egalitarian structures seem to work better than fixed, hierarchical ones. On the whole, churches are not interested in working towards the traditional ecumenical goal of visible unity. It was certainly difficult to generate interest in the proposed covenant in local parishes unless there was already a link with a Methodist church. For Jacky, the new goal needs to be one of 'expressing the unity we already have in Christ as much as possible, for as many churches as possible, for the sake of mission. The new model needs to be based on unity in diversity, to be local, flexible, and founded on relationships rather than structures. It is a network model.' In an ecumenical network of churches a wide range of churches can be involved. A church is not either 'in' or 'out' (as in a traditional Churches Together) but can participate in the network of activities as much or as little as they like. Whilst being glad about the covenant, she hopes that 'both denominations agree to save the energy involved in any further unity moves and direct it instead towards multilateral working together for the sake of mission in the world'.

A CTE report on their 2003 biennial conference for member churches notes that the words which kept occurring in workshops and discussions were 'complementarity', 'hospitality', 'creativity', 'relationships', and 'urgency'. These convey more fluid ways of working than constitutions and covenants. The report comments that the 'old paradigm of structural unity is clearly not working. We need a new paradigm of vision, mission and relationship.'

On the larger, ecumenical front, the World Council of Churches (WCC) has been confronting similar issues. In his farewell address to the Central Committee of the WCC in 2003, the retiring General Secretary, the Revd Dr Konrad Raiser, spoke about the 'need for a new configuration of the ecumenical movement for the Twenty-first century'. In 2002 the WCC faced a serious financial crisis, leading it to reflect on its inherited pattern of organization. It is also trying to make sense of its constitutional mandate to 'further and maintain the coherence of the one ecumenical movement in its diverse manifestations'[2] in a context of rapid globalization. Dr Raiser lists the problems facing the ecumenical movement as follows: 'shortage of funds, increase of bilateralism, growing competition between UN agencies and the NGO community, and defensiveness of governments over against the influence of civil society organizations on the shaping of a new international order'. He notes that: 'Generally there is a trend to respond to the challenges by way of pragmatic organisational and structural changes, hoping to increase "relevance" by adopting "looser, lighter and more flexible structures".' For a Christian organization, however, a pragmatic approach is not enough. It has to formulate a vision and that vision may well be in conflict with the values of globalization. In the WCC the vision that is emerging is one of holding an 'ecumenical space' for participating churches. This space is one where

> trust can be built; where churches can test and develop their readings of the world, their own social practice, and their liturgical and doctrinal traditions while facing each other and deepening their encounter with each other; where they will create networks for advocacy and diaconal services and make their material resources available to each other; where they can continue through dialogue to break down the barriers that prevent them from recognizing each other.[3]

Interestingly, this definition of its vision came out of the deliberations over the participation of the Orthodox Church in the WCC. The WCC constitution, just like constitutions of a small LEP or a local Churches Together, did not allow for easy entry of a Christian group wanting to join. As a result, mission was being hindered.

The notion of ecumenical space conveys the same open and inclusive feel as the words in use at the CTE 2003 conference. It suggests a conciliar model of open participation rather than one depending on institutional membership. While affirming membership of core churches, as it were, it facilitates partnership in mission with a whole range of other Christian groups and agencies. It is very different from the model of the classic car with which I began this chapter. While holding on to the commitment expressed in joint, covenanted ways of being together ecumenically, churches might also look for those spaces where they can work together in a variety of partnerships according to the task in hand. It is such networks of shared activity which will be the ecumenical method for the foreseeable future.

No longer a classic car. More like the different vehicles on a building-site: the crane, the bulldozer, the dumper truck, the lorry – working together to build God's Kingdom.

Further reading

Sharers, Guests, or Tenants? Churches Together in England, London, 2001.

Notes

1 *Sharers, Guests, or Tenants?* Churches Together in England, 2001.
2 World Council of Churches constitution, Article 3.
3 Interim Report of the Special Commission on Orthodox Participation in the World Council of Churches, paragraph 8.4, World Council of Churches Central Committee, document GS4, 2001.

7. Transforming Work

The Parish and the Workplace

JOHN PAXTON

'My church has never prayed for me and my work. In fact, I don't think the Vicar has ever preached about work. He probably doesn't even know what I do.' Unfortunately, this comment is heard frequently by industrial chaplains and others as they ask people about their faith and how it meets their working lives. Why is this so? What can be done?

This chapter will attempt to point to answers, by presenting some case-studies of parishes where the world of work is taken seriously and Christian people are encouraged to make connections between faith, economics and work.

What do we mean by 'work'? Although widely used, 'work' is often misunderstood. Work is more than paid employment. It encompasses voluntary and community activities and work, usually unrecognized and undervalued, done within the home in caring for families. Work is best defined as 'purposeful activity', but recognizing that one person's hard toil might be another person's sport or hobby. How does the Church engage with all this purposeful activity? The Church is good at using volunteers, and millions of person-hours are spent in the community on behalf of the gospel. The Church supports families, particularly when families face difficulties. How can the parish church get to grips with the 25 million people who are employed across the country?

'Work' has been a regular topic for theological debate. The Old Testament pictures work as both creative and as drudgery, as fulfilling and redemptive, as a form of service as well as an opportunity to exploit others. Work is one way of gaining the necessities of life, but also a means of wasting the earth's resources and an expression of greed.

The Roman Catholic Church gives work a high status in human affairs. The Catholic Bishops' Conference of England and Wales has published a statement *The Common Good*, which includes:

Work is more than a way of making a living: it is a vocation, a participation in God's creative activity. Work increases the common good. The creation of wealth by productive action is blessed by God and praised by the Church, as both a right and a duty. When properly organised and respectful of the humanity of the worker, it is also a source of fulfilment and satisfaction. At best workers should love the work they do . . . human work was the primary means whereby humanity was to co-operate with and continue the work of the Creator, by responding to God's invitation to 'subdue the earth'.[1]

The Church of England is, in at least one respect, very privileged. We are everywhere – with people, staff, buildings and resources serving the population of the country in whatever ways seem appropriate. We have more access to institutional life than any other faith community, partly for historical reasons as the established Church, but also because we can more often than others give time to meet representatives of community and national agencies – government, education, leisure and business. We are expected to contribute to Local Strategic Partnerships, community initiatives and working parties because of our experience and expertise. This is a golden opportunity which we reject at our peril.

Everyone in England lives in a parish. A parish is a defined area of land, with a boundary and neighbours. But of course, it is much more than that. It is a presence in a place, symbolized by a building for worship, with a group of committed Christians, led by an ordained minister. The parish in its small way demonstrates the incarnational nature of God, present in the world in Christ. Each worshipping, loving, serving congregation represents, in a local manifestation, his Body. As Christ prayed, taught, served, offered himself, healed, listened, laughed and cried, so the parish church is in the midst of its community, striving to minister in God's name, following the redeeming example of Christ.

When people grew up, toiled and died in the same parish in which they were born (or near enough), the parish was an important factor in their lives. People knew the church building, the priest and the other members of the congregation. With the advent of the Industrial Revolution and the mass movement of labourers seeking employment in the new factories, so the old home-parish was left behind. It is true that the Church rapidly built new parish churches in the cities to provide spiritual, moral and pastoral support, but for many the connection had been broken. The growth of the railways meant that workers could travel further to their jobs, and at work there was no link with the local parish church. The Church of England remained primarily a church for the residents in the area, not a church for those who earned their bread within its boundaries.

As the twentieth century progressed, so that trend continued. People commuted, often for several hours a day; global companies forced their staff to be out of the country for long periods, not least over Sundays; and the new wealth enabled families to enjoy pursuits away from their homes. Residents of parishes, whether rural, sub-urban, or urban, lost touch with their parish church, and the parish church failed to follow its people. Gradually, the connection between the life of worship and service and the daily activity of commerce, industry and trade was broken. Industrial Mission was a belated attempt to keep the link alive, but the Church generally has chosen to ignore the world of work and economics.

Can the connection be reforged? From my perspective, the following stories illustrate some ways in which parish churches have kept the link alive and offer ways forward.

Some parish stories

In 1981 I was appointed Industrial Chaplain in Bolton as a member of the Greater Manchester Industrial Mission, attached to Bolton Parish Church. This was a pioneer post, part of the strategy of expanding this well-established team into the northern mill towns.

St Peter's, Bolton-le-Moors is a large cathedral-like building, with a tower that dominates the town centre, of equal height to the cupola of the Town Hall. Two buildings, complementing or competing against each other – symbols of faith and government in a changing urban environment.

I began to investigate the best place to start workplace chaplaincy. One Sunday, after preaching at the daughter church, Holy Trinity, a member of the congregation introduced herself to me. Dorothy was the USDAW shop steward in the Bolton office of one of the major mail-order companies, based in Manchester. After chatting, she invited me to meet her for a guided tour of the office, so that I could get a picture of a modern mail-order business. At the end of the visit, the manager responded positively to a formal request from me to start regular visiting in his office, among his 300 staff.

I have learned that it is impossible to predict how a chaplaincy relationship will start or develop. From a small parish communion service an interesting and at times difficult chaplaincy grew. Besides offering pastoral support to a workforce which went through some very tough structural changes, I had the opportunity to challenge some traditional understandings of the balance between people and profit. The company was extremely successful in a decade of economic decline, but keeping the human dimension in sight was a challenge at every turn. This relationship between a major local employer and the parish church lasted for nearly nine years.

The 1980s were stressful times for the north-west of England. Unemployment, particularly among school-leavers, was high. Through St Peter's, I was introduced to the General Secretary of Bolton YMCA. We saw the possibility of using some of the increasingly redundant space in his building to provide facilities that might answer the needs of some of the long-term unemployed people in the town. Using funds from the Manpower Services Commission, we employed staff to run individually designed training programmes for unemployed people with some of the severest learning and social difficulties. That four-year partnership demonstrated how a parish church and members of a Christian organization could collaborate to tackle one of the most difficult social problems of the time.

Team Ministry in the Church of England has had a mixed press over the years. Some teams have found difficulty in establishing a vision and a role, while others have collapsed because of relationship or practical problems. Thankfully, however, some teams have thrived and set out on innovative paths of mission, exploring new ways of being the Church in an evolving urban setting. The Southampton City Centre Team Ministry is an example of the latter.

As the population of the city centre moved out, the Church found itself looking after too many worship centres. The bold decision was made to close several, leaving two, St Mary's and St Michael's, but preserving seven ministerial posts, providing a focus for Christian work amongst the remaining residents in the city centre, but also amongst the institutional life of education, local government and commerce. One of the team vicar posts was set aside for an industrial chaplain, sharing ministry with the members of the South Hampshire Industrial Mission. This was the dual-role post I took up in 1991. Although the details of the arrangement have altered, there is still a working relationship between the two teams.

The congregations and the Parochial Church Council were continually aware of the connections between worship, pastoral care and those aspects of city life with which the sector ministers were engaged. All the team ministers, lay and ordained, were expected to worship every Sunday in one of the two churches, sharing in celebrating and preaching as required. A pattern of team worship and meetings ensured that all aspects of the team's work were reviewed and supported. Although the role of the industrial chaplain altered as the city changed, strong links have existed for many years with the retail trade, either as chaplaincy to some of the local stores, or by contributing to debates about Sunday trading, the minimum wage and future shopping developments around the city centre. As economic regeneration grew in significance in the early 1990s, so the chaplain became one of the representatives of the Church in public debates about how best to spend the huge government funds made available to some of the most deprived communities.

This was a model that had a great deal of potential. A group of experienced ministers, working as a team, but with distinct responsibilities, worshipping with people committed to the city, meant that many positive relationships grew. The Local Authority came to see the City Centre Team as partners in a number of city-wide activities. And there lay a problem. The City Centre Parish was seen by some neighbouring parishes as too well resourced, drawing into itself stipends which some felt were unjustified. Personal relationships were good, but occasionally the structure creaked.

However, adjoining urban parishes elsewhere in the country could well look at the Southampton experiment to learn about the focused use of people with expertise working in those fields which influence the lives of residents in our urban areas.

In 1996, I moved again, to the centre of London, to be Senior Chaplain of the South London Industrial Mission and Rector of Christ Church, Southwark. Christ Church is a church which grew with the spread of the city and adapted as the city changed around it. The first building was constructed in 1670, through the generosity of a local businessman, John Marshall, and of the Lord of the Manor of Paris Garden, William Angell, responding to the needs of the rapidly expanding population flooding over the Thames to the 'garden suburb' of Southwark. That building sank into the Lambeth Marsh, but the trustees of the Marshall's Charity erected a much larger church, this time on firmer foundations, which lasted for 200 years. Wartime bombing led to the construction of the third Christ Church in 1959 as both a parish church and an industrial mission centre, formally opened by the Duke of Edinburgh on 24 February 1960.

To demonstrate the focus of this church's mission, the 1959 windows at first-floor level were designed to represent scenes of work, both contemporary and historical. A picture of a master baker is set opposite a woman caring for her children as they play on the grass outside the old fishermen's cottages in North Southwark. An open-plan office (without a computer in sight) is balanced by a window depicting the old Bankside Power Station, now refurbished as the Tate Modern Gallery. In 1984, to mark the twenty-fifth anniversary of the opening of the church, more windows were installed at ground-floor level, picking up some of the themes of working life – trade unions, family businesses, a banking computer centre, a major retail company (the only church window I know which shows a supermarket trolley), and a mosaic picture linking the biblical themes of creation, jubilee, ecumenicity and humanity.[2]

On the east wall, behind the altar, there hangs a huge canvas sheet depicting Wall Street in New York, the heart of the business district. In the middle of this panorama, a large cross has been hung. The symbolism of the cross in the middle of the world of work, of trade and business, of multi-storey offices full of people, speaks volumes. The altar frontal was made by unemployed people in 1984. It depicts the world of people, factories and offices and the ecumenical ship symbol, side by side at the focal point of the house of God.

The bread is broken and the wine outpoured at the place where the world and the cross meet. At the end of the Eucharist as we pray 'Send us out in the power of your Spirit, to live and work to your praise and glory,' the people are already looking at God's world of work, already making connections between their experience inside the parish church and the activity of the commercial offices in Blackfriars Road. Day by day, worshippers and visitors to Christ Church are praying, praising and opening themselves to God in word and sacrament in a context of commerce, industry, creative effort and human relations.

The thinking behind this multi-purpose building was both radical and forward-looking. Industrial Mission had started at Southwark Cathedral during World War Two with the deployment of pastors to the employees of large and small businesses along the Thames. Thus the South London Industrial Mission (SLIM) was established. A network of chaplains and so-called 'key men' grew, organizing meetings, training events and Bible studies, all designed to help men working in predominantly heavy industry to see that the Christian faith does speak to the world of work. Christ Church in Blackfriars Road, half a mile from the cathedral and 300 yards from the River Thames, was the perfect place for the focus of this rapidly developing mission activity. The Revd Alan Weaver was Rector, but he was keen to build relationships with the chaplains, and to open the building to all-comers – trade union meetings, company training sessions, faith and work groups, theological debates and major conferences. On his retirement in 1967, and with the coincidental leaving of the Revd Robert Gibson, the SLIM Senior Chaplain, the Revd Peter Challen was appointed to be both Rector and Senior Chaplain.

The strength of the links between the parish church congregation and the members of SLIM have ebbed and flowed over the years. Chaplains have regularly preached at Christ Church, and been involved in parish activities; church members have attended SLIM events. The congregation welcomed this special dimension to their local ministry, and accepted the particular responsibility to remember working people in the prayers. SLIM has seen Christ Church as its base, and shares in the cost of employing the administrative and support staff with the Parochial Church Council and Marshall's Charity.

The Church's engagement with the world of work in North Southwark has taken two forms:

1. Chaplaincy to companies within the parish boundaries, offering pastoral care to all the employees and a prophetic ministry to the company as an organization. This means building relationships with people, listening to what is going on, and trying to engage in conversations about the values underlying the company. Questions might be raised about stakeholder relations, decision-making processes, the management of change, or people's perceptions about the meaning of the work they do. These are theological discussions, but usually in non-religious language. Concepts like service, relationships, trust, power, creativity, reconciliation and stewardship open channels into both theology and commercial life. The chaplains can help people to explore what faith in its widest sense means in their context, and to make connections between what is important to them and the work they are doing. The last two rectors and a succession of curates of Christ Church have been charged to lead this aspect of the parish church congregation's mission within the parish boundaries.

2. Involvement with the economic issues that impinge on the life of the residents of North Southwark. As the area has changed, so the Church has tried to stand alongside, to support and encourage its neighbours. Since World War Two, housing has been replaced by commercial buildings, and major companies have set up their offices. Shops have been squeezed out, and community facilities have been allowed to decline. In the current draft *Southwark Plan*, the whole area is to be designated as primarily for business use, as a strategy to ensure that sufficient modern office buildings are available to encourage companies to locate in the borough and so provide employment opportunities. Parallel to this, the parish, part of Bankside within London South Central, is experiencing a huge economic and social regeneration programme. The Tate Modern Gallery, the Millennium Bridge, the River Walkway and the Jubilee Line tube station have dramatically changed the atmosphere. Millions of international tourists come through the parish every year and three hotels have opened in the last four years. All of this has altered the residents' lives beyond all recognition. Christ Church tries to help residents to understand these economic changes, it provides a community focal point, and it encourages people to participate wherever possible in the decision-making processes which affect their lives.

This is parish ministry, working out the church's understanding of God's continuing creative process, seeking to bring transformation and redemption, and opening itself to the enlightening power of God's Spirit in the specific geographical area.

Just downstream from Christ Church and in London Diocese is the parish of All Hallows by the Tower. As you walk around the outside of All Hallows Church, the contrast between ancient and modern is clear for all to see. To one side are the gaunt solid walls of the Tower of London, and across the Thames is the glass 'headlamp' of the new City Hall. Traffic and tube trains thunder by, and across the road stone and concrete monolithic buildings jostle each other. Beneath them, a neat sward of grass encircles the Merchant Navy and Fishing Fleet war memorial. This is the parish of All Hallows. With little residential community, the church meets the needs of three groups of people:

- those who come to this church because of its style of worship and its musical tradition
- visitors and tourists
- the business community.

The building is a place of quiet, a space in a busy day. The clergy and staff are available for people who wish to talk. In a nearby building the parish runs the Wren Clinic, providing a ministry of healing and wholeness for a considerable number of people in the City who are often working under enormous stress. Currently, the Clinic is trying to provide counselling and medical support on a contractual basis to local companies.

The Business Houses Association, formed in 1978 by All Hallows, provides a place of friendship and exchange of views in a relaxed atmosphere over lunch, usually with a speaker from business, education or the arts. The Association is a member of the Pool of London Partnership, a private–public regeneration agency established in 1995. This provides an entry point for the Church into the delivery of training and educational programmes in the local area. Finally, the Association sponsors exhibitions and arts events to help provide a balanced and lively quality of life on and around Tower Hill.

All Hallows has close links with churches in New York, Philadelphia and Cyprus and the Gulf. City companies often have staff working in these areas, and the church can provide contacts and support as required. In September 2001, when the World Trade Center was destroyed, All Hallows offered help to the London-based company which lost 600 colleagues in New York that day. The church believes that these international church links are important and could lead to deeper collaboration around common business and ethical issues. David Driscoll, the Associate Vicar, emphasizes the overseas dimension 'in a Church of England that is increasingly parochial'.

All Hallows is the spiritual home of four livery companies, and shares a sunday school with the children of the staff living and working in the Tower of London. It runs a successful programme for local schools, to which City companies supply mentors and literacy assistants.

If all that is not enough, the church hosts approximately 20 carol services each year, which David acknowledges is an extension of the old folk religion, but which helps people make connections between their faith and their workplace. In a parish letter in February 2003, David wrote,

> At a time when so many churches appear to be withdrawing into themselves and increasingly prescriptive about what ought to be believed and practised by their congregations, it is vitally important that there are churches like All Hallows which look outward and encourage people to ask questions. I hope we can provide a home for those who are seekers and still tentative about their faith, and that it is possible to take risks and not be frowned upon! I am sure that many who feel unchurched would find All Hallows to be just the place they are looking for! We need to let them know we are here and would receive a warm welcome.

The active engagement of a parish with its local economic life is a mark of the mission of St Andrew's, South Wimbledon. St Andrew's is a residential parish with only six places of work – local shops. The Revd Andrew Wakefield was appointed priest-in-charge and industrial chaplain in the London Borough of Merton in February 1991. Andrew sees his role as one of priestly ministry to and with the economic life of the borough, and, at the same time, as one aspect of the public face of the Church in the borough. He attends civic events and meetings with the Local Authority, the Race Equality Partnership Board and the Faith Leaders meeting with local councillors.

His theological foundation for this engagement is incarnational and trinitarian – God creates all things, therefore the Church needs to be involved in all things. As Jesus served the people outside the religious structures of his day, so the Church must be outside its buildings. The Holy Spirit vibrates through all things, including the workplace. This, Andrew argues, is a traditional model – moving out of the church to help people: and so he moves out to offer interest in and knowledge of the world of work. 'Proclamation by presence as well as by gift', he states with enthusiasm.

In 1996, Andrew set out along a path which has proved productive and fulfilling. He started attending the monthly networking lunches organized by the Merton Chamber of Commerce. This is a group of mainly medium-sized and small companies, but also includes voluntary organizations in the borough. At the same time, the Government-sponsored Training and Enterprise Councils (TECs) were being established across the country, and Andrew volunteered to join the Special Needs and Equal Opportunities taskforce of the Merton TEC. He brought a pastoral concern for people with disadvantages, plus experience of developing policies and strategies designed to offer the best chances in employment. After two years, Andrew was elected to membership of the TEC Board, the first cleric to hold such a position, and he used that position to become and more involved with local businesses, normally through visiting them as he helped to monitor equal opportunities practices. In 1997, Andrew was elected to the Merton Chamber of Commerce Board, and by accepting invitations and being able to volunteer his time, quickly became involved in a wide range of business issues in the borough. In 1999, Andrew was elected Chair of the Chamber, a post he still holds.

Andrew sees this engagement as part of his priestly role, growing out of his parochial home, 'standing between' the working world of Merton and the Church. Andrew believes that all industrial chaplains should be based in a local church, part of the ministry of word and sacrament, a situation that is becoming more common as church resources are reduced. He attends all meetings wearing a clerical collar. Regular attenders at St Andrew's know of this activity and support it. Andrew is a traditional parish priest in the evenings and at weekends when the congregation members are at home, and undertakes the world of work part of his parish ministry during the week. He believes he is fulfilling the bishop's instructions given to him in 1991 to keep the church and work aspects of his ministry in balance.

The final case study takes us to Chelmsford Diocese. Overshadowed by the Queen Elizabeth II Bridge on the banks of the River Thames, the parish of Averley and Purfleet is a mixed residential and industrial area, whose future will be dominated by the development of the Thames Gateway regeneration programmes and the Channel Tunnel Rail Link.

In February 2001, The Revd Angela Overton-Benge was licensed to the dual-role post of curate of the parish and industrial chaplain in Purfleet. After surveying the industrial life of the parish, Angela wrote to local companies offering her services. This generated no response, so she started knocking on doors, particularly those of smaller companies and transport agencies. They expressed a great deal of surprise, but she was warmly welcomed. One of the proprietors, a Christian, said, after getting over the shock, 'In all the years I have been to church, you are the first person who has ever asked about my business or even cared.' Angela spent two years building up the relationship, which eventually led to her being able to offer pastoral help when the business hit hard times.

After meeting a retired docks chaplain who provided an introduction to the Purfleet Terminal, Angela started regular visiting. After a year, she reports that one of the drivers stopped her and said, 'We don't say much, but we really like you coming. We know that you care what happens here and about us.'

Outside the workplace, but because of her increasing knowledge of the local commercial world, Angela and a colleague established the Purfleet Community Council, part of a response to the Government's directive to local authorities to set up Local Strategic Partnerships. The Council has been operating for a year, and has spent £10,000 on community projects. Angela was surprised at how keen both private and public sector bodies were to have the Church involved in the organization, and how much she was able to feed back into the local church.

As the local parish priest, Angela is able to provide pastoral care to people in their places of work, and at the same time help people in and outside the Church to make connections between their faith, the business world, and community development initiatives. She reports, 'I understand the work of the Church is about seeking God's justice in a situation and endeavouring to discover ways it can be realised. It is helping people find a voice that might bring a determination to their futures.'

The next stage in this expression of the parish's mission is to set up lay teams to widen the scope of industrial visiting. 'It is', she says, 'the work of the whole Church, not just a chosen few.'[3]

Conclusions and wider application

What does the workplace and the economic order say to parishes about our faith, and how does our faith help us to understand the world of work, which is one of the major factors in our lives as individuals, communities and societies? How should a parish church minister to people who are employed or working in the home or in the community or who are beneficiaries of other people's work?

Christopher Baker of the William Temple Foundation helpfully analyses the conceptual gap between how churches see their identity and role within new suburban communities, and the experience of the communities themselves.[4] The churches are operating, he suggests, on the model of the Church as a gathered identifiable social and spiritual entity at the heart of a stable and boundaried community. This attitude is based on a theology of rootedness and lived space which believes that people will come to the Church. He continues, 'Only now is the realisation dawning that the churches need to reinvent who they are without losing their spiritual integrity; to move from being churches of place to be more like churches of flow; flowing to where the people are moving to in their health clubs and shopping malls and themed city centres.' He concludes that churches must take account of the many different life roles, and work and leisure patterns, which people are now engaged in. The churches therefore need, he argues, to be flexible and network-based. Baker proposes that all sections of the community – business, statutory and voluntary – pool knowledge and expertise in the cause of a common resolution to society's problems. Many churches, of course, have been following this course for some time, and local authorities and companies are waking up to the benefits of this partnership approach, but there is still room for improvement.

The William Temple Foundation is one place where strategic thinking is going on. The Industrial Mission Association is a forum where practitioners try to support each other, share good practice and promote the gospel mission in the world of work. Working independently, and sometimes without knowledge of each other, are a number of church organizations which see the economy as the focus of their ministry. Approximately 20 such groups exist in London, but their work is hampered by lack of communication. Most industrial missions are ecumenical by constitution, working with denominational structures as best they can, and across diocesan boundaries where necessary. This is a model for the future as resources become restricted, and where flexibility is required.

What else can churches do? God is creative by nature. How does the Church support the discipleship of lay people who are making things, building community, improving people's health and creating a just society in the course of their daily lives? First, the Church must recognize and validate this activity, and so begin to understand what is happening. Only then can we support at times of trouble, crisis or uncertainty, and, conversely, can we celebrate achievement, progress and milestones reached. Through our theological processes we can link our faith beliefs and values to the work being done, and so lead to gentle questioning of assumptions, policies, processes and practices.

The Church has opportunities to minister to the networks in which people operate, recognizing the multi-focused lives that people lead. For large cities and towns this must mean the Church exploring its mission with commuters, people whose daily employment is topped and tailed by hours of travel time. Instead of a parish putting unfair pressure on its members at weekends, ministers could be leading explorations of the links between employment, travel, home church and city church. Where are the partnerships between suburban and commuter parish churches on the one hand, and town centre and Monday-to-Friday churches on the other? Can they talk to each other? Is there scope for collaborative study and mission activities, all designed to break down the barrier that exists between 'my job' and 'my church life'. How often do suburban clergy visit the congregation's members in their office, shop or factory?

In many areas, parish boundaries are irrelevant, and reflect an earlier age. Churches can work in partnership with neighbouring parishes on agreed topics, such as low pay, work/life balance, redundancy, or a local issue affecting people in several parishes, for example, the controversial development of a factory which might have a significant environmental impact.

In some dioceses, we are witnessing the rapid expansion of the use of parish church representatives, lay and ordained, as chaplains of local companies – for a few hours a fortnight, walking the floors, listening, learning, understanding, asking questions, responding to enquiries and challenges, laughing, loving God's people, and building God's Kingdom in that place. Then, those experiences can be brought into the weekly worship through intercessions, sermons, hymns and activities. The expertise gained can be used to illustrate study groups and Bible studies.

Changes in the economy affect us all, but in different ways. Where major regeneration projects are taking place, do parishes co-operate to improve the quality of life of residents and local employees? Churches must listen to residents and developers, pool information, speak with one voice, plan as partners, and offer resources into a common fund. Where parish churches have built connections with the world of work as part of their mission strategy, the gospel is proclaimed, the community is served and society is being transformed.

Further reading

Rogerson, John W. (ed.), *Industrial Mission in a Changing World*, Sheffield Academic Press, Sheffield, 1996.

Green, Mark, *Supporting Christians at Work*, Administry and LICC, St Albans, 2001.

Notes

1 Catholic Bishops' Conference of England and Wales, *The Common Good and the Catholic Church's Social Teaching*, London, 1996.

2 Christ Church, Southwark, *Windows on the World of Work*, 1985. (Available from Christ Church, 27 Blackfriars Road, London, SE1 8NY. Website: www.christchurchsouthwark.org.uk.)

3 Quotations in this section are from Overton-Benge, Angela, 'Does Industrial Mission Have a Prophetic Voice for the Church?' Unpublished MA thesis, 2003.

4 Baker, Christopher, *Religious Faith in the Exurban Community*, Occasional Paper No. 30, William Temple Foundation, Manchester, 2003.

8. Spiritual Seductions and Spiritual Sustenance

Discovering God's Spirit at Work in the Parish

MIKE HARRISON

'What I need to know vicar, is that my father is in heaven right now, just as we are here right now!' Words spoken to me on a post-funeral visit in the parish a while back. What was I to say? Well, there was the truth of the infinite mercy of God, the truth of resurrection, of the dead held by a God outside of time who was timelessly present to us in time . . . and so on. But no, such pointers were not enough – what was required was the assertion that this woman's father was indeed enjoying the feasting of the Kingdom – 'right now'. I didn't feel I could assent in the cut-and-dried way required, and left feeling that perhaps I had not done my job properly – I certainly hadn't met her need as expressed and anything else I said was so much straw to her. Would it have been so wrong to allow her the solace of believing that which would genuinely bring her comfort? – a bit like those gravestones that proclaim happily and easily: 'together again'?

The life of a priest in the parish is peppered with such situations and our responses can easily go unexamined as we rush on unreflectively to more immediately pressing concerns. And yet our responses can build patterns of speaking and acting which I want to suggest can prevent rather than foster spiritual growth, our own and that of others. And reflecting more deeply on our responses and the motivations behind them can perhaps illuminate more clearly some of the spiritual seductions that are ever-present in parochial life, seductions that can be transformed through awareness into quite different possibilities. It is with such issues as these that the present chapter is concerned.

In relation to the pressure to provide the words sought by the bereaved daughter mentioned above, I am reminded of a story about the Indian sage Krishnamurti.[1] In 1948, a widow of Bombay who had grieved the loss of her husband for some years decided to visit Krishnamurti to see if he might help her. Her daughter went with her.

The daughter was aware that many sorrowful people had visited Krishnamurti and she assumed he would know the words with which to comfort her mother. In fact Krishnamurti spoke in a quite unexpected way to her mother: 'I am sorry, Madam. You have come to the wrong man. I cannot give you the comfort you seek.' The visitors were bewildered. 'You want me to tell you that you will meet your husband after death, but which husband do you want to meet? The man who married you, the man who was with you when you were young, the man who died, or the man he would have been today, had he lived?' The widow protested, 'My husband would not change.' Krishnamurti replied, 'Why do you want to meet him? What you miss is not your husband, but the memory of your husband.' Throughout, Krishnamurti spoke slowly, allowing words to sink deep. 'Forgive me Madam,' he said. 'Why do you keep his memory alive? Why do you want to recreate him in your mind? Why do you try to live in sorrow and continue with the sorrow?' Surprisingly, despite Krishnamurti's shattering refusal to be kind in the accepted sense, the mother was not alienated. Disturbed certainly, and yet despite the words sounding harsh there was a gentleness in his eyes and gestures which communicated authentic compassion. In fact such was his impact that the daughter later became a follower of his and subsequently became his biographer.

Krishnamurti's approach is rooted in an understanding of the sorrow of bereavement as the mind's objection to being left empty, alone and without support. His suggestion is that instead of reacting to that emptiness by trying to fill it in some way, we should just live with it, 'without any reaction, without rationalizing it, without running away from it to mediums, to the theory of reincarnation, and all that stupid nonsense – to live with it with your whole being. And if you go into it step-by-step you will find that there is an ending to sorrow.' Intriguing as Krishnamurti's approach is, its analytical way of proceeding is not modelled by Jesus who, upon realising that his friend Lazarus had died, showed extreme grief (see John 11.33–38). The original Greek suggests that he wept and wept, that he heaved and convulsed with sorrow, such was the gut-wrenching pain of being torn from a beloved friend by death. Being left empty hurts!

But what I do find deeply challenging about Krishnamurti's approach are two things. First is his refusal to give any room to *platitudinous* words of reassurance and comfort, a refusal rooted not in disregard or coldness, but in a tenacious yet gentle pursuit of truth, a truth that he felt would set people free. Within the life of a parish priest the temptations to platitudinous reassurance are many. I began this chapter with one. And to go down that route seems to me dangerous, not because of a single instance where pastoral sensitivity eclipses theological integrity, but because of the habits it subtly develops. These are habits which are looking primarily to *use* the gospel of Jesus Christ in the (intentionally worthy) service of providing solace and support, rather than finding in the gospel sources of solace, support and much else besides. And too easily the same can happen with our notion of priesthood, such a ministry becoming merely a tool to provide comfort and reassurance rather than an iconic ministry which bespeaks Christ's presence – a presence inclusive of comfort and reassurance but with much else besides. In short the danger is good old-fashioned idolatry, being seduced by the idol of the caring pastor who always provides the words people want to hear in ways that bring immediate relief. Wherever we got such an image of ministry from, it was not the Jesus Christ of the gospel.

And the second challenge Krishnamurti presents is related to the first, a certain detachment from concern about how he might appear, a freedom from anxieties about promoting his ministerial status. The Christian tradition has stories which echo such detachment, which are sometimes more extreme. For example, a story from the lives of the Desert Fathers tells of a woman suffering from cancer of the breast who went in search of one of them, Abba Longinus by name, who had the reputation of a saint and healer. She came across him collecting firewood but not knowing who he was, enquired of him where she might find Abba Longinus. Longinus said, 'Why are you looking for that old fraud. Don't go to see him, he'll only do you harm. What's the matter?' She told him, whereupon he gave her his blessing and sent her on her way saying, 'God will surely make you whole again. Longinus would have been no good to you at all.' So the woman went away, confident in the faith that she would be healed, which she was within a month – and she died many years later, quite unaware that Longinus had healed her. So the story goes. Abba Longinus shows a remarkable hostility to concerns with self-promotion, and even as he demonstrates his holiness in healing the woman, he sullies his own reputation to weed out any self-promotion that might be taking root in the soil of his good actions. The question that arises from the example of Krishnamurti and the story of Abba Longinus is: How far is what we are doing motivated by the temptation merely to promote our own 'good' name and how far is it rooted in our gospel convictions?

Of course, there are times when our gospel convictions lead to service which will happen to promote our reputation in particular ways. A careful preparation of a couple for marriage which involves valuing the couple in all their particularity can help convey both something of the priest's concern and something of how the couple's particularity is treasured and rejoiced in by the God whose blessing the couple seek in marrying. So this kind of ministry illuminates both something of God's love for the couple and the priest's pastoral concern for them. But one doesn't have to trawl too deeply in one's ministerial experience to come up with examples where there is not such a neat overlap. Working in a parochial setting which provides open access and which seeks to embody Jesus' radical inclusivity means bringing people of great diversity together who will not always get on harmoniously, be it clergy or laity. And when conflict occurs, the clergy will not always be able to intervene in ways that bring reconciliation, healing and growth, given that frequently the conflict is in part a consequence of established intransigence and inflexibility. Facing the tensions can seem a daunting prospect, but perhaps less so if we have already begun to loosen our white-knuckled grip on our good name.

Detachment of this kind can help us to see the tyranny of plainly erroneous ideas surrounding conflicts in churches, such as the notion that conflict implies poor pastoring, weak discipleship and a loveless fellowship. And what perhaps can sustain us at such a time is recognizing that the way we go about engaging with difficulties matters as much as the facing of such difficulties. Simply to mirror the anger, bitterness or stubbornness when addressing conflicts is like putting out a fire with gasoline, and what seems crucial is that the Christian integrity which led to addressing an issue is not undermined by the style of addressing the issue. Surprising support can be realised in stormy times in the awareness of knowing that one is attempting to keep faithful to the course that led one into the storm in the first place.

Along with the temptations of comfort for comfort's sake and pre-occupation with one's 'good name', temptations around conflict abound. A common one is to bury one's head in the sand, but that will mean not only losing sight of conflicts but also missing possibilities for transfiguration. Take an example. A cold January night, 10.30 p.m. and the Parochial Church Council meeting had just finished – the longest I had chaired as a vicar and probably the least enjoyable. 'Why?' I pondered afterwards, 'What was it about that meeting that made it so long and drawn-out, with such an irritable and irritating atmosphere?' The agenda of the meeting was not especially contentious. Individual members of the PCC were not particularly argumentative or belligerent, far from it in fact, but somehow the evening had steered a course which led to tetchiness, impatience, misunderstandings and a lack of mutual sympathy.

Forget it? Hope it'll be better next time? Well, conversations over the next few days made it clear that I was not alone in feeling ill-at-ease with the dynamics that had developed during the meeting and so I decided against burying my head and visited a few of the PCC members who had made contributions that night. The question for me wasn't 'Who's to blame for this?', often a destructive question in any case, but rather 'How can we better work together as Christians?'

And it seemed especially useful to ask that question, not in some abstract and general way but in the specific context of how we conduct ourselves at PCC meetings. And asking that question of others with any degree of integrity meant also asking it of myself, in the presence of others. There were a number of helpful suggestions in terms of chairing the meeting. We also took on board some standard recommendations from the literature such as ensuring appropriate and level seating arrangements, and it was constructive to lose a large table behind which sat certain august officials.

But what was perhaps most significant in our reflections was the sense in which we felt that somehow, once the PCC meeting had started, we adopted pretty secularized, business-like and managerial personas in order to 'get things done' and 'be professional and responsible'. These personas seemed to contribute to rather abrupt and blunt handling of one another. And beginning and ending the meeting with prayer didn't so much undermine this habit as collude with it, this structure of prayer suggesting to some the feeling, 'Right, we'll start by putting God to one side and we'll end by bringing God back into the picture.' One of the most helpful changes we made to our structure was to ensure that we had a time of quiet prayer about half-way through our agenda. This time of 30–60 seconds was given over specifically to remembering that we are brothers and sisters in Christ and have time to reflect personally on how we might best conduct ourselves here and now to bear witness to this common faith. It also became clear that one of the key challenges for us (and indeed for any of our church groups) was how to handle conflict in a way that did not alienate one another or create division but that was focused on the issues at hand. What we needed to develop was a way of discussing which trusted that those with whom we disagreed were not simply being awkward, obstructive or argumentative, but were those with whom we shared a deep bond, a deep faith commitment, and who happened to see things differently on a particular issue. It sounds obvious, but putting it into practice was and remains far from straightforward!

There are deeper issues here. So much of our life as a parish church can be compartmentalized. We do our worship in church services; we do our discipleship in Bible studies, in cell groups or Christian basics courses; we do our management and business in PCCs, and so on. Such a compartmentalization is spiritually impoverishing when, surely, shot through all that we do as individuals and as groups within the Church there needs to be a readiness and alertness to how we can embody our faith. Put a different way, how can I practise the presence of God in this meeting, or how can I witness to Christ in this situation? In short the issue seems to be all about cultivating mindfulness. If the spiritual seduction is burying one's head in the sand, the

spiritual sustenance can stem from open-eyed alertness, a mindfulness that is not only awareness of what we are doing, but is also
awareness of the way we are going about it, not just where conflict is
concerned but more generally in our relationships with one another,
in the quality of our listening, in our manner of communicating, and
so on.

Of course, even such mindfulness can itself be seductive rather
than sustaining, as we begin to take a pride in our own particular way
of being mindful and half-critically become aware that others are not
mindful in the way that we might be. To give an example, a member
of the congregation pointed out to me once the very different style
that the then curate had to myself when celebrating the Eucharist,
particularly when we were just sat there, behind the altar. She noted
how the curate was alert to everything going on around him, wide-
eyed and engaged with the immediate world in which the liturgy was
unfolding. In contrast I tended to be almost oblivious to what was
going on, with my eyes half-closed – whatever the sermon was like! I
am reminded of the contrast made between the Christian mystic and
the Buddhist, the Christian mystic looking wildly outwards, wide-
eyed, scouring the horizon for the One who promises to come to us in
and through the world, while the Buddhist's eyes narrow, as the way
is pursued through inward attentiveness. Of course the contrast is a
caricature of both Buddhism and Christianity, but what is helpful
about the analogy is that it suggests that both ways are about attentiveness, and that ways of cultivating our attentiveness, internal and
external, lie somewhere near the heart of our spiritual discipleship.
Discussing this with the curate I realised that my danger lay in
dismissing concerns about outward liturgical detail as 'irrelevant
trivia' compared with the significance of inner vigilance during the
Eucharist. The curate's danger lay in dismissing a 'self-absorption'
which enabled a worshipful focusing and concentration of the heart
and mind.

The recommendations of mindfulness and attentiveness I am suggesting don't come easily and never have done. When I was young we
went to church as a family, a fact I took for granted until my early
teens, when I began to find church more and more painfully dull.
Time would go agonizingly slowly during church services, so slowly
in fact that I spent what seemed like an eternity gazing at the church
ceiling, and what seemed an age staring trance-like at other objects
like pews or the pulpit. And I was reminded of these experiences
recently when I read what the Roman Catholic theologian James
Alison had to say about worship. He suggested that when people tell
him they find Mass boring, he wanted to say to them that it is
supposed to be boring,[2] that it is a long-term education in becoming
unexcited, that only such an education will enable us to dwell in a

quiet bliss which doesn't abstract us from our present or our surroundings or our neighbour, but which increases our attention, our
presence and our appreciation for what is around us. And as I look
back I don't feel now that the time I spent staring at the church ceiling
was wasted at all, painfully empty though it seemed at the time.
Something was happening, however obscurely.

Alison contrasts the slow and arduous sharpening of our awareness and attentiveness which true worship is about with the intoxicating excitement of the Nuremburg rally style of worship, worship
which is not about challenging our desires, prejudices and perceptions but which is rather about their uncritical satisfaction. Now I am
not suggesting by all of this that our aim in Christian worship and
discipleship should be maximum tedium and dullness, but that
actually there is no getting round the work that needs to be done in
cultivating our attentiveness, work that by its very nature will for
most of the time *not* be about intoxicating highs. And our readiness to
engage with that sort of work is in part indicated by our willingness to
live with space in the diary, with uneventfulness and ordinariness,
instead of being tempted to inject personal spiritual melodrama, pressurizing engagements or exciting distractions into the situation –
indeed, to recognize the present possibilities of God whatever our
present is. This has some echoes with Zen Buddhism's suggestion that
whatever we are doing, be it sweeping the church-hall floor, preaching, or attending a deanery synod, it is not preparation for something
else, it is practice. As Shunryu Suzuki put it:

> The Bodhisattva's way is called 'the single-minded way', or 'one
> railway track thousands of miles long'. The railway track is always
> the same. If it were to become wider or narrower it would be
> disastrous. Wherever you go, the railway track is always the same.
> That is the Boddhisattva's way. So even if the sun were to rise from
> the west, the Boddhisattva has only one way. His way is in each
> moment to express his nature and his sincerity.[3]

In terms of spiritual sustenance it should also be stressed that cultivating our attentiveness can be revelatory in effect. Writing to a blind
colleague, the philosopher Bryan Magee suggested that the difference
between what the blind miss and what the sighted miss is almost as
nothing compared with what we all miss.[4] What do we miss? Well, I
was rather struck by how it is that in the past 30 years of exposure to
Christian worship I have rather missed the lit candles. It was a lecture
by the producer of Shakespearean plays Peter Brook which flagged
this up for me, a lecture on 'The Quality of Mercy' he gave at the
Temenos Academy in London in 1993. Just before such lectures there
is a tradition that a candle is lit, and Peter Brook commented by way

of introduction that once the candle was lit, there was really nothing much more to say. If we could sit and watch, feel and understand this extraordinary miracle, words would be superfluous. Brook's relating of this to the flame that is the 'quality' of mercy in Shakespeare need not detain us, but is it not true that we barter the gold of this miracle (and others) for the mess of pottage which is something supposedly 'new', 'different' and 'unfamiliar'? And in our greedy search for such pottage we continue to overlook ever-present treasure. So cultivating our attention can be about revelation *and* enrichment.

Part of the problem is, of course, that we are trained to look in ways that reduce what is seen merely to ideas and concepts that become *pre*conceptions moulding what we see. Krishnamurti suggested that the day you teach a child the name of a bird the child will never see the bird again. By that he was perhaps suggesting that initially a child sees a strange object which is alive, feathery and moving, a source of fascination and interest. If the child learns to label the bird as a sparrow then the next day when they see another such object we may find that they have been educated to say 'Sparrow. Got that. I've seen sparrows, I'm bored with sparrows.'[5] Surely this is pertinent to Christians whose faith challenges us to see in surprising ways: for instance, to see in a crucified Jew from 2,000 years ago a man some-how identifiable with the Divine, worthy of worship, or to see in the cross an emblem of worship, to see not just failure or humiliation but also beauty and love. Must we not attend to the way in which we are seeing? For what we see is anything but a neutral, objective act. And the same goes for those within our congregation and parish whom we are enjoined to love. One of the stumbling-blocks to such loving is precisely that way of looking which diminishes the other person in our eyes, a way of looking based on a negative past experience, con-versation or reputation. Look, here comes silly Sue, clever Trevor or Metropolitan Mike. Seeing in that way we will of course find that we see what we are looking for, but we will have been seduced by our loveless diminishment of our neighbour, not noticing that which is changing, that which needs encouraging, that which is lovely, that indeed which can instruct us and strengthen us spiritually.

In relation to this, a year or so ago I was called out late in the evening to the intensive treatment unit at a local hospital, to pray with the family at the bedside of a man who had just a few hours to live. After spending some time there I went over to the nurse to tell him I was leaving, and as I did so I noticed out of the corner of my eye another patient who, when I looked, seemed to be beckoning to me. I say beckoning to me, but she was in such a condition that she was quite unable to lift much more than a finger. When I went over to her I asked if she wanted me to pray for her and she nodded, so I did. I'll call her Margaret – and she lay there helpless, most of her arms and legs uncovered except for various tubes. It could have been a scene which you might have thought was undignified, embarrassing, shameful even. But it was none of these things. In that moment of prayer it looked quite different. In fact the artificial light of the treatment unit falling on Margaret's skin gave it the hue of a new-born baby, so much so that it brought home to me with some force that here on this bed lay not some rapidly failing human organism, but an entirely and unutterably loveable child of God. It also brought home to me how rarely I look in this way. When people come forward to receive Jesus in the bread and the wine at the altar the priest does not sort people into sheep and goats, there is no refusing on the basis of not liking the look of someone. Those who hold out their hands receive. Can we take away with us from the altar that way of looking at one another? A way of looking which sees people (including ourselves) not in terms of degrees of goodness, but as children, children who need to be strengthened, children who need God's help, in the Eucharist and in everyday life, but children who are also unutterably beautiful, unutterably loved?

Reflection on the way we regard one another has wider implications. As a church, both parochially and more broadly, surely we must seek to promote recognition of each other within the Body of Christ, a face-to-face recognition of one another in truth and love. Without it we stand to lose ourselves before the false depictions and diminishments which demonize one another, assuming the worst, reading each other suspiciously, distrustfully and cynically. Such a way empties our relationships of any possibility of realising the Spirit's presence. To give another example from personal experience: In the year I was born the *Sunday Mirror* was still running two-page spreads with titles like 'How to spot a Homo' suggesting that shifty glances and an inordinate love of the theatre were dead-giveaways. I grew up embracing such prejudices and hostility. When I was in my late teens and early twenties I had no time for homosexuals at all. I quoted bits of scripture which neatly condemned all gays and gave the matter little further thought, comfortably oblivious to other ways of reading scripture. I had never consciously known a gay person face-to-face. In my early twenties I found myself being drawn to the Church. And there were two priests in South-East London who were utterly formative of my priestly ministry, by their self-sacrificial example, their preaching and their Christ-like care. The Spirit's presence was obvious to me in both of them. Only later did I discover that each was gay, one celibate and one not. How easily I could have missed God's Holy Spirit, given my readiness to misrecognize and dismiss these priestly vehicles of God's Spirit.

And I am not alone in this parish in having earlier views challenged by later experience. My predecessor at Holy Trinity Church, Eltham was Jeffrey John, who served as vicar from 1991 to 1997. Fr Jeffrey was one whose teaching and preaching convinced many – I know because people have borne witness to it and because I have seen the fruits of his ministry here, growing the church in depth as well as in numbers. He is one by whom many have been enabled to recognize God's presence. That for me indicates a bearer of the Holy Spirit. But there are many who would look at Fr Jeffrey otherwise. His views on homosexuality, for example the view that stable and faithful same-sex relationships should be affirmed by the Church rather than casti-gated, have made him a veritable demon for some. Following his appointment as the Bishop of Reading in May 2003 he publicly stated that he would abide by the Church's present teaching, but that, it seems, was not enough. He was regarded by many as a symbol of all that is rotten within the liberal wing of the Church of England. Evidence to back up this opinion was hungrily sought, and for a time his house was under 24-hour surveillance by journalists, while past articles were picked through with a fine-tooth comb, and he was quoted and seriously misquoted in some national broadsheets. Eventually the pressure put on his appointment proved too great and he stepped (or was stepped?) down.

We at Holy Trinity are in something of a unique position with all of this, for many of us have known Fr Jeffrey personally and have seen in him a person with outstanding gifts to offer the Church. The revelations about Fr Jeffrey in the national media were news to some parishioners, but what has been astonishing to me has been the recog-nition of those who experienced his ministry here, whatever their position on 'the gay issue', that he bore profound witness to the Spirit's gifts and presence. When Rowan Williams addressed the bishops of the Anglican Communion in 2000 he asked the following stark question: 'Are we really prepared to say that we Christians, who are united by our common baptism in the three-fold name of the Trinity, agreed on the authority of scripture on matters of doctrine, agreed on the creeds of the Church and on bishops' ministry, are we really saying that we are not recognizable to each other as members of the Body of Christ when we differ on matters of sexual ethics?'[6] At that time the bishops felt that it would take more than disagreement over homosexuality to bring them to a point where they could not recognize one another in the Body of Christ. And, as Ben Quash points out,[7] what was vital about the bishops coming to this mind was that it was face-to-face dialogue. They were able to see through some of the misrecognitions and the misrepresentations that were being fostered by a media whose lifeblood is conflict and disagreement, and instead were listening face-to-face to one another, acknowledging localized tensions and problems and simultaneously recognizing brothers and sisters in Christ struggling to embody Christ in the world. This was a hopeful sign, but whether this spirit of recognition will flourish or wither remains uncertain at the present time.

One of the Anglican Church's glories has always been its willingness to hold within itself a breadth of opinion and co-ordinated diversity which at its best bespeaks a humility, tolerance and openness which invite the possibility of not only recognizing that the Holy Spirit is at work in people quite unlike ourselves but which also invites us to learn from that presence. The piecemeal reflections that go to make up this chapter are an attempt to embody such an ethos, looking within and beyond the bounds of Anglicanism to those whose insightfulness can help us in our recognition of the Spirit's presence and looking for ways in which we might become more alive to our blocking or embracing of that presence in the parochial setting. If we want to fall foul of the spiritual seduction of blocking the Holy Spirit, of denying God's presence, it is easy. We could, for example, substitute cold comfort for change, burn a pinch of incense at the altar of one's good name, and avoid noticing conflict at all costs. And we could continue by misrecognizing and misrepresenting the bearers of the Holy Spirit around us as aliens and foreigners, by failing to acknowledge each other lovingly, and by failing to see in one another anything that one has not seen before. Better still, combine some of these seductions and demonize or dismiss one another, elevating oneself simply by doing down one another. But if we are looking to be sustained by the Holy Spirit, to embrace the Holy Spirit, then we might do better to be recognizers, able to sit sufficiently loose to our precious self-images to be able to recognize that grace-ful reality which is seen not least in and through the seeming difficulties and dullness of our days. Thus we might become face-to-face loving recognizers of one another as bearers of the Spirit, able not only to see God in one another but also able thereby to reveal God to one another too.

Further reading

Alison, James, *Faith Beyond Resentment*, Darton, Longman & Todd, London, 2001.

de Mello, Anthony, *Awareness*, Collins, London, 1990.

Suzuki, Shunryu, *Zen Mind, Beginner's Mind*, Weatherhill, New York, 1970.

Ward, Benedicta (tr.), *The Sayings of the Desert Fathers*, Mowbray, London, 1975.

Notes

1 Jayakar, Pupil, *J. Krishnamurti: A Biography*, Penguin, London, 1996, pp. 1–3.

2 Alison, James, 'Worship in a Violent World', unpublished talk for the Ceiliuradh, Christ Church Cathedral, Dublin, June 2003.

3 Suzuki, Shunryu, *Zen Mind, Beginner's Mind*, Weatherhill, New York, 1970, p. 54.

4 Magee, Bryan, and Martin Milligan, *Sight Unseen*, Phoenix, London, 1998, p. 37.

5 de Mello, Anthony, *Awareness*, Collins, London, 1990, p. 121.

6 Quash, Ben, 'The Vocation of Presence and Anglicanism', in *A Questioning Authority: The Anglican Witness to the World*, Third Millennium 5: The Journal of Affirming Catholicism, 2002, p. 64.

7 Quash, 'Vocation', p. 74.

9. Art and the Sacred Space

Art and Architecture in the Parish

NICHOLAS CRANFIELD

Churches are preserved so long as people like them, even if they don't like them much (John Betjeman).[1]

Sacred definition

Well away from the tide of the Thames and the pursuit of the Third Millennium, this chapter opens on the mountains of mainland Greece. For across much of Greece, and elsewhere, both in its islands and in Turkey, one comes across small chapels, often quite remote, on hilltops. More shrine than meeting place for large numbers of worshippers, these distinctive places are quite commonly dedicated to Ag. Profetas Elias – Elijah, the Prophet.

This strikes the visitor from the Western Latin tradition as strange. Few of our churches have dedications to any of the 'Old Testament' patriarchs and prophets. And why Elijah? Often a clue is to be found in the archaeological rubble at the sites: re-used columns from pagan temples and shrines show that the place had originally honoured Apollo. And where better to do that than in a high place at which the rising sun is visible? The association of Elijah with Apollo becomes obvious when we recall Elijah's departure from earth in a fiery chariot (2 Kings 2.11).

It is not, of course, only in the ancient Greek world that Christianity overlaid and then changed pre-existent beliefs. In some cases this may have been a subtle spiritual shift while in others it was as the result of deliberate attempts to Christianize a site, as at the famed Necromandeon on the west coast of Greece where a much later church sits oddly atop the reputed labyrinthine hell mouth. Elsewhere there seems to have never been such luck. Worshippers of the mystery cults of Eleusis continued into the nineteenth century and when the cult statue of Demeter was stolen from there in 1801 by Professor E. D. Clarke from Cambridge University the devotees of the cult foretold the wreck of his ship; the ship duly ran aground off Beachy Head but the statue is still in the Fitzwilliam Museum in Cambridge. No church was ever built on the house of mysteries.[2]

At Ephesus, long after St Paul had preached there, the known world's largest temple was raised, to the Egyptian god Serapis. In Rome the existing twelfth-century basilica of S Clemente is built on the site of an earlier, fourth-century church; beneath that lies a Mithraeum. Mithraism was one of the last of the oriental mystery cults to reach the West and it was only in AD 307, under Diocletian, that the god Mithra, popular in the Roman Army as the unconquered Sun (*Sol invictus*), was heralded as 'protector of the Empire'. In central London, yards from the church of St Stephen Walbrook, an early Mithraic temple was uncovered after Second World War bombing.

In the heart of Thessaloniki, north of the ancient Roman *agora* (market place), there was a complex of public baths where, according to one account, St Demetrius was first imprisoned and later martyred, under the emperor Diocletian. The basilica that was raised over the site (fifth century) was seized by the Muslim Turks in 1493. Although they converted the church into a mosque (*Kasmiye Camii*) they left Christians a corner of the Roman baths in which to worship undisturbed at the shrine of St Demetrius. After the 1912 liberation of Greece the mosque was restored to Christian worship. The Muslim tradition of tolerance and generosity has not been matched by subsequent Christian use of the building.

Unless we think naively that the coming of Christ and the early mission of the Apostolic Church led to a massive or immediate shift in beliefs, this much is obvious. The emperor Constantine's proclamation of the Edict of Milan (AD 314) and the adoption of Christianity as the official religion of the Empire, while marking the end of the Age of the Martyrs, did not lead to mass conversions or to enforced Christianity overnight and no doubt in remoter places traditions remained in parallel for many decades.

Such examples that we have begun with suggest something about the importance of the sacredness of a site, and often of a building, that lies beyond its use by any one specific religious group. This should be borne in mind when we consider our own church buildings, their function and their purpose. For even in Britain, on the fringe of the known Roman Hellenistic world of Jesus' own lifetime, there are clear examples of churches raised over earlier cult buildings, whether Roman or Celtic. If the traditional orientation eastward of so many churches is such that the priest and people face Jerusalem, we too should recall where the sun rises.

Church building today

Part of the importance of churches in the life of the parish today is simply that they are places that are holy, sacred in the eyes of many, as well as public houses of prayer. This does not necessarily make them the only holy sites within a community (not least for the Christian perception that the true heart of faith and the most holy place is to be found in the Body of Christ, the people, and not the building). It does, however, suggest that for many, believer and unbeliever alike, the physical structure of the church is a sign of sacredness. The church therefore becomes, both theologically and pastorally, a meeting place.

Any active church will want to meet the demands made on it by a regular core who come to worship as well as those who attend occasionally and those who are casual visitors whose own desire and reasons for being present may be known to them, or may not. Those appetites may not all be fed in the same way or nurtured with the same expectation. There may be no clear way of meeting all the demands, and we should remember that it is not only the architectural historian who might decry what has happened inside some of our own buildings in the cause of accommodating liturgical reform. There is also the broader question of the likely need to provide meeting rooms, dedicated access, kitchens etc.

My opening emphasis on the sacredness of space may at first seem at odds with our own experiences in a post-industrial Britain in which even the 'God of concrete, God of steel, God of piston, God of wheel' now seems to be outmoded by new technologies and the service industries and in which conceptual art threatens to outwit the minds of diocesan chancellors. But the sacred remains a core element in the demands of the pilgrim people of God for a place in which to order their lives.[3]

Nor in making this emphasis do I distance myself from more recent church buildings, or from churches built in new communities, although not all are successful. Such buildings have always been the bedrock and first foundations of church life. As the Roman *titulus*, the house where a Christian lived which became the focus for a small meeting of Christians, only later became a church building, so many church communities only later built recognizable (and often architecturally distinct) places for worship. To this day the Society of Friends retains a strong sense of this in using the very name 'meeting place' for their place of worship.

An anecdote about the famous Airforce Academy Chapel in Colorado is instructive. It is a fine structure whose architectural shape viewed along the east/west axis looks like the fingers entwined of many praying hands. When it was completed there were no paths leading to it across the military campus. When quizzed about this the architect, Walter Netsch, later made the point that he had deliberately waited a couple of years before laying paths in the tracks and footprints that had gradually worn away the soil at various points.

While that is not uncommon for track-laying (a vigorous policy of extending the infrastructure of roads in England, Wales and Scotland in the past forty years has only now begun to erode the links between main highways and older drove roads and the like) it is also somehow true of churches. Leaving aside the example of Christ the Cornerstone, in Milton Keynes, where a new ecumenical church was planned as part of a new urban development, it would almost be better to leave new communities to find their own theological and spiritual meeting places before building them into solid structures.

The distinctiveness of God

But if we take that as a given, what kind of buildings, and what kind of art are needed now to proclaim a place sacred to the God of our Lord and Saviour Jesus Christ? A preliminary answer must in part be about distinction, or 'distinguishing features' in the language of our Passport Office. It is perhaps only the survival of so many ancient buildings across these islands that leads us to anticipate tower and steeple norms for designating a church. Even the Ordnance Survey marks distinguish between them.

But that is a characteristic of our landscape that would not be as visible in Scandinavia or in parts of Germany, for instance. In England, in particular, it may owe more to the unusual prevalence of surviving rural mediaeval buildings and the fanaticism of Victorian revivalists, or to the expansion of the Empire in an age of classical building that then 'exported' such designs to the colonies, than to any theological, spiritual or sacral purpose. How can we make distinctive the place in which, Sunday by Sunday, day by day, priest and people join together at the very entrance gates to heaven?

When Augustus Pugin's friend Bishop Willson was appointed to be Bishop of Van Dieman's Land, as Tasmania was still known in 1843, both men were concerned, in Bishop Willson's words, 'to introduce the proper church style in this distant land . . . with a variety of things which I hope will tend & promote God's glory'. We may smile or scoff at the idea of pattern books, vestments, models of churches of the most simple form, and even head-stones for graves being sent out to transplant English Gothic into the unlikely field of convict hearts thirteen thousand miles away, but we should not as readily dismiss the conviction that the church building is itself a *signum Dei*.[4]

Are we now to carry on building distinctively or should our buildings mirror and reflect the existing architecture of the communities in which they are settled? Which is to ask, in another sense, How is the face of God revealed in our day? Does this need to be limited in any way to a Christian context? At St Hugh's, Bermondsey, there are five paintings by the artist Adam Boulter which were commissioned in 1998 and dedicated in the year of Jubilee. They use images drawn from five of the major faith traditions, reflecting multicultural life at the end of the Second Millennium in Bermondsey.

The churches and religious buildings of South-East London, like many in similar industrialized and urban landscapes, show many signs of the changes of the past 150 years. There are, of course, many ancient foundations and there are still scenes, in Kent in particular, that bear the hints and traces of architecture known to pilgrims on their way to the shrine of Thomas à Becket in Canterbury Cathedral. But the coming of the railways and the gradual shift from the River Thames being the main nexus and transport link with its wharves and its warehouses running downstream from the Liberty of Southwark through Surrey Quays and out to Deptford (a route known as well to Christopher Marlowe as to Henry VIII and Elizabeth I) led to change and destruction long before that caused by the wartime bombing.

Bishop Cyril Garbett

In the inter-war years the rapid expansion of the housing estates south of London led to significant alterations in existing church buildings and to new buildings, at the behest and with the extraordinary vision of Bishop Cyril Garbett, and provided the opportunity to rethink the sacred space alongside a much frequented artistic community. Bishop Garbett's is perhaps the clearest voice that we can listen to instructively, for, as Kenneth Richardson has recently shown so persuasively, his was the ecclesiastical voice which, in hearing Lloyd George's General Election call in 1918 to build 'A land fit for heroes to live in', realised that God's people deserved churches.[5]

Garbett became Bishop of Southwark in 1919 and, faced with housing deprivation, inner-city poverty and the prospect of rapid population migrations, he established the Diocese of Southwark Twenty-five Churches Fund, with a view to building new churches for the new housing estates. Such a fund deliberately followed earlier models. Under Queen Anne, Parliament provided for the insufficiency of accommodation for worship in London and drew on the likes of Nicholas Hawksmoor[6] and James Gibbs as principal architects for 50 new churches. Post-Napoleonic England saw the 'Commissioners' Churches' (or 'Waterloo Churches') built throughout the 1820s after Parliament had voted The Church Building Act (1818), known as the 'Million Act', to provide a million pounds for new churches in expanding areas. The Church Building Society, largely a product of the Evangelical movement, had been founded in 1818 to construct and maintain Anglican churches across England and Wales, and it remained the spiritual godparent of the many churches built by the Act. Nearly three hundred new churches were provided between 1819 and 1830, largely from the public purse.

Unlike both previous funds, Garbett's initiative had to be funded from non-Parliamentary sources as the Commons had long since begun to discuss disestablishment for the Church in Scotland and in Wales. Nonetheless more than a quarter (£25,000) of the sum envisaged had already been raised by 1925. It is a signal testimony to his episcopate that Bishop Garbett was able to contemplate such an appeal at all without any opportunity of raising funds from Parliament.

His philosophy was simple, if not always popular with architects. In the RIBA Journal for May 1930 he wrote a piece, suitably entitled 'Bad Taste in Churches':

> The Church had an unrivalled opportunity for taking the lead in setting a high standard of artistic excellence. Zealous, but ill-instructed restorers had sometimes worked more fatal havoc than the deliberate iconoclast. The interiors of some of the best of their churches were damaged, sometimes half ruined, by tasteless colour, stamped by machine-made ecclesiastical designs, windows with insipid and unreal figures, colours on the walls and floors which were in violent discord, . . . cheap and conventional vases and lamps were found in many of our churches and made persistent progress against the worship of God in the beauty as well as in the holiness. For their sins against beauty they should sometimes have litanies of penitence.[7]

This lament, or perhaps episcopal charge, may have been resented at the time, but the fund that Bishop Garbett established brought to the Diocese of Southwark architects such as J. D. Sedding's pupil, Sir Charles Nicholson (1867–1949), who was responsible for the first of the Twenty-five at St Dunstan's, Bellingham (1924–5), and who became delightfully playful in his early Christian basilica for St Barnabas', Downham (1927), before returning to a healthy sobriety for St John's, Catford (1928). It also brought the younger Nugent Cachemaille-Day (1896–1976), best known for St Saviour's, Eltham: the first church to be built in London to depart from mediaeval precedent and which is always said to owe much to German Expressionism as if it inhabited a cityscape in a painting of Ernst Kirchner.

Garbett's insight, rather than his episcopal oversight, was driven by a personal conviction of the pastoral demands of a people for finding places of holiness, a proper obsession in a bishop and one which dogged him until his dying day. In November 1955 he wrote of his wish to raise an appeal for new churches in the new housing areas of his Province, a project of which the Archdiocese of York was robbed by his death on New Year's Eve. It was in no way marked by any personal agenda or demand for standardization of forms of worship, ceremony or religious expression, and in this Garbett was a striking modernist; in his charge for his Primary Visitation of 1924, when he personally visited every single parish in the diocese, he wrote: 'We are quite mistaken if we imagine that in the Middle Ages there was any-thing like a rigid uniformity either in belief or in ceremonial . . . The comprehensiveness of the Church of England is one of its glories, and will be of value in promoting further reunion.'[8]

What Garbett wrote in 1930 is the more remarkable not because it sounded like the appeal eighty years before of Bishop Robert Willson but because it firmly stated a conviction about Art and the Sacred before John Betjeman and John Piper had begun looking at churches and because it predated the arrival in Britain of Nikolaus Pevsner from the Germany of the 1930s, three men who in very different ways celebrated churches as houses of prayer and places for excellence. It is simply about 'the beauty of holiness' as the Psalmist repeatedly calls it (Pss. 29.2 and 96.9) in all its intricacy and profusion (Exod. 19).

Two South-East London churches

The Downham housing estate was announced by the London County Council in 1920 to provide housing for 35,000 persons. Downham was originally part of the parish of St John's, Catford. Immediately after the Great War in 1919 the parish had a population of some thousand souls. Six years later it included the district of Bellingham with a population of 12,000, and of Downham. Work on the estate was begun during 1924 with a sprawling, almost village-like run of houses along the side of the hill. By 1928, when the population had reached 15,000 and the increase showed no signs of abating, the only public building on the estate was Nicholson's hall/church (opened in 1926), a deliber-ate dual-function building that would, at the completion of the permanent church the following year, revert to single use as a popu-lar parish hall. By 1928 more than 2,500 children had enrolled in Sunday school classes which had to be held in relays in the church hall to accommodate the numbers. Whenever I am in Downham Way this demand from numbers always reminds me of the first Pentecost (Acts 2.47).

Sheer pressure of numbers and the need for swift building could have driven down standards, but instead Sir Charles Nicholson, who had already built St John's, Catford in a very different style, provided an almost idyllic rural village hall, faced with 'Old English' Sussex stock bricks, to remind the burgeoning population of the rural world then being put under construction all around them. Inside, the timber frame rafters span the hall without it ever becoming threatening or overpowering. It remains today a striking moment along Downham Way, humanizing the scale of urban development that carries on relentlessly for miles around while offering a hint of yesterday and a quieter age inside.

Next to the hall, Nicholson pulls off one of the best of theatrical coups in South London. The exterior of the church building, although never finished to his final plans for want of money, is dressed in the same brick as the hall, and although the west-end rose window and little belfry give it away as being the church the similarity between both buildings is clearly intended to deceive. And to deceive more than once: from the outside both buildings, although very different from the housing stock around them, respond to their environment closely. In 1911 Nicholson had worried that 'the state of divorce existing between civil and ecclesiastical architecture is an evil'. He went on to wonder, 'would not an occasional excursion into ecclesiastical art be a salutary change for the man whose life is spent making telephone call-rooms and mayors' parlours'.[9] At Downham he ruefully seems to comment on this missing link between the mundane and the divine, between the holy and the ordinary.

Once inside the church, far from finding a domestic- or even village-scale building, the visitor finds that a large, airy space opens up with Tuscan columns forming a basilica-like interior, as grand and as moving as the famous basilicas of Rome herself but bare of decoration. All of it is achieved with the minimum of decoration and a simple trust in the stateliness of the worship that will fill the place rather than in the over-decoration of some Victorian forbears. Nicholson himself admired the great G. F. Bodley, commending the latter's church at New Bilton in Rugby where he had made 'a cheap church, absolutely devoid of ornament yet perfectly dignified and harmonious', an achievement that led him to espouse a single creed: 'Proportion is, of course, the real secret of architectural dignity.'[10] He preferred plain, simple plastered walls to unfinished brick or stone, eschewed murals and opted for a classical emptiness in which the soul can take wing.

Seventy-five years on, Nicholson's church in the heart of Downham stands as a testament to his fidelity to the God of Proportion and of Order, to the unity of the Spirit and the Body, to the Holy and the Ordinary. It is a rare achievement well matching the spiritual demands of its first congregations and holding still, with a decently restrained modern liturgy, the balance between building and temple. The exterior aspect has been recently enhanced with a beautiful rose garden and the introduction of an avenue of trees, making sense of Nicholson's rural vision and offering an oasis of calm in a busy suburban estate.

If Nicholson was nurtured by the Victorians among whom he had grown up, the young Nugent Cachemaille-Day positively revelled in rejecting the same antecedents. Better known now for the scatter of his later churches in and around Metroland in outer West London (in particular St Anselm's, Wealdstone, and St Paul's, Ruislip) and for the bastion of Anglo-Catholicism at St Thomas's, Ipswich, Cachemaille-Day built perhaps the most successful Expressionist church in what had been the royal forest at Eltham Palace. St Saviour's, Middle Park Avenue, Eltham was built in 1932 and in 1933 won the RIBA London Architecture medal, a rare distinction among churches.

The royal palace at Eltham had been largely neglected after the reign of James VI and I and a once thriving community around its park fell into decline, while the palace at Greenwich, the much-loved Placentia of Henry VIII, continued high in the favour of the Tudors and Stuarts because of its access to the river Thames, so that its community, around the shrine church of the martyred St Alfege, throve instead. In 1931 the local council decided to build some 2,000 homes on part of the former royal park and Bishop Garbett at once set about providing for church plant in the area. The church was built inside eight months by which time only four hundred of the locally planned houses had been built; it could seat five hundred. Using reinforced concrete cased in brickwork and sticking to a rectangular plan it breaks all traditions of church architecture that so often respond to cruciform shapes or to the harmonious links to be made between square and circle.

Although it is now surrounded by rows of pre-war housing, from a distance this church still looks like a recklessly laden barge even if it is now safely anchored to corporation pavements. It has reminded many of a fortress-like stronghold from a bygone age, the latter aspect enhanced by the solidity of the square tower at the east end that is raised above the sanctuary. It is disconcerting and confrontational and although it clearly has Presence one would say as much for Durham Gaol. It does not appear in any way to be designed to elevate the mind or to enhance the soul. But what so often is mistaken for a debt to Expressionism (and the angularities derive singularly from that school) is also part of a complex game in which the architect has sited the church in the landscape of memory.

By the 1930s the old royal palace was in much disrepair and Sir Stephen Courtauld brought in Seely & Paget to make it habitable and to build a very 1930s house, deliberately set at odds with all that survived of the Great Hall. It was left to Cachemaille-Day at the parish church to provide a solid mediaeval bastion, a reminder of the former history of the area and the identity of the land itself from which the church has been extruded.

The church has not always been popular (and even the comparison with the cathedral at Albi seems to be begrudged), with its long windows making it look like some outsized shoe-box that has been tied with string, and it seems to have caused some parishioners to be scandalized. But it is not the simple *jeux d'esprit* of a youthful and untried man, even though Cachemaille-Day was not yet 40 and was still serving in a practice (Welch & Lander). He achieved a more monumental and memorable building than the neighbouring *faux palais* surrounded by its ancient moat by buying into the history and spirit of Place and then reinterpreting it within his own day and culture.

Inside, the effect is even more an honest tribute to mediaeval precedent without ever once becoming mediaeval; bare brickwork and a singularly cold nave lead to a chancel where light and colour (predominantly the effect of the piercing, blue stained-glass lancets and of a richly worked hanging cross in gold and silver, black, red and green) predominate. Since the church seems to come to an abrupt halt with a solid grey concrete reredos, the eye is immediately led upwards by the coloured linearity. Here is the very gate of heaven. Incongruous as it may seem, much of what the church shows is that in Eltham there was a past age, maybe not golden, but very much a part of the Christian heyday of England.

The art of God

From the architecture and building I want us to turn, at least in part, to the artistic decoration placed inside churches. And in this I do not wish to overlook the very real fact that many churches, and even cathedrals, simply cannot afford to commission art and have become adventurous with design, often using locally associated fabric to enhance the décor. At St Paul's, Thamesmead, cloth obtained cheaply (by UK standards) from the market of Dakkar has been used to dramatic effect. It not only reminds some worshippers of their home but is also celebratory of the inclusiveness that is such a distinguishing mark of that church community.

Almost all Christians have agreed that worshipping inside a structure is both amenable and necessary, but the place of art in those churches remains contentious, not only as a matter of artistic choice (Garbett's position and that of Pugin) but of belief. For there are many Christians who believe that art of itself is a contravention of the Second Commandment prohibiting idols. The Christian tradition has had its own periods of iconoclasm, some as violent as the acts perpetrated by followers of the Taliban, while others would more

moderately aver that the presence even of a simple cross can draw the
emotion and deceive the believer from true worship. It is argued that
if we persistently worship God with the aid of material media, our
religious life will be confined to the lowest element in our soul, the
sensuous, and we will never truly know God. Others, however, in
hoping to share in the prodigality of the gifts of creation, have richly
followed a long tradition of observing that beauty and holiness are
intrinsically what we offer to God as we seek to bring to him all that is
best, in our music, our words, our art and our liturgies.

A remarkable artist

Perhaps no single artist has had such a profound effect on the Diocese
of Southwark as a whole as the late Hans Feibusch, who was born in
Frankfurt am Main in 1898 and had exhibited in the famous
Degenerate Art Exhibition in Munich in 1937 before coming to live in
England. When he died, a few weeks shy of his hundredth birthday,
he was undoubtedly the best-known religious muralist in Britain.
He had painted in priory churches as grand as Christchurch in
Hampshire, where his great *Ascension* (1967) lifts off above the Jesse
screen behind the high altar, reaching to the very vault of that great
church. But it is in the many war-damaged inner-city churches that
his real triumphs emerge.

Of these his most notable work is to be found in the church of St
Crispin with Christ Church, Bermondsey. The church itself is in the
form of a single Greek cross with a central dome. It was designed by
Thomas F. Ford in 1958–59, to replace two earlier churches, that of St
Crispin in the district of the leather industry of Bermondsey (aptly
enough, as Saints Crispin and Crispinian are the patron saints of
cobblers and leather workers) which had been bombed, and the
demolished church of Christ Church. Inside, the dome is decorated
with a mural of the sky and of clouds; the singular dignity of the
building is matched by depicting the *arca coeli* in this simple manner.

Feibusch worked regularly with Ford, redecorating the interior (in
much disputed pink and orange) of Sir Giles Gilbert Scott's bombed
Naval Dockyard Church (St Barnabas, Eltham), at All Saints,
Woolwich Common on Shooters Hill (1956: another post Second
World War church built on a Greek Cross plan with a mural in the
central dome) and at St Mary the Virgin, Welling (1954–55) where he
supplied an Ascension to a building that, according to the dismissive
note in the gazette of *The Buildings of England*, 'epitomizes all that
mid-c 20 architecture ought not to be, yet one at least feels that Mr
Ford got a kick out of designing it'.[11] Elsewhere the two worked
together at St John's, Waterloo Road, at St James's, Merton, at Christ
Church, Battersea, and at Holy Trinity, Rotherhithe (1960).

Who has ever seen a phoenix? Where Thomas F. Ford built, assiduously and caringly, in the bombed terrain of a destroyed London, Feibusch sought to bring some sense of colour, albeit with a thin pastel palette in many cases, to suggest that the grey London skies, once lit only by the trails of falling bombs, were a thing of the past. Those who had lived through the Blitz and the bombing of the dockyards and naval yards along the Thames and who had seen their sacred spaces destroyed by enemy action, were being offered, by the artist, a theology of hope, the exultant expectation of joy. And, in the circumstances, who better to employ than a German-born artist who in his world becomes the bearer of the message of Christian reconciliation? In many such cases, of course, the murals now appear dated (and some need conservation) but the strength and conviction of the artist is never in doubt; God is reigning in the heavens.

The Diocesan Advisory Committee for the Care of Churches

This short introduction to the possibilities of art and the sacred space intentionally began far from the Diocese of Southwark, both in time and place. It was argued that, for many, the profound attachment to a sacral area has led to the continued occupation of sacred sites, often across millennia and certainly across traditions and faiths. For that reason the discussion of modern architects was limited to those who set about church building *de novo*, where no earlier place of mystery asserted itself. The inter-war years seem to have shaped the area of South-East London sufficiently to justify their being chosen. There would also have been no shortage of choice of an artist to represent the many, known and unnamed, who have continued to decorate so many of our churches, but Feibusch's nationality and his contribution so widely across the area demands that he be better known.

So what kind of buildings would now best express our faith and how might we set about determining suitable art for them? It is less and less likely that new churches will be set on the site of earlier shrines and places of prayer. Rather, as in so much of the past 150 years across the industrialized nations, land is at a premium, and Christians will have to pay good market prices for whatever land they can obtain; but, as Nicholson pointed out nearly a century ago, that is no reason to cut corners: 'Our aim should most certainly be dignity rather than picturesque-ness, especially in town churches.'[12] If we could regain a little of the earlier Christian conviction that churches are built for eternity to the glory of God then we might more readily ensure buildings of worth.

In the matter of commissioning a work of art for a church there is always a range of hurdles that lie behind private tastes or the idiosyncratic wishes of a donor, but it is certainly helpful if there is early consultation between the artist and the congregation and if the terms and conditions are readily understood by all parties (including the donor, where there is one, or the testator's representatives).

In many cases it will help the parish – both priest and congregation – to feel more convinced if they have had time to explore what are their own common expectations and to assert their own views about works of art other than the intended commission or gift. It might be as well to organize a study day, either of the particular artist's work if the artist is willing to afford the time and demands of such an inspection, or to go to study a completely different work of art and then try to discuss its pros and cons as a group. To that end there are usually enough opportunities locally as well as in national collections or in temporary exhibitions, but one should not overlook the very real treasury of art of all periods which is already in our cathedrals and churches. Such an exercise, which is quite different from going on a National Art Collection Fund outing or attending a National Gallery lecture, will give individuals who may never before have thought to find a voice about art, or about Art and the Sacred, a chance to develop their own confidence.[13]

Before any substantive changes can be made in or outside any church building in the Church of England, a faculty has to be granted by the chancellor of the diocese. In every diocese the chancellor will take advice from the Diocesan Advisory Committee for the Care of Churches ('the DAC'), and the early support of the archdeacon and of the DAC for a proposal can often help to shape the application to ensure a more likely safe passage without recourse to the litigation of church courts.

The DAC (and the chancellor) will have in mind whether the proposal is fully supported by the Parochial Church Council and across the wider church family as well as by the parish's architect and, where appropriate, by local representative groups, conservation societies, and other interested parties. Churches that have received grants from Lottery funds or from English Heritage may also be legally required to gain the consent of those bodies for intended alterations and additions, even where there is no obvious or direct link between the project and the earlier funding.[14]

The DAC and the chancellor will also wish to establish the suitability of the architectural or the artistic proposal to the place, and for large works will insist upon a site visit as well as upon drawings and designs. There will be broader questions, such as: Does the proposed design obstruct or enhance the worship that is offered in the church? Is it distinctively Christian or could it be misunderstood for a secular piece of art? What does it say theologically? Whom might it offend? Does it sit well within its intended context? Does it create a precedent (often a concern about memorials)? Might the congregation be better advised to try again?[15]

While such a close and legalistic path can seem off-putting, there are good reasons to pursue it as the Church of England, currently under Parliamentary allowance, is largely exempt from planning permission. There are many architects and artists willing to work in churches, and in seeking to choose to commission one the parish should be clear about the sort of requirements, both pastoral and spiritual, that they have in mind, and be prepared to be explicit with the architect or the artist (and the donor if there is one).

The only unhappy side, to this writer's way of thinking, is that we still live under a shadow cast by Victorian revivalism and by later conservatism such that the bold experimentations and the blatant inconsistencies that so enliven and enrich many of our ancient churches and churchyards are now being standardized to a level that will make many wary of accepting a commission at all. Serried ranks of similar headstones now line our cemeteries, worked to prescribed dimensions and in suitable stone, in place of the riot of invention and style that makes earlier yards such a pleasure to disport the soul in. The interiors of churches are also now at risk of being standardized within too many narrow definitions.

Case exercise

It will be a brave church that takes on the diocesan chancellor over a statue such as the Nicola Hicks sculpture *Chowl* (Flowers Central Gallery, June 2002). Wherever artists explicitly or tacitly portray the death agony of the God-man Jesus it is bound to provoke a mixed response. We might as a closing exercise try to imagine how to defend the installation of just such a piece to the DAC.

The work itself is clearly Semitic in origin: indeed, the striking life-size figure[16] is called by what the artist explains is a Hebrew word. It means sand, and as well as self-referencing the medium of its expression, this also suggests the whirling force of shifting sands and might recall the Palestine in which Jesus shared in an earthly home. What Hicks forbears to state is by way of the obvious: the English form of the word in the title contains within it the howl of agony. The Seven Last Words have passed. 'It is finished'. Can any one word hold the Word? Theologically this discussion might persuade the authorities.

With knees drawn up and arms outstretched this body seeks to rise above and out of the world, in which we are passers-by, and at the same time to contain us as the Body of Christ. This too suggests that resurrection and ascension both derive from and are intrinsically part of crucifixion. Profoundly, there is no crown without a cross, and the wood of the cross, which here is notably absent, becomes the very throne of the Godhead.

But against that it can be objected that the emaciated, tortured form of mediaeval pious contemplation, which is the model for this style of the dejected God-man, is not here. Here rather is a solid figure of a man, All Man, a model familiar from earlier pieces by Hicks, *Evolutionary Tale* in 1988 and even the earlier *Crow Man* (1995). But this would be a vapid objection since figures of the Crucified come in all sorts of shapes and sizes, and styles have evolved across traditions with telling distinction. The great *Christ in Majesty* at Lucca is very different from the dying man of Cimabue and Duccio, models that became so widely copied.

Rather more persuasively, it could well be argued that this sculpture bears no scars in hand, feet or side; in other words, that there are no signs or clues that it is Him. It is, surely, just a sculpture of a randomly naked man in an overtly recognizable posture? If that is the case then only the context begins to suggest that the sculpture itself might have a sacred purpose to it. And here we need to be clear about the power of context to shape and transform.

No one would suggest for a moment that the individual elements of the 'Apostles', a series that Damien Hirst included in his recent show Romance in the Age of Uncertainty (White Cube Gallery, September 2003), were Christian. The artist himself rejected the idea that he had become religious and claimed only to appropriate Christian symbols. The 'Apostles' was a series of sculptures representing the deaths of the Apostles and the ascension of Jesus. It included 13 wall-mounted glass and steel cabinets in the series with mirror backs and glass shelves, 12 of them littered with the detritus of laboratory glassware, crucifixes, rosaries, a candle and some hammers and swords. In front of them, on the floor, were 13 boxes containing formaldehyde, in 12 of which were the flayed and skinned heads of cattle. The thirteenth, like the wall-cabinet above it, remained empty.

The gallery has sold the works separately, thereby endorsing the artist's view that he is not working in a Christian context. For whereas Caravaggio's martyrdom of St Matthew (S Luigi dei Francesi, Rome) or the Rubens Crucifixion of St Peter (Peterskirche, Cologne) might stand alone, it was only the spatial layout at the gallery that made sense of Hirst's concept. In the large, white, top-lit gallery, the empty tank and cabinet were placed on the end wall, between two largely blue gloss-paint canvasses. On the walls on either side were placed the remaining cabinets, six on either side with their respective heads in front of them placed in such a way as to represent column bases of a central nave (the Apostles as pillars of the Church) with outer aisles, the walls of which seemed to hold reliquaries. Such a physical disposition allowed the sculptures to make sense as a whole.

The sculptures would not retain any symbolic meaning once the individual pieces are scattered since the context, not least the colour of the gallery which suggested so strongly a chapel or a church, would be lost.

So with the Nicola Hicks dramatic sculpture of a man wracked in agony; in a church or a chapel it would convey a sacred meaning, which may or may not have been the artist's intention. A figure such as this tells the universal story that stopped the world amid the drifting sands of time and once and for all has saved us.

Further reading

Cherry, Bridget, and Nikolaus Pevsner, *The Buildings of England – London 2: South*, Penguin, Harmondsworth, 1983.

Richardson, K., *The 'Twenty-Five' Churches of the Southwark Diocese: An Interwar Campaign of Church-Building*, The Ecclesiological Society, London, 2002.

Buchanan, C. O., *Mission in South-East London*, Diocese of Southwark, London, 2002; and *Follow-Up in 2003 to Mission in South-East London*, Diocese of Southwark, London, 2003.

Notes

1 Betjeman, John, *Church Poems*, Murray, London, 1981, preface. The author is grateful to Phillip Broadhead, Bob O'Dell, Ila Burdette and Fred Shriver for their professional comments on the draft of this chapter, and to Rupert Thompson, as always, for driving him to some out-of-the-way churches.

2 Lane Fox, Robin, *Pagans and Christians*, Penguin, London, 1988.

3 Bocock, Robert, *Ritual in Industrial Society: A Sociological Analysis of Ritualism in Modern England*, London, 1974.

4 Andrews, Brian, *Creating a Gothic Paradise: Pugin at the Antipodes*, Hobart, 2002, pp. 55–6.

5 Richardson, Kenneth, *The 'Twenty-Five' Churches of the Southwark Diocese: An Interwar Campaign of Church-Building*, The Ecclesiological Society, London, 2002.

6 du Prey, Pierre de la Ruffinière, *Hawksmoor's London Churches: Architecture and Theology*, University of Chicago Press, Chicago, 2000; and Hart, Vaughan, *Nicholas Hawksmoor: Rebuilding Ancient Wonders*, Yale University Press, New Haven, 2002.

7 Smyth, Charles, *Cyril Forster Garbett, Archbishop of York*, Hodder & Stoughton, London, 1959.

8 Garbett, Cyril Forster, *After the War*, Primary Visitation Charges, 1924, p. 87, quoted in Smyth, *Garbett*, p. 176.

9 Nicholson, Charles, and Charles Spooner, *Recent Ecclesiastical Architecture*, London, 1910, p. 6.

10 Nicholson and Spooner, *Architecture*, p. 7.

11 Cherry, Bridget, and Nikolaus Pevsner, *The Buildings of England London 2: South*, Penguin, Harmondsworth, 1983, p. 152.

12 Nicholson and Spooner, *Architecture*, p. 12.

13 Day, Michael, *Modern Art in English Churches*, Mowbray, London, 1984; Thistlethwaite, David, *The Art of God and the Religions of Art*, Carlisle, 1999.

14 The current legalities are discussed knowledgeably enough in Dawtry, Anne and Christopher Irvine, *Art and Worship*, London, 2002; but the early assistance of the archdeacon cannot be too lightly set aside when it might prove invaluable.

15 de Gruchy, John W., *Christianity, Art and Transformation*, Cambridge University Press, Cambridge, 2001, pp. 213–54.

16 173 x 217 x 50 cm.

10. Purposefully Going

The Parish as a Community in Mission

BRUCE SAUNDERS

As a university chaplain, I worked for several years with students. Their relationship with the Church, if any, had largely petered out through apparently mutual indifference. My job was to find ways to show that Christianity was worthy of their interest as young adults and to help to create Christian community within their cultural environment. What I was doing was very different from my previous experience in a parish. There were fewer road maps, it was riskier, and I felt more personally exposed. Perhaps that is why I got irritated at deanery synods and chapter meetings when clergy working in traditional residential parishes described themselves as being 'at the sharp end' of mission. They were probably not claiming that parish ministry has stiletto-like qualities of penetration, nor that it was at the dangerous edge where universes meet. More likely, they were referring to its heavy and constant level of demand. Perhaps more 'coal-face' than 'sharp end'.

Working again subsequently as a parish priest, I became fully aware of the strengths of the parish system. Living as part of the communities they serve, clergy and their families share in and are affected by local issues, the quality of local schools and health services, traffic, and crime. They are generally there for long enough for trust to develop and for relationships to grow, not just with individual parishioners, but with civic institutions. Standing in worship behind the altar, facing a congregation, some of whose most personal joys and sorrows I have come to know and share over the years is, for me, one of the great privileges of priesthood. All that trust, all that history, all that experience of common humanity is made part of the sacramental offering. And this relationship and process, which might almost be called incarnational, is mirrored in the multi-faceted life of the congregation. Through them, 'the Church' grows links and builds bridges between 'Sunday' discipleship and the wider communities in which congregation members live and work. Such relationships provide the raw material for the offering of the life of the world that goes into the chalice. And they are the veins and arteries through which mission and evangelism can flow.

Some, of course, argue that the parish system and the territorial Christendom assumptions on which it is based are no longer fitted to twenty-first-century life. The revisions to the Pastoral Measure proposed in 2003 are in part a recognition of the number of people who already shop around and go to their church of choice, regardless of parish boundaries or even of denomination. For them and for people who ring up a vicar in relation to a baptism, marriage or funeral, the legalities and protocols of parish boundaries can seem archaic, bureaucratic and unwelcoming. The proposals make the crossing of boundaries more possible for marriage and other occasional offices, and this flexibility might encourage the imaginative development of new patterns of Church that suit contemporary lifestyles and might provide a medium for the flourishing of the informal networks of Christians which already exist below the radar of the institutional church and which have been described as 'England's version of Base Ecclesial Communities'.[1]

But in many suburban and larger rural communities, there is still life in the old model. However mobile and multi-centred people's lives may be today, home for many is still a centre of gravity where life's issues find their hub and where contact with a local Christian community (even if it is not their nearest) makes most sense. For all the hopeful work of those scanning the horizons for new ways of being Church, there is nothing yet with the critical mass to offer an alternative to the Anglican Church's 'High Street' presence in places of population. Nor do I believe we should willingly relinquish it. Once lost, that footprint in the life of the community will not be regained.

But the very advantages and strengths of the parish system can cushion and blunt the edge of mission. The process that roots priests in congregations can also gradually condition the priest's perception, leading to an acceptance of the status quo. Over time, sharing in the most intimate joys and sorrows of a congregation, the priest's involvement and identification can lead to a shared acquiescence in the preferences of the congregation and a sense of the inevitability, immovability and even the holiness of the familiar.

Perhaps through the same kind of over-identification a suburban congregation can become as bland and comfortable, an inner-city congregation as stressed, a rural congregation as isolated as the communities they serve and thereby lose their distinctive, prophetic, missionary edge.

There are those who see these dangers as terminal, arguing that the shelf-life of the parish system is well past expiry, and that continuing to hope in and invest resources in the inherited ways of being Church is not only wasteful but hostile to the exercise of mission. John Cole summarizes this view:

> Ironically it is our traditional congregation life . . . into which denominations pour the greatest proportion of their resources, that show the least evidence of making a positive missionary impact for the sake of God's Kingdom.
> There is now so much of society that congregations simply cannot reach.[2]

A Canute-like refusal to take seriously the tides of cultural and demographic change would be arrogant and stupid, particularly in new housing areas where new opportunities for co-operation, new ways of building congregations and new ways of being present in the community may offer themselves. But I am not persuaded that the problem in most communities lies in the parish system, if 'the system' is a network of thousands of local congregations. Indeed it could be argued that in a post-modern cultural environment, it is precisely organizations with de-centralized, local, flexible expressions that can provide the adaptability and diversity that contemporary society requires of its religious institutions. And Church history shows that the gospel can flourish in such a context.

Nor do I believe that the deployment of professional clergy is in itself the problem. For all the horror stories of clergy who die at forty but retire at sixty-five, and for all the dangers of congregational dependency, most other voluntary and community-sector organizations who also rely heavily on a volunteer workforce envy the Church's theologically trained, politically articulate and practically resourceful professional local leadership. Christian ministry is by nature collaborative and it is increasingly the norm for local communities to be nurturing their own additional ministerial resources. But removing the stipendiary priest has not generally been found to be a recipe for sustained growth or greater missionary engagement.

Given greater flexibility, the parish system – a nation-wide network of local churches – has many potential strengths and advantages. But whether it lives or dies is not a structural matter: rather it depends on whether parishes can regain a sense of missionary purpose.

After six years as a diocesan missioner, exposure to current missiological thinking has persuaded me as never before of the essentially missionary nature of the Christian Church. The word 'mission' is understandably an unpopular word for the Church, even though it has been born again in secular use. I use the word in its widest sense, that is, to mean the Church's willing partnership with God in God's own purpose for creation.

Whether or not parish ministry is at the sharp end of anything, it certainly needs a point. Working with scores of local church groups in recent years and reflecting on my own time in parish ministry, I have come to believe that the critical factor in whether a parish is likely to be effective in mission is its sense of purpose. Just as we individual Christians are called to account for the faith that is in us, so churches must be able to answer the question 'What are you for?'

Following a 2002 survey of attitudes to mission in his parishes, the Bishop of Woolwich observed that too many churches seem to believe that 'being there' is somehow enough. This approach, even when expressed in quasi-sacramental terms, is, he suggests, 'insufficiently missionary'.[3]

For a consistently imaginative and exciting expression of a more adequate sense of missionary purpose, I am indebted to the later work of John V. Taylor, and not least to *The Uncancelled Mandate*,[4] a powerful reminder that for God, creation is not merely an act of self-expression but is purposeful. And that purpose, the *missio Dei*, repeatedly summarized by St Paul, is an open secret – nothing less than the reconciliation to God 'of all things' (Col. 1.20), of 'the world' (Eph. 1.10). The project is breathtakingly comprehensive: 'that is, in Christ God was reconciling the world to himself' (2 Cor. 5.19). It was that impulse of the divine nature to pour itself out in the love that longs for and evokes relationship that first called life into being – the overflowing generosity of One who is, in David Bosch's lovely description, 'a fountain of sending love'.[5] Through the turbulent history of the Hebrew people, we see that relationship repeatedly damaged by their infidelity, but God repeatedly calls them back, like a wronged but forgiving lover, into the chance of a new beginning. As one of the Common Worship Eucharistic Prayers puts it:

> As a mother tenderly gathers her children,
> you embraced a people as your own.
> When they turned away and rebelled
> your love remained steadfast.[6]

We see the same relational impulse in the life of Jesus – the incarnation itself a profoundly loving and imaginative act of reaching out to humanity. Many of Jesus' parables are about the restoration of good relationships between estranged fathers and sons, debtors and creditors, masters and servants. Many of his healing miracles not only confer physical healing, but call religiously unclean or economically useless outsiders back into proper relationships in human society and back into relationship with God. And all the big words in the Christian theological dictionary that struggle to account for the breadth and depth of God's love poured out from the cross are relational too – atonement, salvation, communion.

It is God's own commitment to relationship-building, to communion in all its many forms and faces, personal, political, social, spiritual, that is entrusted to the Church as its mission. As ambassadors, with the authority to act and speak for God, those who have themselves been reconciled to God are enlisted in this ministry of reconciliation. The Church is invited to become a community where God's love is not merely talked about as an echo or a memory, but where Christ-like love happens now, where people can see it, feel it, touch and be touched by it in the quality of the relationships within the Church, between the Church and the community and in the relationship between what goes on in church on Sunday and in the other parts of the lives of Christians during the week.

> The Church empowered by the Spirit is itself part of the message it proclaims. It is a fellowship which actualises God's love in its everyday life and in which justice and righteousness are made present and operative.[7]

As Diocesan Missioner, visiting parishes, leading workshops and conferences, offering supervision to individual clergy, I have found that kind of articulated sense of theological purpose to be the most frequently missing piece at the centre of parishes that are otherwise taking good care of the practical aspects of parish life.

I would not wish to draw too clear a distinction between maintenance and mission. I believe the Church does need buildings, administrative systems and other resources, all of which need to be sustained. But whether by temperament or training, many clergy seem to fall into what can properly be called a pastoral model of ministry. This seeks to meet human needs and, in ways that reflect God's love, somehow to hold the joys and pain, the memories and the longings of a community. This essentially responsive style of ministry makes many parish clergy superb opportunists, able to use the merest chance encounter, local event or unexpected phone call for the gospel. But I am all too aware from personal experience how, after frighteningly few years, creative response can become mere reaction, and the diary starts filling itself up, sometimes to the extent that survival strategies are needed to keep demand at bay. A sense of purpose is hidden under the weekly routine. The question 'What is the point of this?' becomes a cry of exhausted desperation rather than a helpful, routine, tactical question.

The discovery or rediscovery of a more fundamental sense of purpose is a more demanding process than simply brain-storming a mission statement for the notice-board. It requires nothing less than members of a congregation, individually and collectively, answering for themselves the question about God's own purpose for creation. A rediscovered sense of atoning, reconciling, relationship-building purpose, which flows directly from the divine nature, is more than enough to kindle in a congregation an awareness of its own vocation in the fulfilment of that greater purpose and at the same time tells it what kind of community it has to be.

I have been encouraged to see a variety of evangelism and mission strategies from different denominational and theological traditions coming to the same conclusion about the essential primacy of this sense of focused purpose, which acts as a visionary standard, an organizational watchword and a self-critical tool.[8] Re-equipped with a sense of purpose that is first theological, then strategic, parish congregations have, I believe, enormous potential for engaging constructively with the Church's mission task. In many communities, the initial practical priority may well be preparation for the task.

For some quite understandable reasons, many Christians are hesitant about the language of mission and evangelism. But sadly they not only steer clear of the language, they lay aside the concept and the need for missionary activity. Or they opt for the only partly true adage that actions speak louder than words. That may have been true in a culture that knew how to read and understand the meaning and motives of action, but our action today sometimes needs to be labelled. People may not need to know that this is a 'Christian' jumble sale, but they may need something to help them understand actions that are based on a view of the world that prefers forgiveness to revenge, generosity to selfishness. In former Christendom days, when we could assume that everyone was Christian, such views were the common currency, even if implicit. Today, there are strident alternative value systems. Today, people of faith have to argue their position and that may mean making our motives and values understandable.

A congregation of people who know one another, worship together regularly, have some kind of unwritten, long-term contract of trust and who may share all kinds of common interests in the local community is the ideal training forum for safely taking the first shaky steps in faith-sharing. Sharing aloud the history of God's love in each person's life, hearing biblical echoes and making connections with those stories, getting used to the sound of one's own voice and finding ways of telling the story in personal and natural ways are all best practised among friends. The spirituality of congregational life is almost inevitably enriched by such a process. And that spirituality, that passionate sense of being loved by a passionate God, is the flame from which all missionary activity is kindled.

Equally important for many Christians, and part of this same process of preparation, is the need to recapture a sense of the big picture. So much Christian education, chiefly in school and Sunday School (and that is the nearest many Christians ever get to systematic teaching) has been about the individual jigsaw pieces of the Jesus story – this miracle, that parable. But ask many Christians to step back from the detail and describe the whole picture – what the life, death and resurrection of Jesus is about, and many resort to familiar religious shorthand phrases ('He came to save us', 'He died for our sins') which they find hard to unpack or articulate in other terms, and on doing so can find those phrases fail to represent their own experience of God. It is striking how little use St Paul makes of stories from the life of Jesus, but, as when talking to Greeks in Athens (Acts 17.22ff.), is able to tell the story of salvation in big-picture terms that connect with their experience and capture their imagination. Typically, he is able to show how the death and resurrection of Jesus is not a one-off phenomenon but is part of God's great loving purpose that has been unfolding from before creation began. This process of learning to see and articulate the larger picture of the mission of God, crucially expressed in Jesus Christ, is again fruitfully explored in the laboratory of a congregation wanting to equip itself better for mission.

There are many ways of telling the God-story. The model used in the Old Testament – God acting in and through the history of the Hebrew people – is only one. Telling the God-story from a relationship-building trajectory seems to me to be the way that best registers within the cultures of our time. This is good news for Christian congregations in a parish setting, for many Christian people are already engaged in precisely that task in a host of ways, in family life at home, at church, at work, with friends, and through voluntary engagement in the community.

A church that can get on to the front foot in this way no longer merely waits for opportunities for relationship but creates them. And most churches, in urban, suburban and rural communities, are richly provided with such opportunities within their own fellowship and in the wider networks of community contact which they have as churches. But these opportunities are also created most significantly through the 'secular' lives of their own congregational members. At a recent training event with a dozen Parochial Church Council members from a small church in rural Surrey, I listed about forty local organizations and projects with which those people were already personally involved.

Looking for opportunities for relationship, converting mere contacts into relationships, and empowering congregational members to make creative use of their opportunities all become front-line mission tasks. This is not only about teaching, but about supporting the missionary lives of the congregation with prayer, and making their work and the lives they lead outside church all part of the spiritual and sacramental offering of praise and thanksgiving to God. How often do the prayers of intercession dutifully include far-distant corners of the globe and remote parts of the Anglican Communion while failing to take account of the old-people's homes, the schools and hospitals, the offices and businesses, the charity shops and voluntary projects, some at least of which will be in the parish and in which local Christians spend their working lives? And what of the Church's prayerful solidarity with health-visitors, police, teachers and council workers who are also engaged in Kingdom activity with the wider community?

Far from replacing the existing pastoral, catechetical, diaconal and liturgical aspects of the life of a local church, the understanding of mission expressed as a sense of purposeful relationship-building integrates them and highlights their value and their inter-connectedness. Instead of the departments of church life becoming the prerogative and, too often, the possession of different and separate groups (servers, Sunday School and house-group leaders, musicians, people with prayer or pastoral ministries and those actively involved in practical social-care projects with homeless people or refugees), all need to see themselves as engaged in aspects of the same task, all needing to know and care about one another as complementary pieces of the whole, with worship as the centre where all these aspects meet, are celebrated, affirmed, and offered to God.

Everything we know about the churches and congregations that are proving attractive to new Christians and are rekindling the faith of others is that they pay attention to relationships, not only creating an environment in church that is welcoming, attentive, human and honest but also seeing as vital the relationship between worship and the rest of life, church and community, Sunday and the working week. Such congregations have a palpable sense of purpose, detectable in the smallest things, even in the way people sing, the way they pray, the way their expectations of themselves, of one another and of God are raised. The process begins with a question about God's purpose, and develops with an assumption that the Church's purpose must be the same.

Reflecting on how the Church's mission task cascades from the nature and purpose of God, a group of Ordained Local Ministry trainees recently decided that since God is love, and since love needs an 'other', they could confidently assert that it would not be in the nature of God to keep love to himself. Love overflows from God generously. And in giving himself to his creation, God necessarily longs for human beings to be in God-like relationship with one another. They went on to assert that a Church which signs up to this understanding of itself will itself become generous and self-giving, not just 'friendly and welcoming' but pouring itself out in love. It will need to know the world well enough, with the intimacy that comes from daily engagement, to be able to offer it to God in prayer and worship. Such a Church will want others to experience the love of God because there is no other way towards the fullness of their humanity. It will want others to play their part in God's purpose for creation. And in its own life, the Church will be a living example of divine love.

It is a bold claim for the Church to aspire to being like God. Such an ambition, such a sense of vocation, leads Christians deep into the business of reconciliation, of the healing and nurturing of Christ-like relationships with self, with others, with the created order and with God. Christian tradition and scripture provide us with hosts of images about what this reconciled creation might look like: a casting down of golden crowns around a glassy sea; seeing face to face; the restless heart finally finding its rest in God. The eschatology implied by these images feels decidedly posthumous. Even those who turn their prayerful longing for the coming Kingdom into a daily struggle for peace and justice might today hesitate to locate the fulfilment of their longing within the timescale of human history.

But the Church is called not merely to be a signpost towards some far-distant fulfilment of God's reconciling purpose. Through the mystery of the Church's sacramental now-and-not-yet, here-and-hereafter nature, we are also called to be the here and now household of God. And where better for a seeker to look for such a community of holy living than in the extended family of a local congregation? It is one of the few meeting places for people of different generations, where people from widely diverse social backgrounds kneel side by side. It would, however, require no small culture shift for some congregations to become such churches. And some will certainly not be willing even to set out on the journey. There are plenty of people in the Church who have a vested interest in keeping things the way they are.

Those willing to embark on the adventure will find that they have already been provided with most of the resources they need: the scriptural witness of those who have shared this adventure before us, a rich inheritance of liturgical prayer and action which addresses and articulates human experiences at its highest and lowest points, a footprint in every community and a workforce, voluntary and professional, which most other organizations would kill for. Some of these precious gifts have become dust-covered with familiarity and under-use. We have become far too ready in our acceptance of the tired and second-best. (Look how a parish Eucharist perks up when the BBC arrive!)

Managing that change will require much skill, courage and vision. But the rewards are immense and there will be plenty of people, in the Church and currently outside it, who will welcome the chance of contributing to the task.

This is not an argument for continuing to do what we have always done – however excellently. Some of the attitudes, values and habits of the past will find no place in a Church that is fit for the people of our time. Assumptions about living in a Christian country, with Christian values embedded in and protected by the institutions of the state and where everybody is Christian underneath, have to give way to a sense of being a missionary Church, just one of a number of options in the spiritual market-place.

A missionary Church will not allow itself to depend on default social attitudes which do or (increasingly) do not bring people to the church door in prams, wedding limos and hearses. They will put aside the hierarchical, pompous, arrogant and authoritarian attitudes which they learned from the Constantinian court rather than from the man from Galilee, and they will allow to be pruned away any attitudes to priesthood which have become overgrown with those alien life-forms.

In a missionary context, opening the door, putting on a smile and waiting for people to come will no longer do. The threshold into the Church and into its self-referential culture is too high a step for most people either to attempt or achieve. Accessible entry points must be deliberately provided. But access is not only about initial points of entry. It is also about cultural compatibility, about our being able to articulate the good news of God's love and the story of salvation in other people's language, not simply requiring them to learn ours. And recent experience has encouraged many churches to enjoy discovering that faith is more like a journey than a parcel or a library. For established as well as new Christians, opportunities for continued adventure and discovery are wanted.

This has a radical effect on how clergy might spend their time, how PCCs might spend their money, how the gifts and experience of congregation members are exercised and on the kind of lay leadership that is modelled by those selected or elected for public office. Everything from the state of the toilets to the music the choir sings is either part of the problem or part of the solution. (And I do not mean that 'good' has to be complex. Simplicity is capable of greater beauty than unrealised ambition.) And if the local church is not to disappear into the plug-hole of its own domestic preoccupations, the congregation cannot simply be a gathering of people who like worshipping together. An essential part of their discipleship will be the rhythm of their day-to-day lives being brought to the altar for renewal in self-offering, intercession and penitence alongside the commission to go in peace to love and serve the Lord. One clever church dismissed the congregation with the words 'Our worship is ended. Our service begins'.

To help congregations move towards missionary mode, I sometimes use this matrix and ask them to indicate on both axes where they believe their church currently stands, then to join up the two points to indicate which quarter of the matrix they occupy.

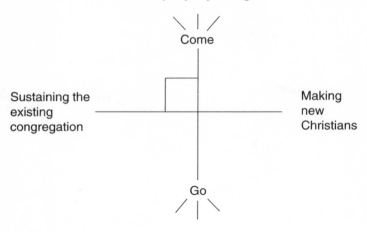

The extreme positions on each axis are not alternatives. Most local churches will be doing some of each, both sustaining existing congregations and offering something for new Christians. And there will be examples of both 'Come' models of evangelism, with an emphasis on drawing people into the life of the church, and also of 'Go' models, which take Christians into other people's territory. But in most cases the centre of gravity on each axis will not be hard to identify. This will indicate in which quarter of the matrix congregational life predominantly lies. The traditional church is likely to have the profile illustrated above, welcoming but primarily concerned with its own. Churches would need to move towards the bottom right-hand quarter in order to become more missionary.

I have enough faith in the inherited patterns of parish life to believe that such a move towards missionary purpose requires no fundamental revolution in many parishes. The instinct for relationship-making is deeply embedded in the genes of the Anglican parish system and in the motivation and values of many clergy and congregations. The move towards mission seems to me to be more about remembering than inventing. I have been greatly encouraged, among the parishes I have visited in recent years, by how little one has to dig in order to find these instincts and convictions.

Christendom was a world where Christians and the Church could take a lot for granted. People understood. Things could be left unsaid. It is no longer so. Churches are full of worshipping agnostics for whom it is a struggle to relate the language and images of hymnody and Sunday liturgy to the weekday God they falteringly pray to and seek to know. The Bible is largely unread at home. People in contemporary European cultures, even those who go to church, often lack the theological tools to make for themselves the connections which kindle a sense of purpose, so their religion remains in the zone of personal private preference.

Yet where better than within the life of a congregation to reflect, explore and discover the rich veins of purpose that run through our inherited corporate life as Christians? A community of learning, prayer and service, with a multitude of subtle human and institutional relationships with the wider community, all ready to be celebrated, used and offered to God. If parish churches didn't already exist, we would have to invent them!

Further reading

Morisy, Ann, *Beyond the Good Samaritan: Community Ministry and Mission*, Mowbray, Oxford, 1997.

Tomlin, Graham, *The Provocative Church*, SPCK, London, 2002.

Taylor, John V., *The Uncancelled Mandate*, Church House Publishing, London, 1998.

Notes

1 John Cole in *The Unity-in-Mission Agenda*, The Church of England Council for Christian Unity, London, June 2003. See also *Encounters on the Edge*, a quarterly series of reports by George Lings at the Church Army's Research Unit in Sheffield www.encountersontheedge.org.uk; Hinton, Jeanne, *Changing Churches*, Churches Together in Britain and Ireland, London, 2002; and Hinton, Jeanne and Peter Price, *Changing Communities: Church from the Grassroots*, Churches Together in Britain and Ireland, London, 2003.

2 Cole, *Unity-in-Mission*.

3 Buchanan, Colin, *Mission in South East London: The Practice and Calling of the Church of England*, Diocese of Southwark, London, 2002.

4 Taylor, John V., *The Uncancelled Mandate*,Church House Publishing, London, 1998.

5 Bosch, David, *Transforming Mission*, Orbis, Maryknoll, 1997, p. 392. 'Mission has its origins in the heart of God. God is a fountain of sending love. This is the deepest source of Mission. It is impossible to penetrate deeper still; there is mission because God loves people.'

6 Prayer G, Order One, *Common Worship*, Church House Publishing, London, 2000.

7 Bosch, *Mission*, p. 157.

8 In this country chiefly Warren, Robert, *Building Missionary Congregations*, Church House Publishing, London, 1995, and his subsequent work for Springboard; and the Churches Together in Britain and Ireland, *Building Bridges of Hope Project*, Church House Publishing, 1998.

11. A Seed of Youthful Hope

Young People in the Parish

RICHARD BAINBRIDGE

How we live now – the social and cultural context

Growing up is not what it used to be. Our society is going through a time of rapid change and the whole social and cultural context for young people growing up today is different from that of their parents. It used to be said that the past is a foreign country. People in their forties or fifties look at the lives of young people and experience a similar sense of distance. Young people seem to inhabit a different world from the one in which we grew up. It is worth noting this changing context before looking at an example of work with young people at parish level. Of course it is not only young peoples' lives that are changing. Youth cultures do not exist in isolation from what is happening in the wider society. It is the changes in the whole culture that shape young people's experience and expectations.[1]

Consumerism has bitten deep into our culture and our consciousness. There is a sense in which we are what we buy. We live in the world of the market-place. We have moved from a culture where identity came through production and the work-place to one where we are defined by our personal choices as consumers. One significant writer on the shift to post-modernity writes: 'Modernity extolled the delay of gratification; . . . the postmodern world . . . preaches delay of payment. If the savings book was the epitome of modern life, the credit card is the paradigm of the postmodern one.'[2] Teenagers do not have credit cards, but they are very much part of the consumer society. They are used to a world in which identity is constructed through consumer choices. Individual choice has replaced over-arching ideas of progress. Part of the ideology of consumerism is that we have a right to consume. 'Consumerism proclaims pleasure not merely as the right of every individual but also as every individual's obligation to him or her self . . . the pursuit of pleasure untarnished by guilt or shame becomes the new image of the good life.'[3] Although this consumer heaven is offered to all, not everyone has the money to participate. Social inequality in this country and world-wide has been increasing.

Consumerism also has far-reaching impact on attitudes to religion and spirituality. It is easier to dive into and out of different scenes or spiritualities. 'Young people appear to consume the Christian scene in roughly the same way they consume other scenes. That is, they move from one to the other fairly easily and construct their identities from whatever takes their fancy.'[4] The transition from youth to adulthood has always presented challenges, but the social and cultural context of these challenges is changing in significant ways. Cray identifies three transitions that are generally needed: 'from school to work; from singleness to marriage or cohabitation; and from the parental home to a place of one's own'.[5] Each of these transitions is in a process of significant change.

More young people are staying on at school and entering higher education. They are under great pressure to succeed academically, both from their school and from parents. At the same time the employment opportunities for young people have declined. Earlier routes into work through apprenticeship schemes have virtually disappeared. For increasing numbers of young people the transition to employment extends into their twenties, thus prolonging the time of at least partial dependence on their parents.

While there is evidence of the earlier onset of puberty and physical maturity and indications of sexual activity beginning at a younger age, the age of marriage or having children is going up. Marriage itself is increasingly seen as one possible lifestyle option rather than the norm. If we look at my parish, Good Shepherd with St Peter, Lee in South-East London, we can see these trends at work, even if the sample is too small to be significant on its own. Taking marriages in the parish church for each of the last three five-year periods, the total number of marriages declined from 46 in the years 1989–93 to 21 in 1999–2003, a decline of over 50 per cent. There was also a marked change in the age of marriage over this period. In 1989–93, 33 of the couples, or 69 per cent, were both under 30. Nine of the couples were both under 25. Ten years later, out of the 21 marriages, only five of the couples, or 19 per cent, were both under 30. There were no couples where both were under 25.

The high price of housing in London makes it harder for young people to move out of their parents' homes. This is aggravated by increasing levels of student debt.

These developments mean that adolescence is full of new pressures and uncertainties. This is the background to the experience of a very modest development of a new youth club in one South-East London parish.

Where we are living – the local context

The parish has a population of around 12,000, it is bounded in the south by the South Circular Road, and it has good rail links to central London. If London's development is thought of as a series of layers, like an onion, then the parish straddles the outer ring of pre-1914 housing, both terraced and large detached, and extends into the layer of characteristic 1930s semis and into an attractive post-World War Two modern estate. It is a residential area with no significant industrial premises. Most of the parish falls into two wards, Lee Manor in the Borough of Lewisham and Sutcliffe Park in the Borough of Greenwich. It is a comparatively comfortable area, with a higher proportion of owner-occupied properties than the average for the two boroughs as a whole. The Greenwich end of the parish has a number of sports fields and the Lewisham end has an attractive and well-used park. Both ends of the parish are predominantly white, more so than the boroughs as a whole. There is very little provision for teenagers. Young people say to us 'Where can you go to be with friends and meet new people if you are too young for the pubs?'

The Youth Club is re-born

The phone call came on one of those dark winter days when Christmas and New Year are over but the winter seems to stretch ahead. 'Hi, it's Mia. Me and my friend Lou want to start a youth club at the church.' I could hardly believe what I was hearing. We talked and I promised to get back to her. In a small way, this was a breakthrough. Fifteen-year-old Mia was one of our servers, but like many other teenagers she was hanging on to Church by her fingernails. Her friend, Lou, had at one time sung in the choir, but was no longer involved with the Church.

I reflected on the history of youth work in the parish. Typically this had gone through different stages in the recent past. First there had been an open youth club for 9 to 13-year-olds run by the church for young people of the neighbourhood. This included young people from the church but all were welcome. Started in 1990, it offered sessions on Sunday evenings with table tennis, football and other activities. Numbers never fell below 15 and were sometimes in the 20s. Apart from the usual difficulty of finding sufficient helpers, problems developed with behaviour. Young people excluded for anti-social behaviour then started to retaliate by throwing stones to break windows. According to one of the key helpers, 'It was like acting as an extension to the local authority's youth service, but without the money or the staff resources.' Given the pressure on the few helpers, there seemed to be no alternative to closing the club. This happened two years later in 1992.

A second approach had been geared more closely to the nurture of young people attached to the Church, not least young members attached to a thriving music scene and church choir. There were meetings after church, trips to the local Noodle House, and from time to time the young people contributed to the main Sunday worship. They also joined with the Scouts for events like the firework parties in the vicarage garden. From 1995 onwards there was always a group of teens and twenties who went together to Greenbelt, the Christian arts and music festival. The annual Walk the City, a sponsored event for Christian Aid in May, was also a regular fixture for some. Through the previous vicar a link had been established with a Lutheran pastor in Berlin. Visits have been made and friendships established which have been kept up over a number of years. Young people from Lee have visited Berlin and the German young people have visited us, slept in our hall and been cooked for and welcomed through an impressive team effort.

I arrived in the parish in 1999, by which time the old youth club had long been closed. As most of the young people had reached the stage of university or college, the pool of teenagers in the church had shrunk. Young people were dropping out of regular church worship at a younger age. However, the uniformed organizations were still thriving, although numbers dwindled after the age of about 12. These attended and contributed to the flourishing monthly Family Services at both churches, which are sometimes called 'church parade'. Otherwise the uniformed organizations mostly operated fairly separately. Relationships were cordial and interest and support from the clergy was welcomed, but these groups were not primarily concerned with the Christian nurture of the young people they served. A parish visitation by the Bishop of Woolwich in late 1999 had singled out the development of 'Christian teenage work' as a big gap and challenged the parish to develop a strategy to fill it.

While there was no organized youth group, contact with church young people continued in less structured ways. Food, as always, was important. Two pizza lunches were held at the vicarage, a Noodle House and bowling trip was arranged after a Sunday service, and a short drama was put on in the service at both churches in the parish. Some of the young people were involved as servers or in the music, still strong, but affected by the moving on of a talented director of music. The aim was to organize a special activity or outing twice a term and encourage participation in worship and other existing activities, but some of these never materialized because of lack of support or interest. With very erratic attendance, small numbers and the busy life of teenagers, it was hard to keep any momentum. It sometimes felt like starting from scratch every time. However, Greenbelt and the annual Christian Aid Walk had sufficient adult help to continue. Skating and bowling trips also worked well and young people joined in the active parish support for the Jubilee 2000 campaign to break the chains of third-world debt. The idea of joining with others in the local Churches Together Group was suggested. The nearby Roman Catholic Church had a reasonably flourishing youth group. After a good deal of informal contact with their leader we were invited to a special youth praise service at their church, but the response from our parish was only one young person plus myself. This did not seem an adequate basis on which to build inter-church co-operation, but we may want to return to it in the future.

Music was another area in which some of the older young people and young adults could contribute. The Good Shepherd has had several gifted youthful organists in recent years and the choir has helped to nurture a number of young people in faith. Several older teens/young twenties began to meet in one of the local pubs. They always sat round the same table and had in-depth discussions over drinks about the nature of worship. They became known as the Worship Group. They wrote some highly original dramatic presentations, taking responsibility for the liturgy of the word in the main Sunday service at both churches on several occasions, until key members moved away for work or further study.

This then was the context in which I received Mia's call. She acted together with her friend Lou. I would like to say that I and many others had faithfully prayed for the youth work. I am not sure our prayer was so specific, but God is good. From this call we began to move forward. The first step was to gather anyone who might be interested, both young people and potential adult helpers.

First we listened to the young people. They wanted a place to hang out with friends, somewhere away from home where they could also meet new people. Having plucked up courage to express their request, they were naturally keen to get going as soon as possible. A series of planning meetings followed – what might be called inter-generational negotiation. The adults involved initially were two of the clergy and parents. The different agendas involved were explored. The aims summed up at the first meeting by the young people were 'to have fun and meet other young people'. There was also the desire to build relationships with and nurture in the Faith young people who were linked with the Church. Then there were what might be called the infrastructure needs. In order to run a safe, secure space for young people there would have to be adequate adult presence, child protection procedures in place, and appropriate insurance cover. The young people preferred the idea of young adults nearer their own age as helpers. The involvement of parents was discussed. By making it clear that this was to be the young people's group and that they should own it, some of the sensitivities over this issue were resolved. There is a wide range of adult helpers, almost all from the Church. Parents have continued to form one important element.

Over a period of about three months plans began to take shape. Sometimes the pace of progress seemed slow and it was a measure of the commitment of the young people that they stuck with the process. The organizational needs of even the most modest venture seemed daunting. Once we opened we would need to be able to draw on at least two and preferably three volunteers for each session. Initially, meetings would be fortnightly on Sunday evenings, but weekly sessions would be held if enough volunteers could be found. All volunteers would need basic training in child protection procedures and appropriate ways of working. There was no Diocesan Youth Officer in post at this time and we felt this lack of support keenly. A little later the new DYO, Dean Pusey, started work. A valuable source of ideas and advice in writing this chapter, he will shortly be working with us to review progress so far. However, we were fortunate that in the initial stages valuable consultancy was provided by Nick Shepherd of Greenwich Youth for Christ. At a volunteers' training session run by Nick we were asked how we felt about the prospect of opening the club. Pleased, proud, content and pressurized were all mentioned. I think I was the one who felt most nervous. The general feeling was 'content' and we agreed that this was a good place to be.

One more question had to be settled. Who was the club for? The answer to this would dictate how it was publicized. One option was to start with existing contacts and their friends and work out from there. The alternative would be wide publicity and open invitation to any local young people. The general feeling was that enough young people were already involved or known to start the club. Bigger events could be arranged from time to time. Not only would this help to keep the link with the Church and the young people already involved in some way with the Church, but the volunteer team wanted the chance to work themselves into the job slowly. We did not want to face the prospect of being overwhelmed by numbers on the first night. Having agreed this, it soon emerged that one of the young people put notices about the club's opening meeting on trees all down a nearby street. These were soon taken down and the reason for this explained. However, publicity in the Church of England secondary school attached to the parish went ahead.

Fifteen young people came to the opening session, which included a mobile phone marking session with the local police. This response was very gratifying, enough to make it seem alive but not too many to cope with. A few days later there was a difficult moment at the Parochial Church Council (PCC). Although they had been kept fully informed about the plans for the club they had never been formally asked to approve them. I realised that for insurance purposes this was needed. However the agenda for the meeting simply specified a brief report. Members of the council were very concerned that there was no constitution and some had grave doubts about giving backing to the club. This was understandable. To take responsibility, the Council needed to know that all was in order. But how could the club have a constitution if it was at such an early stage of development? Eventually it was agreed that it should be adopted temporarily and reconsidered at the next meeting.

Before the next PCC meeting there was some encouraging news to report. Mia and Lou, whose initiative had led to the founding of the club, had been nominated by one of the volunteers for a Lewisham Young Citizens Award, organized by the police. The nomination was accepted and they were presented with their awards at the town hall. They came along to the next Parochial Church Council meeting and showed their award and talked about the club. As vicar I was approved as chair of the youth club. Still the constitution was not ready, but the broad outline of it was emerging. It was finally agreed in the club in September and ratified by the PCC. The club was to be an intrinsic part of the wider community of the Church of the Good Shepherd and St Peter's Church. 'It encourages all members to engage with the Christian faith and make their own distinctive contribution to the life of the church.' The overall aim of the club is 'to provide a safe environment where young people can enjoy themselves, meet others, grow spiritually and fulfill their potential'.

By the time of the Church's annual meeting in April 2003, it was reported that over the first eleven months average attendance had been 8, drawn from about 15 members, and that 14 volunteers had been recruited and trained. Over the year one of the members had been baptized and two had been admitted to Holy Communion. Two of the members were on the rota of servers. Two have recently begun a Christian basics course which may lead to confirmation.

Why this way? – the value base

Two rather different traditions can be seen in Christian youthwork, according to Pete Ward.[6] The 'inside-out' approach starts with young people who belong to the Church. It seeks to nurture them in the Faith and provide a safe place for them to be. Although it starts with young people who belong to the Church and have some Christian commitment, it also seeks to attract other young people and draw them in. One of the limitations of this approach is that the social and educational background of the young people can limit the group's effectiveness in reaching people who are different.

The 'outside-in' approach begins with those outside the Church and seeks to draw them towards Christian Faith. The previous youth club in the parish was close to this model. It is very hard to operate ⁺his model in a way that engages young people with the Christian Faith. They may be interested in the club, but not in what it stands for. An open club is accessible to young people from a variety of social backgrounds. This is a strength, but it can be challenging for church-based work. The previous youth club in the parish could not sustain the pressures of this work over the long term, despite heroic efforts. The two traditions have different starting points, methodologies and assumptions. However, Ward also recognizes that these are theoretical models. Work on the ground does not necessarily fit tidily into this scheme.

The starting point for our youth club was the often expressed view: 'We have to do something for the young people.' This has been said on numerous occasions in our parish, not least by the Bishop of Woolwich after his visitation in 1999. Unless there is complete flight from reality, this must be a concern in every church. Without handing on the Faith to the next generation the Church cannot survive. However, the agenda implied does not always face up to the needs and concerns of young people. If young people are to find a place in the Church then they need to be listened to. A Church with active young people will not be the same as one entirely made up of adults.

Our club is closest to the inside-out model in its origin. We have started with the young people we have and worked from there. Yet the sessions of the club are in practice social. It is a place to be, rather than an occasion for specific Christian teaching. We do not have worship or an epilogue, but we do seek ways of drawing the young people into participation in the main Sunday worship. Recruitment has been through the church young people, through their friends in the area, and through the Church of England secondary school linked to the parish and other miscellaneous contacts, such as a group of boys who have persistently used the church garden as a football ground but find it hard to sustain interest in anything else.

In terms of its programme and stated aims the club operates with some features of the 'outside-in' tradition as well. Young people are valued for themselves. This is the core value of the youth club, to support and befriend young people and through this to encourage them to engage with the Christian Faith. They have a place in the church community, even if they find it hard to feel comfortable with frequent attendance at Sunday worship. The club has to run as a co-operative effort between the adults and young people. Parents of some of the young people join with other adults in their concern to support and value the young people at this stage in their lives and do so within a Church-related setting. Good communication across the generations is vital. In order for them to have a safe and secure place to relax and meet friends, the young people need the time and help of adults. A gift of flowers for the adult volunteers at the end of the first meeting of the club from some of the young people was a touching sign that they recognized this, and a sign that they considered the club to be a venture which they owned for themselves. The adults in turn are very clear that this is the young people's club. This is one of the ways in which they express their valuing of the young people and the young people in turn have to take responsibility. Young people share in decision-making and the programme of activities depends on their ideas. They help to set up and put away, and recruitment of new members depends to a considerable extent on their efforts.

The club rests on a vision of the Church as a community of faith, a community of people who are called to offer support to each other, this mutual support being an aspect of the Church which was high-lighted in a recent Parochial Church Council discussion. It draws on biblical images of the Church as the Body of Christ and our Lord's command to love one another. The Church as a community can be seen as something of a cliché. I am sure I am not the only one to have mixed feelings about being called a 'faith community' by local and central government in their efforts to promote social solidarity. 'We're not a faith community,' I feel like protesting. 'We're a Church!' Yet the idea of a church as a community of faith can be very fruitful. This idea has been usefully explored by an American evangelical writer, Rodney Clapp.[7]

Few would disagree that we are leaving behind the time of Christendom. 'Constantine was the first in a long line of emperors, princes and presidents who saw Christianity as the unifying force that might bind and discipline their . . . subjects'.[8] In this situation 'Christians . . . too readily equated the Church's work with religious sponsorship of the status quo'.[9] The Church of England was formed around the role of pastoral chaplain to a Christian society enforced by the state. The Anglican Church of the Reformation did not even con-ceive of citizens outside the Church.[10] Even though this inheritance still deeply marks our pattern of church life it is very clear that we have been rapidly moving away from this situation. Part of the cost of this is that the Church 'lost a sense of itself as an alternative way of life'.[11] In a highly pluralist, post-modern consumer culture this approach does not work. The Church cannot act like the religious department of the National Health Service. Rodney Clapp suggests that the Church needs to be seen as a culture in its own right and calls for the return of the Church 'to an existence that can become distinc-tively, exhilaratingly christian – a social and political existence quite like that of the church in its earliest days'.[12]

Where we are heading

We need to recover anew the sense of the Church as a community, not
a collection of isolated individuals each on his or her own private
spiritual journey. To recognize that we are communal beings is in
itself counter-cultural. The friendship of the adult helpers for the
young people and their desire to meet can be seen as a way of affirming this sense of community. But we need to be more than a community. We need to be a Christian community, a community that shares
the Christian Faith and seeks to live out its discipleship. According to
its constitution, the club is an intrinsic part of the wider community of
our two churches.

The challenge to us as a parish is to become what we are called to
be: to assert our Christian identity in our worship and to find ways of
living Christianly in our culture. We are called to be communities of
loving resistance to many of the assumptions of our consumer culture, or, to use Clapp's term, a community of 'sanctified subversion'.[13]
The young people can be offered the chance of belonging to this community. The needs they have expressed are for a place to meet and
relax. The Church is able to offer a physical space. Although we do
have a separate hall, part of the parish church has been partitioned
off, with opening soundproof screens. This makes a sizeable multi-
purpose space. It can be interesting when the door between the
worship space and the hall space is left open. Some of the young people wander in and explore the church and simply spend a little time
there quietly. This can be a metaphor for the invitation to engage with
the Christian Faith. But the Church is not just a physical space, it is a
community. By belonging to the club the young people are part of the
wider community of the Church. They are offered the chance to
belong in a more active, committed way and part of the task ahead of
us is to make this theoretical invitation a reality.

At first sight the young people's expressed needs could be just
another chance of consumption for personal pleasure. Yet behind this
there is also a wider sense of the need to belong and contribute to the
common good. The Church can offer them the chance to think how
they can be useful, how they can show a Christian serving spirit and
challenge the Church where it needs to live this out more deeply.
What the young people can offer the Church is their energy, their
questions and their demand for the chance to participate and be
heard. They also offer their networks of contacts. Friendships going
back to primary school have been especially significant. Part of living
Christianly is for all ages and backgrounds to feel accepted and to
experience being valued. If in Christ the barriers between Jew and
Gentile are broken then barriers of age should be capable of being
bridged. This in itself can be powerful, a gift that the parish can offer.

Opportunities for young people to be part of a cross-generational community are not so common outside the Church.

Perhaps this sounds more like an agenda for the club's future development. We have built on a deeply felt concern for supporting young people as well as a concern to pass on the Faith. This enabled us to respond positively when the opportunity arose. The request for adult helpers has tapped into considerable energy and commitment which I as the vicar had been unaware of. It is still very new, small in scale, and modest. Our life so far will need to be reviewed and reflected upon. We are on a journey, a hopeful journey, but at least we have started and are involved with some young people.

Further reading

Youth Apart: Young People and the Church, National Society/Church House Publishing, London, 1996.

Taking A Part: Young People's Participation in the Church, National Society/Church House Publishing, London, 2000.

Yoder, John Howard, *The Politics of Jesus*, Eerdmans, Grand Rapids, 1972.

Notes

1 Cray, Graham, *Postmodern Culture and Youth Discipleship*, Grove Books, Cambridge, 1998. I have drawn heavily on Cray's brief analysis of the cultural context of young people for this section.

2 Bauman, Zygmunt, *Life in Fragments*, Blackwell, Oxford, 1995, p. 5, quoted in Cray, *Postmodern Culture*, p. 6.

3 Gabriel, Yiannis and Tim Lang, *The Unmanageable Consumer*, Sage, London, 1995, p. 100.

4 Ward, Peter, *Mass Culture*, Bible Reading Fellowship, Oxford, 1999, Introduction, p. 26.

5 Cray, *Postmodern Culture*, p. 11.

6 See Ward, Peter, *Youthwork and the Mission of God*, SPCK, London, 1997.

7 Clapp, Rodney, *A Peculiar People – the Church as a Culture in a Post-christian Society*, InterVarsity Press, Downers Grove, 1996.

8 Clapp, *A Peculiar People*, p. 23.

9 Clapp, *A Peculiar People*, p. 22.

10 See for instance the Report on Christian initiation *On The Way*, Church House Publishing, London, 1995, p. 51.

11 Clapp, *A Peculiar People*, p. 75.

12 Clapp, *A Peculiar People*, p. 82.

13 Clapp, *A Peculiar People*, pp. 199–204.

12. Making it New

Regeneration in the Parish

GRAHAME SHAW AND MALCOLM TORRY

Jerusalem, Jerusalem, the city that kills the prophets and stones those who are sent to it! How often have I desired to gather your children together as a hen gathers her brood under her wings, and you were not willing! See, your house is left to you, desolate. For I tell you, you will not see me again until you say, 'Blessed is the one who comes in the name of the Lord.' (Matt. 23.37–39)

'Regenerate': invest with new and higher spiritual nature; improve moral condition of, breathe new and more vigorous and higher life into, (person, institution, etc.); generate again, bring or come into renewed existence . . . Hence 'regeneration'[1]

From its beginnings the parish has been involved in regeneration: of individuals, of communities, and of the built environment, mainly through the building and running of schools, hospitals and other institutions. During the nineteenth century, parish churches and their clergy were often influential in the replacement or upgrading of slums and in the building of a generation of church schools funded by the National Society; and during the first half of the twentieth century parish churches were often involved in welfare projects.

Our story begins in South-East London during the mid-1960s, at St Catherine's, Hatcham, at New Cross. The Labour government was promoting neighbourhood councils as the way to renew communities, the parish hall was on its last legs, the parish was unusually cosmopolitan (it is where many of the earliest people arriving from the Caribbean during the 1950s and early 60s had settled), the community had experienced more than its fair share of violence (mods and rockers and otherwise), and the parish priest, Allan Auckland, saw an opportunity for the parish church to serve its community. The hall was demolished, half the vicarage garden was sold for housing, some of the churchyard was sold to the Borough Council so that a library could be built on it, Bishop Mervyn Stockwood was petitioned for a faculty (bypassing the chancellor, with whom he had fallen out), legalities were sidestepped, a ten-thousand square-foot community centre was built inside and around the back end of the parish church, and a neighbourhood council was set up to run it. For nearly twenty years an elderly people's lunch club, youth clubs, a playgroup, uniformed organizations, community events and a bar generated considerable activity and much community participation – and Lewisham Borough Council paid most of the bills. It might not have been called 'regeneration' then, but that's what it was.

The Telegraph Hill Centre was built during an era of considerable optimism. Human nature was sufficiently trusted to allow the chair of the neighbourhood council to be elected at an open meeting of the entire community, and the building was designed on the assumption that oil would always be cheap. In 1988 the borough withdrew its grant aid, the Telegraph Hill Neighbourhood Council decided that it could no longer cope, and the Parochial Church Council recognized that it had a moral (but not a legal) obligation to rescue the centre. The top two floors were let to a housing association for office space, and the playgroup, lunch club and youth clubs were relocated into the ground floor. Though the lunch club soon departed, and activities have changed over the years, the centre must be one of the longest-standing parish regeneration initiatives, providing opportunities for community involvement (the management committee still contains representatives elected at an annual meeting of the whole community), for community activity (the annual arts festival and other community events use the space), for youth work, and for much else.

In Lorrimore Square in Walworth, the rebuilt St Paul's Church contained the first Albermarle Youth Centre, a partnership venture with Southwark Borough Council. This too was to collapse during the early years of 1980s Conservative government. In the midst of much hand-wringing over the cost to the community of dismantling traditional community provision, in much of which parish churches were partners, St Paul's recognized that a new world of social care was on the way, and the parish contributed to the new infrastructure required by the Community Care Act by establishing the Lorrimore Centre, a multi-profession centre to serve people with mental illness. The voluntary sector in general was becoming professionalized as it responded to the invitation to be service-providers in a world in which local and other authorities are purchasers rather than providers, and St Paul's and its parish priest recognized the role the parish church could play as it responded to social need within the structures on offer, in much the same way as St Catherine's, Hatcham had done twenty years previously.

A significant contribution to the process was made by the report *Faith in the City*, published in 1985, which encouraged parishes to carry out audits to discover social and other needs to which the parish might be able to respond, and which led to the establishment of the Church Urban Fund to support projects designed to meet the needs identified. The report, the audits and the fund stimulated activity at parish level, but also more widely, and in South-East London Borough Councils held *Faith in the City* conferences to encourage new partnerships to evolve, and the Diocese of Southwark set up its own housing association to enable surplus church land to be used for social housing. Whilst the Church Urban Fund has been a significant stimulus to new projects, we suspect that the report's call for parish audits might be its major long-term contribution to the Church's relationship to regeneration, for such audits are still being carried out – and the process has now been extended to larger areas, and related to consultation and planning processes managed by boroughs and by the Greater London Authority. An excellent recent example of such an audit is *Regeneration in London South Central*: a wide-ranging research project which seeks to understand the needs of local people across a large area of inner London, to map current and future regeneration activity, to document the work of faith communities, and to explore responses which faith communities might be able to make to expected changes in their areas.[2] What has been particularly significant about *Faith in the City*, the *London South Central* report, and many individual church initiatives, is the importance they have given to *social* regeneration. Economic regeneration can have a variety of effects: it can enable new social regeneration to occur, or it can damage existing communities and thus require new injections of social regeneration. If economic regeneration encourages new gated communities, and the people who move into them don't use local schools, other local services, or local churches, then building community can become harder rather than easier. The Church's role here is surely to encourage the kind of economic regeneration that might promote social regeneration, and then to pursue a social regeneration agenda with all the partners it can find.

One of the early Church Urban Fund projects was in East Greenwich, where the doubtful future of the large Christ Church building, the existence of the fund, a parish audit, and the need of local organizations (such as Greenwich's Association for People with Disabilities) for space from which to operate, led to the building of Christchurch Forum, a centre for integrated living. Inside the old building new floors were put in, offices and meeting rooms were built, and lifts were installed, and a new worship space was built on one end of the building. Here a particular need had been identified and provision for meeting it made, and for fifteen years now the Forum (now the Forum @ Greenwich) has been providing facilities for people with disabilities and for the community generally.

In each of the initiatives we have listed the parish has been the initiator. Always the parish priest has taken the leading role, and the congregation has either agreed or acquiesced. Sometimes there has been a handful of members of the congregation who have participated enthusiastically in the process, but sometimes the important group has been the priest working with members of the community who do not belong to the congregation. Similar patterns can be seen in other initiatives, such as the Copleston Centre in Peckham and Christ Church, North Brixton. It has not always been plain sailing, of course. Sometimes the parish church has had to fight to remain engaged, and sometimes it has had to re-engage, as at St Catherine's, Hatcham. Always the relationship between the regeneration activity and the parish church has to be constantly renegotiated. Given the differences between religious and secular institutions it is no surprise that tensions often arise in the relationships between them and that in a changing world in which all institutions change all the time relationships sometimes become fraught.

There are always new opportunities for engagement: and it is often those parishes that have previously engaged in regeneration activity which re-engage when the world changes. At Lorrimore Square, St Paul's is now the home (both physically and otherwise) of the Lorrimore mental health 'Drop in' but also of the London Ecumenical Aids Trust. Many Christians and people of other faiths or of no faith were committed to the growth and development of Southwark Community Care Forum, a major infrastructure organization committed to an increased professionalism within the community care arm of the voluntary sector. At St Peter's, Walworth, the crypt of which was an early conversion to community use, a new multi-use centre called 'Inspire' has just been opened. This is another project which started with a parish audit, and in this case the audit identified a need for facilities for training for the arts, and also for community events. The crypt has been reordered accordingly.

Now there is a new felt need: to engage in the planning stages of regeneration of the built environment. There has been plenty of such regeneration, and there will be much more. In the Rotherhithe area the old docklands area has been transformed; Canary Wharf has been built to the north of the Isle of Dogs and this development is still spreading southwards and eastwards; and the 'Thames Gateway', on both sides of the river from Greenwich to the sea, is a vast regeneration area. The challenge now is twofold: for our parish churches to respond locally, and for the strategic planners of our faith communities to respond with resources as well as with hope and goodwill.

On the Ferrier Estate in Kidbrooke, Church Army Captain Nick Russell has been supporting tenants as they face the redevelopment of the entire estate. English doesn't have an adequate word to describe his role. He is an *animateur*, providing a focus for debate of the most politically sensitive issues, such as tenants' right of return to the place from which they will have to be moved. Here the Church in the form of the Church Army and the parish to which Nick is attached is relating not only to its own need for facilities from which to serve the new community (though it is doing that), but is also relating to the *whole* of the regeneration task: the new built environment, and the community which will evolve within it.

At the Elephant and Castle a variety of regeneration schemes have come and gone during the past forty years. Nothing has come of most of them, but the parish church has always been involved, and still is. It might be said that much time has been wasted at meetings which eventually lead nowhere, but that would be only half the story, because for the parish church to be engaged with other social partners brings its own rewards in terms of opportunities for service, and at the Elephant the parish church has made a major contribution in terms of community development.

One of the major successes was the Coin Street development on the south bank of the Thames between the Oxo Tower and Waterloo Bridge. There a vigorous local campaign during the mid-1980s saw off a large office development and led to the building of high-quality social housing, and the parish (and not just the vicar and curate) were a vital part of that campaign. The vicar David Wickert's role at the public enquiry remains memorable.

A similarly high-profile approach was taken by the parish adjacent to what became Canary Wharf on the Isle of Dogs, with the vicar leading a coffin-carrying procession round the island to represent the death of the existing community. It is an open question as to whether this was the right thing to do. In terms of identification with people's often legitimate concerns about the impact of a large office development on their community, the parish might have regarded its reaction as relevant; but in terms of building a relationship with an inevitable development in order to contribute to what the local community might get out of it the approach was rather counterproductive. The situation has not been helped by the development being in three different parishes, all with different attitudes to Canary Wharf: from a desire to evangelize individuals to a concern to relate the development to a changing residential community. But now there is at least dialogue between parishes and with the company running Canary Wharf, and a multi-faith prayer-room is a tangible result of this co-operation.

Lessons have also been learnt in Thamesmead. West Thamesmead is currently seeing massive residential growth, and the Diocese of Southwark decided (on the basis of a consultant's report) to build a clergy house in the new housing area but no church building. With hindsight this might have been a mistake. Cyril Garbett, when Bishop of Southwark during the middle of the last century, organized the building of a couple of dozen church buildings in new housing areas in South London, so that as the housing was built there was already a parish infrastructure. Yes, it might be possible in borrowed buildings or in people's homes to gather Christians to form a congregation so that that congregation can relate to the growing new community of West Thamesmead; but without a physical focus it might be difficult to do so. A recent initiative in the Millennium Village at the southern end of the Greenwich Peninsula has experienced precisely this difficulty.

Which brings us to the rest of the Greenwich Peninsula, where we enter a whole new regeneration world. In the past, development masterplans have been written by Borough Councils or by such quangos as development corporations. But the masterplan for the entire Greenwich Peninsula has been written by Meridian Delta Ltd. (MDL), a consortium of global companies. The Borough Council's role is to give permission for the development after negotiating as much planning gain as it can, and this Greenwich Borough Council is doing.

If all goes to plan, by 2006 the Millennium Dome will have become a sports and leisure complex, hosting concerts and sports events. A hotel next to the Dome will follow, then new homes, and by 2021 there will be around 10,000 new homes, enough office space to fill two and a half Canary Wharf towers, some light industrial units, retail and service facilities, and a new secondary school.

In August 2002, after initial contact between staff at MDL and some local religious leaders, a meeting was held at which possible models for relationships between the development and the faith communities were discussed. Further discussion revealed MDL's and the borough's wish that the faith communities should work together on the new development, and explored the possibility of a building being provided. At a meeting in March 2003, to which members of Greenwich's Multifaith Forum and Greenwich's Ecumenical Borough Deans were invited, Meridian Delta and the borough offered the Greenwich Pavilion to the faith communities to manage for their own use and for that of the wider community, and asked for a single person to be appointed to liaise between the borough, MDL, and the faith communities, and for a site chaplain to co-ordinate chaplaincy arrangements during the construction phase and beyond. The Anglican Team Rector was appointed to undertake both of these tasks, and a small steering group was appointed to guide the project. Also appointed was a group of religious leaders to ensure good communication between the faith communities' work on the Peninsula and faith community leaders. The steering group keeps this leaders' group informed of its activity and continues to consult with the Ecumenical Borough Deans and the borough's multi-faith forum. It has educated itself in possible models for its activity by visiting the Canary Wharf prayer room, the London Inter-faith Centre at West Kilburn, and Bluewater, and it is represented on MDL's Business Planning Group and wherever else it might be useful to participate. On 23 September 2003 a consultation was held for faith communities in Greenwich: an opportunity for representatives of all the borough's faith communities to hear presentations by MDL and by the steering group, to see the Greenwich Pavilion, to ask questions, and to make suggestions. This project is in its early stages, but already there is the possibility of a wide-ranging relationship between the developer, the new community, the borough, the faith communities, and other social institutions. In this situation the parish church is a partner, offering volunteer help, its clergy's time, and possibly in the future the nucleus of a new congregation. In this situation the parish church is only going to be there if it is a partner, for the masterplan makes no provision for stand-alone church buildings or for stand-alone buildings for any faith community.

To return to our definition of 'regenerate': 'Invest with new and higher spiritual nature; improve moral condition of, breathe new and more vigorous and higher life into, (person, institution, etc.); generate again, bring or come into renewed existence.' As we have seen, there have been many opportunities for a parish to participate in regeneration activity: in regeneration of the community through education, healing, welfare provision, and other forms of social care, and through contributing to debate and other activity on the built environment. There are still many such opportunities, and there will be more, but the means which have been employed in the past, while still relevant to regeneration within existing communities, might not be quite so relevant in relation to future large-scale developments. Whereas the parish has often in the past been a major partner in the process, in the future a partnership in which there is greater equality between the players might be required. There will still be a need for the traditional skills: consultation, planning, budgeting, fundraising, and above all the ability to negotiate a tangle of institutions, pots of money, and sets of values; but we shall need new skills too. We shall need to learn to structure our activity so that global companies can relate to it. (This will include, as on the Greenwich Peninsula, the appointment of an individual to liaise between the private, public and faith communities; it will require the faith communities' ability to trust that single channel of communication; and it will require that individual to be able to consult widely.) We shall also need the ability to relate on equal terms with other denominations and other faiths. (On the Greenwich Peninsula we are taking a multi-faith rather than an inter-faith approach, that is, we shall be doing together everything which every party can do together in good conscience but not otherwise: so, for instance, we shall be managing a chaplaincy team together, but not worshipping together.)

We suspect that, as in the past, the parish priest will remain a focal person in the relationship between the parish and regeneration activity, whether that activity be of the traditional or of the newer type. The priest is the parish's visible representative, and is a natural channel of communication. The priest's position as a member of the congregation, as a representative of the congregation, and as a person with a particular role in the wider community, will always mean that much power lies in their hands. This means that careful consultation and the using of existing representative structures and the setting up of new ones if necessary will be essential elements in the parish's relationship with regeneration. What also seems to be important is a parish priest's willingness to stay. One of the parish priest's own particular gifts to regeneration processes is their place in a variety of networks of people and institutions, and this only develops with time – though this point applies elsewhere too of course, for Malcolm Cooper, a Methodist minister on the staff of the Kent Industrial Mission, has been as effective as he has been at Bluewater, the large retail project near Dartford, because he was there before it started and he is still there.

Developments are now often large or they are elements of larger projects. So it might be thought that parish boundaries have become irrelevant. We are convinced that parish boundaries are still relevant, because they define responsibility: they ensure that the congregation knows that within these boundaries they have a responsibility to relate to the community, to the built environment, and to the community's and the environment's regeneration. Problems occur where a large (or even a small) development crosses parish boundaries, for in this situation it is not clear who is responsible, and tensions frequently lead to inactivity, as they did in Canary Wharf for many years. What is needed in such a situation is the redrawing of parish boundaries,[3] not their abolition. On the Greenwich Peninsula we are in the fortunate position of the entire site being in one Anglican parish and in one Roman Catholic parish, meaning that the two territorially-minded communions can spend their energy relating to each other, to other churches, to other faiths, to the developer, and to the borough, without having to cope with interparochial relationships.

One lesson which seems to us to emerge from the regeneration projects that we have discussed is the importance of the parish structure as a whole: the boundaries, the priest (or in the case of the Ferrier Estate the Church Army Captain), and the building. Where there is no identifiable building (whether it be a parish church or a clearly defined, jointly used building), relationships amongst the faith communities and between those communities and other institutions become difficult. Religions are constituted by their gathered congregations, and congregations need homes, preferably visible and identifiable homes. It is congregations and their pastors that relate to regeneration and that offer physical space for use as community centres and centres for social care, and this will continue to be the case.

But the provision of physical space, while an important contribution to the regeneration of a community, is not by any means the only contribution that a parish might bring to the regeneration process. A parish brings an identifiable congregation: a relatively coherent body of people with skills to offer and decision-making and plan-making processes to deploy in the service of their communities. A parish brings an identifiable person, the parish priest or similar figure, through whom communication can flow and who can enable relationships to occur. A parish brings consciousness of a wider community (and one of the debates to which we have been able to contribute on the Greenwich Peninsula is the question as to whether what is being built is a new community or an extension of the existing community of East Greenwich). A parish brings its own contribution to a network of relationships between public, voluntary and private institutions. And a parish brings with it a gospel of a transcendent God, an involved God, and a God who brings in a future community of justice and peace. If to 'regenerate' means to 'invest with new and higher spiritual nature; [to] improve moral condition of, breathe new and more vigorous and higher life into' a community, an institution, or a development project, then the word itself invites every parish that can do so to involve itself in the regeneration of its area, for the parish (along with other faith communities) has an element to bring to its partnerships which other kinds of organization cannot bring. This is not to suggest that God is not already there, at work in secular regeneration processes: rather it is to suggest that the Church in the form of the parish has a particular contribution to make, for the parish is a sacrament of a God who is incarnate in our suffering and hopeful humanity.

At the head of this chapter we have placed Jesus' weeping over Jerusalem: a city then and now in need of regeneration. We end the chapter with the seer's vision of a regenerated city:

> Then I saw a new heaven and a new earth; for the first heaven and the first earth had passed away, and the sea was no more. And I saw the holy city, the new Jerusalem, coming down out of heaven from God, prepared as a bride adorned for her husband. And I heard a loud voice from the throne saying,

'See, the home of God is among mortals.
He will dwell with them;
they will be his peoples,
snd God himself will be with them;
he will wipe every tear from their eyes.
Death will be no more;
mourning and crying and pain will be no more,
for the first things have passed away.' (Rev. 21.1–4)

This is the ultimate regeneration for which we hope. In the meantime, it is the *pen*ultimate regeneration for which we work, so that our city might be a sacrament of the city to come.

Further reading

Davey, Andrew, *Urban Christianity and Global Order: Theological Resources for an Urban Future*, SPCK, London, 2001.

Hamnett, Chris, *Unequal City: London in the Global Arena*, Routledge, London, 2003.

The Archbishop of Canterbury's Commission on Urban Priority Areas, *Faith in the City: A Call for Action by Church and Nation*, Church House Publishing, London, 1985.

Notes

1 *The Concise Oxford Dictionary*, 5th edn, 1964.

2 Robertson, Catriona, *Regeneration in London South Central*, Southwark and Newington Deanery, London, 2002.

3 A conventional district is often formed when there is a new development. By this means a territory, sometimes crossing parish boundaries, can be designated as an area in which a particular priest has responsibility rather than any one of the existing parishes. Parish boundary changes can then be considered at a later date when the pastoral situation has become clearer.

13. Travelling Towards Faith

Evangelism in the Parish

MIKE MARSHALL

Three parish churches; one a large neo-classical building occupying a site at a busy London crossroad. The second a new-built brick structure set in a side street in a cosmopolitan residential area. The third a tall-spired Victorian neo-gothic building standing on its own island.

These are the three churches in which I have served in South London over the past twenty years. The first and latest, St Mark's, Kennington and St John's, Blackheath, while clearly identifiable as parish churches, are nevertheless buildings isolated from their nearest neighbours; visible but architecturally aloof. In the middle church, where I served my first incumbency, St Alban's, Streatham Park, I had the privilege of serving in a new building. There were many wonderful things about the structure, not least its pristine condition, but there were also one or two drawbacks. The building itself, constructed in modern material, was tucked away in a side street and did not have a conventional church appearance. In fact, a number of people told me that they passed it by for many years before they realised what it was, having assumed it to be a squash court. It will be useful to refer back to these buildings shortly.

In this chapter, we are looking at the parish and evangelism. It is not my intention, though, simply to list a number of good or not so good ideas. What I will attempt is the provision of a framework in which to understand the task of evangelism, what the nature of that task is when viewed from the perspective of the parish church, and one or two examples of that pursuit in real situations.

Since most parishes have at least one worship centre or church, I will assume that our expectation is that evangelism will in some way increase the number of people going to that worship centre as a result of the activities which we term 'evangelistic'. I doubt very much, though, whether anyone would want to see evangelism defined as merely getting people into church. Moreover, the Church globally is not always organized in territorial communities such as the Anglican parish. Non-community-based outreach will always have its place.

Clearly we must see evangelism in much wider terms than those of the local church. Nevertheless at this juncture our focus is on the parish.

Evangelism is, to use a working definition, a proclamation and living out of the good news of the Kingdom of God accompanied by a divine invitation to be part of that Kingdom. Millions of words have been written about the practical outworking of that task, and many means and methodologies have been employed down the years in pursuit of it. It is a subject that arouses great fervour in some, dread in others, and a degree of uncomfortable guilt in many. It is an area of church life that many have felt was 'not for them' but rather one for the especially gifted, the called, or the just plain potty. I would want to suggest though that evangelism is not only best pursued from the base of a local community of Christians, such as the parish church, but that it is that very missionary task which defines the existence of a Christian community and circumscribes its activity.

On a practical level the Church must involve itself in evangelistic outreach for the very purposes of survival. The decline in Anglican church attendance is well documented and however the figures are buoyed up by the influx of faithful Christians from other communities (for example, the arrival of African Anglicans into South London Churches) the Church will be robust and healthy only in so far as it is successful in drawing into its life those who customarily have little or no contact with it or historic relation to it. Times have changed. People don't *have* to go to church any more – if in London they ever did. There can no longer be any credible expectation that there will be a stream of people growing into adult church life through Sunday school, etc. Those churches that do not have a realistic strategy of 'recruitment and retention' will find their planning for the future to be merely an exercise in staving off the inevitable point of closure.

While such practical considerations might be important, I would prefer to present an argument for an evangelistic outlook as a matter of theological conviction.

Paul exhorted the Corinthian church in the following manner: 'We are therefore ambassadors for Christ, God making His appeal through us' (2 Cor. 5.17).

Insomuch as this exhortation applies to the Church in general it surely applies to the local parish. It is in the local parish, and in setting out from the weekly worship in the parish church, that the average Christian man or woman encounters those who are unchurched. Put another way, it is the daily contact of the many 'ordinary Christians' with other people in the neighbourhood, work or home that provides the largest interface the Church is likely to have with non-affiliates. A body of Christians worshipping together in a distinct geographical area, therefore, is called to play an ambassadorial role. The parish church is an embassy of the Kingdom and provides a focal point for the ambassadors and a centre of operations for those who gather there. Evangelism is not just about 'getting people into church', but bringing people into church, involving them in a Christian community and introducing them to the good news of the Kingdom may well result in Christian commitment. How a church operates and how the parish's worshippers order their activities will have a direct effect on whether it is a numerically growing church. And whether or not the church grows could well be determined by how fully the members of the local congregation embrace their ambassadorial role.

But let us go back to the parish churches I mentioned at the start and use those buildings as a metaphor in helping us to delineate the evangelistic task. The buildings themselves, the piles of brick or stone that we call 'churches', provide useful illustrations that can demonstrate how the church itself might be seen in the community, and might help us to see how the church might therefore pursue its role. The church in the parish needs to have a high profile, and it must be visible to those who have no affiliation with it or little affection for it. Those who are to be reached with the good news of the Kingdom need to know that the church is there, so the church needs to be prominent, like the two churches that I have served which are built on their own plots of land, and which are distinctive and highly visible. The local communities are certainly aware of them: indeed, they are landmarks. In contrast, the church where I served my first incumbency, St Alban's, was tucked into a side street. There was a danger that it might be overlooked, that people would not find it even if they were looking. In a similar manner the living congregation, the church, may be subdued, quiet, indistinct and lacking in profile in the community and thus limited in its task of engagement.

But visibility must not be achieved at the expense of accessibility. People may know the church to be there, but can they get to it? What are the barriers that lie between the inside of the building and those who don't habitually attend? Furthermore, when the effort is made and barriers are crossed, is it possible to enter? Is the church welcoming? Is there a cultural accessibility even when there is an actual open door? These are questions we can ask about a physical building but they serve very well as metaphor for the church community and the church community as representatives of the Kingdom of Heaven which seeks to invite others to be part of that Kingdom. An analogy that might help us to orchestrate our evangelistic task might be one of 'gradient'. If a church is to have a high profile in the community – and I am suggesting that this is necessary – then there will be an inevitable gradient between the inside and the outside. The evangelistic task requires us to make this gradient as gentle as possible, providing stepping stones along it for people to make progress in small increments, and creating multiple entry points into the church so that access can be as varied as possible.

This gradient approach to evangelism need not be in contradiction of some of the more stereotypical views of what evangelism is. I am fully aware that there are numerous anecdotal examples of those who have taken a large leap and landed with both feet comfortably in a local congregation as a result of some evangelistic crusade. It seems to me, though, that for most people movement into the Kingdom and into Church is through incremental progress up the gradient from the outside to the inside with subsequent incorporation. My personal conviction is that 'becoming a Christian', the point of incorporation, of inclusion of an individual in the Kingdom of God, is a specific event. The actual location of that event, however, may well be indiscernible. The identification of it may be God's alone. Although a crisis event such as a conversion experience may be pastorally very helpful and fix a certainty in someone's mind, for most people the journey to faith is a process, however tangible the 'crossing of the line' may or may not be. Thus evangelism addresses people at all and every stage on their journey. Evangelism aimed at only one point of that journey, or evangelism solely designed to achieve an effect or 'decision', might well prove to be ill-targeted and counter-productive. Evangelism must be a continual and continuing process. It is must be one of attitude and numerous small tasks rather than just a large, loud and periodically explosive endeavour. It may well use 'crisis' as a means of growth, but 'company and care' are at least as important.

If the parish church and its community is to pursue creatively an evangelistic task, encouraging people to take steps along a gradient, one of the first requirements must be its self-understanding. Those who consider themselves part of the church community need to be aware of who they are, where they are, and what they are about.

At St Alban's, where I was first an incumbent, the one with a low profile, we took time as a congregation to set ourselves a mission statement. The phrase we took was from Paul's letter to the Colossians: '. . . to present everyone mature in Christ' (Col. 1.28). We were recognizing that our role as a church was to see people grow in their Christian Faith. Of necessity, that included seeing people come into Christian Faith in the first place, so an integral part of our mission statement was an understanding of the evangelistic task. At the church where I am serving my second incumbency, St John's, when I suggested we had a mission statement there was a groan of anguish! Everybody was fed up with mission statements from work and public organizations and didn't want one in church, so we compromised. The PCC, after much discussion and prayer, formulated 'not the mission statement'. We simply described what we were doing with three phrases. We were to:

1 'Look up' – looking up to God in worship and praise

2 'Look in' – looking in to the support of one another as we walked in faith together

3 'Look out' – A call to look out in service and proclamation to the world around us.

This formula was one which then informed all the smaller groups in the church. One of the church members wrote a song that incorporated the ideas and which is used regularly in worship. Every small unit in church has adapted these statements as fundamental to their existence, whatever their task is.

The point is that in both these cases, because we had a clear statement of what we thought we were doing, everything we did in church was evaluated in this light. The underlying understanding in both these cases was that we were members of the Kingdom of Heaven. We were here on earth, a band of pilgrims who were journeying to heaven carrying the conviction that our journey incorporated an ambassadorial role. We were to invite others to join us on the way. That is why we were journeying through the communities in which we were placed (otherwise we might as well already be in heaven!). It was a particular delight when someone remarked that they had never thought before of the gardening team as being 'evangelistic' but now they had begun to think of ways in which it might be!

Surely congregations of all historic traditions would do well to have a similar self-awareness. I hope that this may increasingly be the case. While taking a recent holiday I went to two very different churches. The first was a small rural church in Cornwall and the second a cathedral in an urban area. What was so encouraging was that at both these centres of worship there was an emphasis on evangelism. This was neither aggressive nor overt, yet in the way the service was shaped, in the explanations we were given of what was happening, even in the welcome to a cup of coffee after the service, there was clearly planning for and preparation to welcome someone making a transition into the worshipping community.

What then about specific evangelistic activity? Clearly, from what has already been said, everything that is done might be considered evangelistic if it has already been decided that the congregation's reason for being is to be ambassadors. But what specific things might be done if our congregations are to be bodies of people committed to growing? – to adding to their number?

Perhaps we should begin by looking at our buildings themselves, not now as metaphor but as hindrances or helps in evangelism. What do our buildings look and feel like? What are they saying? In the light of the opening to the chapter, one of the first questions we might ask is: do the buildings themselves announce our presence? Do they give us profile? If ever we are involved in the building of a new church there are some very important architectural and locational considerations to be borne in mind. Too many congregations have given up prime locations on the high street (with a high visibility) following a lucrative offer from a chain store or supermarket to help with a rebuild round the corner. The solution to antiquated plant has often been achieved at the expense of prime location.

It isn't just location that is important, for we might ask the question: 'What should a church look like?' I was fascinated to attend a new church building in America recently in which the building was, well, 'just like a church'. Given the technical innovations incorporated into the building, I was a bit surprised at the lack of architectural adventure in the new structure. When I questioned the people responsible for this there was a ready answer. They pointed out that many people in this particular area were coming back to church, returning after perhaps a generation away. The evangelistic endeavours of this congregation had been particularly fruitful, hence the need for a new, larger building. They explained to me that while clearly there was no 'correct' architectural form for a building for Christian worship, those in their area who were looking for a church wanted to recognize what they were looking for. Fascinatingly, the foremost consideration in the building of a new worship centre for this congregation was: 'What will make it easiest for the newcomer to find us and join us?'

We may not be able to do much with the external architecture of a building that we have inherited (though if the building isn't 'working' then that should always be considered). What we can do, though, is to aim to make the inside of our main parish building somewhere that is comfortable, the kind of place where those who are not used to church might be ready to stay for a while and learn. Why should people come to a place where they are cold and uncomfortable? Without being prescriptive of any internal style it seems to me that our buildings must be attractive and welcoming, whatever our church tradition. To spend money on the comfort and aesthetics of our building is in itself a mission project. When we reordered the present church of which I am incumbent at a fairly high cost there was one person who said they were very uneasy about spending this amount of money 'on ourselves'. The reordering involved new heating, lighting, seating, sound system, video projection, carpeting and internal decoration (and an expensive consistory court sitting to gain a faculty). The PCC's reply was robust: This money was not being spent on 'ourselves', it was being spent on making the building an effective evangelistic tool. If we wanted people to come to church and to be receptive to what was being said in church, then the distractions have to be minimized. The welcome we purport to profess verbally must be supported by the place in which we meet.

But what about the external profile? What if people pass by and don't even know the church is there? They are hardly likely to engage with a church and hear what is being said if they are unaware of it. There is, of course, more to profile than architectural visibility. In St Alban's, where I served my first incumbency, the church that some-one thought was a squash court, we decided we needed to let the local community know we were there. We needed to become more visible. We had a team of four young people working with us at the time (all full-time volunteers) and rather 'tongue in cheek' I always main-tained that one of their major contributions to us was their energy, irrespective of what their activity was. They were constantly coming in and out of the building. The building was clearly alive. You might not be able to see a spire from a distance but you couldn't go past the building without knowing it was a presence. It had profile. Since there was such activity, part of the profile-raising was to give constant explanation about that activity – good notices in the windows or on the notice board and inventive artwork and provocative news-sheets were all part of our profile-raising tactics.

At my present church we use a church magazine that is thought-fully targeted. It is written in such a way as to engage the attention of the non-churched reader with information and articles intended to draw that non-church reader's attention to the existence of the local church community. Moreover, this is not a magazine that is sold but one which is hand-delivered free to every house in the parish (why collude with the convenient myth that the Church is only after your money?). Engagement is invited. We ask for comments and letters back. This heightens the awareness of the 'there-ness' of church. A personal ambition I have is to provide an official graffiti board outside the church where dialogue can be entered into with any passer by!

But if the Church raises its profile, heightens its visibility, it must surely not remain content with sitting on an island waving flags or bellowing messages with megaphones saying 'Come in number 7!' The Church needs to move to where people are. The congregation needs to step down the gradient to meet people, needs to lay down stepping-stones on the path and set up signposts that point to the entrances and turn what is so often inward-looking outward.

I was once walking along the sea front at Brighton.

'Are you a Christian?' yelled a fervent young man whom I had tried to walk past, looking straight at me.

'Yes,' I replied, deciding that it would be churlish just to keep walk-ing. Obviously a little nonplussed he rallied and said

'Ah, but are you saved?'

'Yes,' I replied again.

'Are you born-again, though?' he tried with a little more desperation, 'and have you been baptized in the Holy Spirit?'

Resisting the temptation to say that, whilst I admired his zeal, I found his assumption that the average passer-by would understand his esoteric language to be naïve, and that for the sake of the Kingdom of God and the comprehension of all, perhaps he should attempt to master a more creative cultural hermeneutic, I merely replied

'Indeed I have.'

But it was a sticky moment!

We have all, no doubt, had the experience of wondering how to negotiate the street preacher. Indeed, many Christians I know find the thought of open-air meetings, especially evangelistic ones, really daunting. If such activity can make committed church members cringe, what might it be doing for those who have an antipathy towards our activity? But there are more subtle ways of being 'out there' with a profile-raising intent and an evangelistic purpose. Indeed there is a rich heritage in all traditions of taking what is normally inside outside. If the correct explanations are supplied then we might find that when we 'beat the bounds' (walk the parish boundaries), go on a Good Friday 'Walk of Witness' or undertake a 'March for Jesus', then we are doing very similar things.

Some less traditional ideas can also work extremely well. Our youngsters have worn church T-shirts and been involved in neighbourhood 'good deeds': street cleaning, window cleaning and car cleaning (for free) for example. We have often advertised particular services in the main shopping areas, not lobbing 'tract grenades' at people but genuinely seeking to woo people into worship by taking worship outside. A profile-raising activity we have tried that has surprised many of us with its effectiveness has been the setting up of a 'prayer station' on a street on a Saturday morning. People are invited to fill in a card requesting prayer either for personal matters or more public ones at a prayer table. Few of these events in themselves will bring people to faith but that is not their intention. While the event might have obvious intrinsic value the main intent is to heighten the awareness of the Church and signal the presence of the worshipping community. Creating stepping-stones, putting up signposts, lessening the gradient, so that the seeker after faith might cross the various barriers and come to a place of receptivity.

Once the profile has been raised, once there has been an attractive wooing, what do we have at our disposal to invite entrance? What are the means we might use to convince the agnostic that our doorway might be entered? That this 'way of faith' is the one to accompany us on?

I once played squash with a marketing executive from Unilever. We were having a drink in the bar afterwards and he, as you do, started asking me questions about my job. He was genuinely interested and once he pressed the buttons we were rapidly engaged in a quite serious theological discussion. As we had another drink, he said to me, 'You really do have product confidence, don't you?'

Rather shocked at the crude-sounding commercial edge he was giving our discussion I asked him what he meant. He told me that one of the key assets his company needed in their marketing department was people who believed in the product they were handling and who had a real commitment to it: people who had confidence in the product they were responsible for. 'Not always easy with margarine,' he added wryly. But how right he was. How can we engage with the community around us and proclaim what we believe unless we have confidence in that belief and are equipped to articulate it? Moreover, does the way we hold our faith and express it carry that same confidence? For example, when people do join us in worship, when they negotiate the barriers and cross the road to enter the church, what do they see? Do they see people who are motivated and excited by what they are doing? People who are caught up in what they are practising? Do we appear so convinced about the legitimacy of our activity that we clearly want to make it accessible to others so that they too might be caught up in the vibrancy of our activity? Is our pilgrimage one which radiates the message to the onlooker: 'Hey, we believe that what we are doing here is coherent and true: why don't you walk along with us?'

So often I fear that when people make the bold move of entering our arena of worship the message they hear is: 'This is private, we are special, this is not really for you, you wouldn't understand.' Or worse: 'We are not quite sure what we are doing here so please don't ask too many questions.'

I am appalled by the possibility of the 'Dibley index' – that is, the degree to which any gathering of regular Anglican worshippers conforms to and therefore confirms the expectations raised in the mind of the casual observer that *The Vicar of Dibley* represents Anglican worship in its standard form!

I seriously suggest that we should look at the way we worship Sunday by Sunday. Whatever our 'house style' may be the question we should be asking is: Does it lead those who don't yet worship into worship of God? Does it contain such a sense of the numinous that the experience demands an explanation? A right but difficult question has to be: Are we facilitating faith or merely indulging our own cultural preferences? Before we criticize innovations in approach and style, and before we automatically bow to Thomas Tallis and shudder at Matt Redman, we should ask about the effectiveness of what we do in the pursuit of our given evangelistic mandate. The reality is that so much of our worship is alien and foreign. It simply is not accessible to the unchurched seeker after God. If we are serious about evangelism we must be serious about access.

What then about explanation? Supposing a hunger has been awakened. Supposing a gradient has been climbed, obstacles traversed, and entrance made: where is understanding to be gained? Whose job is this? The vicar's? The licensed preacher's? Well, yes. Our sermons must engage people and lead them forward in faith. Good, coherent preaching has to be a major tool in our evangelistic endeavour. It is easy to devalue the role of teaching and explanation, treating it as merely a perfunctory part of the overall ritual. It need not be. The age of the sermon is not over, but the sermon must be made to work. Why not use Power-Point? Could an illustrative video clip be helpful? Story telling will never die. As long as we are human we shall value narrative (if we doubt this we should listen to Billy Connolly), so let us use narrative more to illustrate our explanation and proclamation. I believe every sermon should have 'appeal', and by that I do not mean, as someone once supposed, an old-fashioned 'altar call', but rather a draw, an attractiveness which brings understanding and an alignment with the overall message which the Church is giving.

The vision I have is of a church service in which the worship, liturgical and musical, is so engaging, so stimulating of the spirit of the unknowing enquirer, that they hang on the words of the preacher in order to understand what it is they are responding to. I am not advocating a particular style here, or a particular churchmanship, but simply the best practice of the congregation that we belong to. I was thrilled recently to be at a service in a cathedral where the preacher stopped in mid-flow of an engaging and informative sermon and asked members of the congregation to talk to one another about how they came to faith. It was an unexpected, a provocative, and for some people an uncomfortable, dialogue, but it was an entirely appropriate device in the context of a coherent service. It made us think. For those with a firm faith the interjection arrested complacency. For those who had happened upon the service without any clear faith position there was a provocation to think properly and personally about how what was being said related to them. It also gave members of the congregation opportunity and permission to engage in conversation about faith, and perhaps be involved in the process of evangelism there in a service.

Just as we must take proclamation outside of the boundaries of the church walls, so also we need to take explanation beyond the remit of the clergy. Perhaps one of the biggest mistakes in the pursuit of the evangelistic task is to clericalize it. You would think we might know better by now. It is every church member, every pilgrim, who assumes the role of ambassador. It is every member of our congregation who requires product confidence and a readiness to engage in their community as an envoy. For too long we have caricatured the 'evangelist' or witness as a particular type of person – the ecclesiastical equivalent of a pushy salesman (or the aggressive street preacher). But the biblical pattern is so much more subtle than that. The Divine became human in order to win humanity to heaven. The Body of Christ is called upon to express humanity and to inhabit humanity in a diverse manner in order to proclaim the gospel. If only we could get this picture. If every member of every congregation could see themselves as the uniquely placed, sociologically specific ambassador for Christ, in the place they inhabit, in the particular socio-economic niche they occupy, then the Kingdom proclamation would permeate many more levels of society than it does at the moment.

Of course not everyone can preach, though perhaps we ought to identify those who are good at it and use them without insisting they put on a clerical collar. And of course, not everybody can argue and present a coherent apologetic. But everyone can have product confidence and can speak with enthusiasm of their faith and of the place and community in which they express it.

In our churches, we need to have programmes in place to encourage this confidence. A good question for every church member is: If a neighbour were to ask you, 'How can I have a faith like yours?' or 'How do you become a Christian?' or (to make it thoroughly biblical) 'What must I do to inherit eternal life?' what would you say? How would you deal with it?

Perhaps it is worth mentioning the Church Pastoral Aid Society course 'Lost for Words', which seeks to tackle this. Our army of envoys needs to know what they are doing and needs the confidence to do it. They need to have the heart of Philip who, when he invited Nathanael to come and meet the Messiah, in response to the cynicism of Nathanael was able to say 'Come and see for yourself' (John 1.45). We need to have congregations full of people who are prepared to say: 'Come and see.'

When people do come to see, they need to be able to encounter more than just a good service of worship, and need to be offered more than a good explanation from the pulpit. They need to be offered avenues of exploration. There are many of these that can be used off the shelf such as the Alpha Course, the Emmaus Course, and various diocesan courses. I have often heard in criticism of some of these courses that they are 'not quite the right thing for us', or that they are 'too evangelical', 'too simplistic', 'too patronising', 'too middle-class'.

(The last comment, by the way, is a criticism I have often heard levelled at the Alpha Course. Having personally run this course about 20 times in Streatham as well as in Blackheath I have only ever heard the criticism from those who could be described as middle class!)

How complacent can we be afford to be? These courses have normally been developed by individual churches, found to be effective, and then generously published and offered to the wider Church to use if they find them helpful. That is all. I have found that all kinds of courses can be used effectively. We just need to be using something. If we don't like Alpha (which has helped thousands of people, and which has the distinct advantage of national profile), what course are we going to use instead? Perhaps we ought to be constructing our own course that contains the particular nuances we are happy with. If we spent as much energy devising teaching courses for explaining the faith to others as we sometimes spend criticizing what others have used then we might be in better shape.

In passing, one of the things that I believe has contributed hugely to the success of the Alpha Course has been an activity I did not regard very highly at first, and that is a meal. Never underestimate the power of the palate! For those who don't know, the Alpha Course is often based upon the starting point of sharing a meal together. Having eaten, the group then studies and discusses the topic for the evening. The meal does far more than nourish people physically. It is the point where friendships are made, anxieties alleviated and the 'safety' of the group established. It is the device which facilitates the working of the whole group. Initially it is this meal which I thought was superfluous and could be done away with. How wrong I was! And how easy it was for me to forget Jesus' precedent of making the central event of history unforgettable by anchoring it to a meal!

A meal is so versatile. At my current church we once identified quite a large group of men whom we felt would simply not respond with any enthusiasm to an Alpha group. It is not that they wouldn't find it helpful, it is just that we knew they wouldn't come! One or two of us decided to have a series of six beer and lasagne evenings. These were held in someone's house and we sent written invitations and invited a group of about 12 men to come to a 'no holds barred' discussion on faith. Each evening began with eating and drinking together and then there was a provocative opening talk of five to seven minutes often summarizing what had happened at the previous meeting. A free-flowing discussion then followed. Nothing was forbidden, nothing was assumed, but the intention, effectively accomplished, was to lead and direct people towards faith while knocking down some of the prejudices held by those who consider themselves to be 'above all that sort of thing'. One of the best moments was when someone loftily informed us that they had given up on faith when they had come to realise that it was no longer scientifically credible. In response to this, another invited member, who happened to be a chief government scientist, responded saying that that was very interesting since it was only as his career had developed in the scientific world that he had come to and grown in faith in Jesus.

If we use explanatory courses in church, clearly no one course will do for all. The question is: What is it that we *are* offering? I think it was Billy Graham who said something like: 'You might not like my style of evangelism but I am more comfortable with the evangelism I *am* doing than with the evangelism you are *not* doing.'

Have I described this gospel task in too commercial a way? Is this particular imagery one that fuels all our worst fears about evangelism? Does it seem that once again we are encouraging people to be 'salespeople for Christ'? Is there the attendant danger that if we do this then we shall bring the good news of Jesus into disrepute?

I hope not. One of the key things I want to emphasize is the need for sensitivity, and I do not mean only sensitivity to the comfort and feelings of those to whom we seek to bring the gospel. One of the exciting things we continue to discover together about evangelism is that this actually is a divine task. Congregations are not sent out by God to cold call: rather we find that the proclamatory task is one in which God invites us to co-operate with what he is already doing. It is a divine/human partnership. There are myriad anecdotal examples of people who, having prayed, having in part embarked on this evangelistic trail with some degree of trepidation, have been astonished to find that the Holy Spirit has gone before them. It is such a common story that we hear related in many different forms – how having decided to invite someone to church, summoned up the courage and tentatively made a (frequently bungled) invitation, the person they had been longing to invite had been waiting for just such an invitation. God does not send us out on fools' errands. This in itself is so faith-affirming for so many people. There is genuine positive feedback here. It is exciting for hesitant church members to discover that the faith they profess is not merely a philosophical creed of words but an active life in which the work of the Holy Spirit can be seen and experienced. God is ready and willing to work through them. It is this very experience that gives 'product confidence'.

One last lesson to mention: although it is commonly accepted that we are in a post-Christian society, and that ignorance of the gospel is profound, the reality is that because we are all made in the image of God the human longing for the divine, whatever the degree of ignorance about him, is still very much there. That is why praying with someone is such a powerful evangelistic device. It is not just myself as a clergyman but many members of the congregation who have discovered that at work, in the home or in the playground, when difficulties and calamities have struck, the simple offer to pray with someone or for someone, even the most apparently irreligious, has been received with gratitude rather than ridicule. The exhilarating and simple discovery for all of us engaged in evangelism is that people want to know God! Once someone begins to pray and once someone begins to receive answers to prayer then the explanation of what is going on and who it is who is answering our prayers comes naturally and inevitably. We soon find that we are doing the work of an evangelist.

Might this then be a model for the parish church and its evangelism?

Clear apprehension of mandate
   Building of profile
      Attention to 'appeal' of practice
         Provision of stepping-stones along entrance gradient
           Clear means of explanation by all
              Ready acceptance and incorporation

It was Bob Jackson, an incumbent with a lot of parish experience, who recently wrote a book encouraging 'hope in the church'.[1] When he was a theological student he wrote a report on a church where I was serving as director of evangelism (a lay post). He entitled his report: 'What's a nice church like you doing in a place like this?' A very good question for every congregation, I suggest. I pray that all might answer it with confidence and clarity.

Further reading

Pippert, Rebecca Manley, *Out of the Saltshaker and into the World: Evangelism as a Way of Life*, InterVarsity Press, Downers Grove, 1999.
Lawrence, James, *Lost for Words*, Bible Reading Fellowship, Oxford, 1999.
Watson, David, *I Believe in Evangelism*, Hodder & Stoughton, London, 1984.
Jackson, Bob, *Hope for the Church: Contemporary Strategies for Growth*, Church House Publishing, London, 2002.

Notes

1 Jackson, Bob, *Hope for the Church: Contemporary Strategies for Growth*, Church House Publishing, London, 2002.

14. Being and Doing

The Priest in the Parish

MALCOLM TORRY

For by the grace given to me I say to everyone among you not to think of yourself more highly than you ought to think, but to think with sober judgment, each according to the measure of faith that God has assigned. For as in one body we have many members, and not all the members have the same function, so we, who are many, are one body in Christ, and individually we are members one of another. (Rom. 12.3–5)

The other chapters in this book contain a good deal of material on the priest in the parish. In this chapter I attempt not to repeat what has been said elsewhere, so to that extent this chapter might appear somewhat unbalanced. After discussing what the priest *is*, my aim is to examine and illustrate some general attitudes the priest might adopt, in order to offer a realistic and practical introduction to the role of the priest in the parish.

So what *is* the priest? The problem with this question is that answers given to it are generally in terms of what the priest *does*. In the second chapter of his book *The Christian Priest Today*, Michael Ramsey (before the days of women's ordination) defines the priest as 'the man of theology . . . the minister of reconciliation . . . The man of prayer . . . the man of the Eucharist . . . displaying, enabling, involving the life of the church'[1] – and, under each heading, it is how the priest *does* these things that is discussed. But there are *some* aspects of the priest that are more about what the priest *is* than about what the priest does. The priest is designated by the Church as a particular kind of person, and the (not insignificant) sign of this designation is the clothes which turn the priest into a visible representative of the Church. And since what we are addressing here is the priest *in the parish*, what the priest *is* is a person whom others can approach, someone who will hear, someone who will share what they hear with no one but God. (Just before this was written someone I met said to me: 'You're a priest. Can I tell you . . .?' And they did.) The priest is a sacrament of the Church, and in some sense simply a sacrament: an outward and visible sign of a gracious God. Yes, every Christian is that, and the Church as a whole is that, but the priest's visibility as the person appointed by the Church to serve the parish gives to him or her a role that is not merely about what they do but is also about what they are.

We *are* what we do, so it is surely right to answer the question 'What is a priest?' with a description of the priest's activity. As the current ordinal states:

> A priest is called by God to work with the bishop and with his fellow-priests, as servant and shepherd among the people to whom he is sent. He is to proclaim the word of the Lord, to call his hearers to repentance, and in Christ's name to absolve and to declare the forgiveness of sins. He is to baptize and prepare the baptized for Confirmation. He is to preside at the celebration of the Holy Communion. He is to lead his people in prayer and worship, to intercede for them, to bless them in the name of the Lord, and to teach and encourage by word and example. He is to minister to the sick, and prepare the dying for their death. He must set the Good Shepherd always before him as the pattern of his calling, caring for the people committed to his charge, and joining with them in a common witness to the world.
>
> In the name of our Lord we bid you remember the greatness of the trust now to be committed to your charge, about which you have been taught in your preparation for this ministry. You are to be messengers, watchmen, and stewards of the Lord; you are to teach and to admonish, to feed and to provide for the Lord's family, to search for his children in the wilderness of this world's temptations and to guide them through its confusions, so that they may be saved through Christ for ever.
>
> Remember always with thanksgiving that the treasure now to be entrusted to you is Christ's own flock, bought through the shedding of his blood on the cross. The Church and congregation among whom you will serve are one with him: they are his body. Serve them with joy, build them up in faith, and do all in your power to bring them to loving obedience to Christ.[2]

Every parish is different, so how all of these things are done will be different in different places, and no one can tell anyone else how to do them where they are; so, in this short chapter, all I can do is discuss how some of these things have been done in parishes that I have served.

First of all, because it *isn't* in the ordinal, and it isn't in Michael Ramsey's list: the priest is, in practice, an administrator, a fund-raiser, a surveyor, a plumber, an electrician, a postman or postwoman, an editor, a typist, a printer, and a poster, leaflet, service-sheet and notice-sheet designer. Amongst my first tasks as a curate at the Elephant and Castle in South London was learning how to empty the coin-operated gas meters of the tenants in the old vicarage; and one of the constant tasks of being a curate was (with others) the writing, editing and organizing of the monthly community newspaper. And since then there have been toilet seats to mend, shelves to build, duplicators to coax, stationery to order, computers to repair, building projects to plan, funds to raise, pianos to move, jumble-sale tables to put up, jumble-sale tables to take down – for the priest is a member of the congregation as well as being its pastor. So if the priest possesses skills, and if others do not have those skills, or if the priest has a more flexible diary than others, then those skills must be used: for the priest is a member of the Body of Christ, and if a drain needs clearing then that's what needs to be done.

As an incumbent at both New Cross and Westcombe Park, I have been blessed with congregations in which many different skills are represented – but they are also congregations in which people with certain skills lead very pressured lives. So when the jumble-sale posters need printing, I do it; and I paste them up, too, because it is amazing what people will talk to you about while you are standing in the churchyard with a paste brush in your hand. Being visible matters, and being known matters, and that only happens when the priest walks the parish, and goes to the places where people are. And listening matters: listening to what needs doing, and listening to what people tell you. Sometimes, of course, people won't tell the priest what they are thinking, but they will tell someone else, so listening to *that* person is what is needed.

This is particularly true when a priest arrives in a parish. This is no time for 'vision', because the new priest's vision is bound to be inappropriate in some respect or other. What is needed is *listening*. When I arrived at St George's, Westcombe Park, it was quickly apparent from the state of the building and from what people were saying to me that 'something must be done'. A small group chosen by the Parochial Church Council – a group with some of the longest-standing members of the congregation on it – was what was required. Apart from asking questions, I listened, because I was new, and they had been there a long time and some of them, and possibly all of them, were going to be there after I had gone: and, most importantly, their deep knowledge of the relationship between that particular congregation, that particular building, and that particular community, was something which I wouldn't have for a very long time, and in some respects would never have.

The plans that emerged were radical: we turned the whole building round inside, built a new kitchen, bought a new second-hand pipe organ, unscrewed the pews from the floor, built a new vestry in an old porch, and turned the old vestry into a meeting room – and these changes have served the congregation and the community well and will continue to do so. Yes, as the parish's incumbent, I have helped it all to happen, but so have lots of other people – and it started with listening: to the situation, to the community's needs, to the congregation, and to possible futures.

And this particular exercise shows just how important it is for the priest to care about *buildings*. Our parish churches are the homes of our congregations, they are home to our communities, and when they are shared and welcoming they are expressions of the gospel: they are *themselves* such expressions, and not simply the containers of activities that express the gospel. For five years now the St George's building has been shared with a nursery school. This makes the whole building warmer and more welcoming. Just as importantly, it means that the bills get paid. In an area where congregations are not wealthy, the congregation needs a public space in which the Eucharist can be celebrated, and the priest, being a member of the congregation, must use whatever skills he or she has to enable the building to survive and to be maintained, insured, lit, heated – and, if necessary, rebuilt. For whilst a congregation without a building is a possibility, and in some cases it is a necessity, a parish church is the focus of the community's relationship with the congregation, with its activity, and with the gospel it represents.

It is that community and that congregation that the ordinal is all about. But the ordinal's declaration begins not with the priest's tasks but with the requirement that the priest should work with the bishop and with other clergy. This is often a pleasure. While there is an inevitable sense of competition between clergy, to which the lack of control we have over whether our parishes prosper or disappear inevitably contributes, incumbents are all different, and curates are too, and there is a wealth of experience, spirituality, theology and commitment to be tapped into. I was somewhat perturbed to hear from a former curate that they had been told at theological college that clergy chapter meetings are a waste of time. They can become so, but they aren't intrinsically so; and, particularly if clergy tackle important issues together, chapter meetings can be a source of inspiration. An important piece of work in our area recently was a good-practice agreement worked out between clergy and funeral directors, a project which is bearing fruit in terms of improved practice and better relationships. It has worked because we did it together.

The same applies to our relationships with our bishops. In East Greenwich and Westcombe Park we have seen our fair share of them recently, mainly because we have the Millennium Dome and the Greenwich Peninsula in the parish. It is the incumbent's task to work with the bishop and the archdeacon, to invite them (and not just wait for the occasional visitation, however valuable that might be), to involve them, and to keep them informed. If the relationship goes wrong, it must not be the incumbent's fault. Our last two bishops of Woolwich, Peter Hall and Colin Buchanan, have both been well involved in what concerned their parishes, and Bishop Colin's survey of mission activity in his area has been a particularly engaged piece of work.

But the bishop's role is changing. A world full of organizations run by chief executives encourages society at large to see bishops in the chief executive role, and the necessity of a certain amount of line-management control of clergy (for example, in relation to child-protection provisions) means that the bishop's role as well as our perception of that role is changing. As far as the parishes are concerned, the relationship must remain one of mutual respect and mutual listening and of a balance of power between parish and bishop. An important element of the Church of England's parochial system is a local autonomy that enables the gospel, the congregation and the community to relate to each other in ways appropriate to each different place. The priest's relative autonomy in relation to the bishop is an essential element of the parish's autonomy, and its loss would be serious. Whilst an element of line management is bound to intrude on the relationship between bishop and priest, it will be important to draw clear boundaries round it so that line-management presuppositions don't seep into the heart of a relationship which must continue to be characterized by mutual trust.

When it comes to proclaiming the Word of the Lord – the first specific task in the ordinal's declaration – parishes will, of course, do it differently. The priest's task is to listen to the community, to listen to the congregation's skills and its likes and dislikes, and to work with others to find *that* parish's method of proclamation. In New Cross, the arrival of a couple of opera-directors in the congregation led to a performance of *Joseph and the Amazing Technicolor Dreamcoat*, to other drama productions, and to the continuing annual Telegraph Hill Arts Festival. In various ways over the years this bridge between the community and the congregation has enabled proclamation to occur: sometimes through the productions themselves, sometimes through the art, sometimes through the Festival Eucharist. And at Westcombe Park an existing drama tradition was revived, helped along by the occasional paid-for professional director. Productions of *Godspell*, *Pop Goes the Passion*, *Joseph . . .*, *Guys and Dolls*, and *A-lad-in a Manger* all tell the Christian story one way or another. The Greenwich Passion Play, to which this parish gave birth, was for its audience and cast a life-changing telling of the gospel in South London during the millennium year.

The priest's role is to listen, and to help a congregation to work out what *its* way of proclaiming the Word of the Lord might be. And there are some who have heard *Pop Goes the Passion*'s 'Who killed cock robin?' during the crucifixion, and some who stood at the foot of the cross in Greenwich Park on Good Friday 2000, for whom 'repentance' – to which, according to the ordinal's declaration, the proclamation of the Word of the Lord is to lead – might mean more than it once did. *Anyone* who has thought afresh about issues, who has changed their mind, has 'repented' – for that is what it means: to change one's mind.[3] Sometimes what someone turns from is a sin, and felt by them to be so: confession, individual or corporate, formal or informal, *is* good for the soul, and absolution is *the* proclamation of the good news. But sometimes it is not clear that what has been turned from is sinful, yet there is still a changing of the mind, a new beginning, new actions, new ideas. So these are the priest's tasks: to hear the call to confess their own sin (especially where the priest hasn't listened, or hasn't exercised a servant role); to hear the call to do new things; and to encourage others into confession of sin and into doing new things too – to call people to repentance. This goes both for people's under-standing of the Christian Faith and for the way they live out their faith. Thus the priest's proclamation of the Word of God must be a matter of listening to what people think and do, and to his or her own thinking and doing, and must be a seeking of change according to God's will, change which might not be entirely predictable. Both at New Cross and at Westcombe Park, study groups planned and led by participants have been part of this process – sometimes using materi-al from elsewhere, sometimes planned entirely from scratch by par-ticipants or by leaders appointed by the Church Council. The same process has worked for confirmation classes. Sermons that are participatory have also been part of this process, sermons with loose structures which have enabled flexible response to people's responses to questions. The teaching of Christian doctrine in a col-laborative manner has been part of this process, with the teacher pro-viding the raw materials and a framework to the discussion, and the group working out what it believes and why. In the whole life of the Church the priest can encourage such widespread participation, and in the parishes I have served an important focus for this approach has been rotating the chairing of meetings so that we learn from one another and so that everyone, including the incumbent, can take part in the debate.

The key to *all* of this is *listening*: to God, to the congregation, and to the community – and it is as important to do the listening to God in a participative fashion as it is to do anything else participatively. Different parishes will develop different patterns of prayer. I have served in parishes where there is a daily (or almost daily) morning Eucharist and daily evening prayer, and in parishes where that doesn't work and where everything happens on Sunday. Here, planning a Sunday evening event which is a Bible study, a prayer meeting, and a discussion group, was the right thing to do. The priest's concern is to enable the parish to work out the right way for that parish, and also to fit his or her own life of prayer into the pattern which evolves in the parish. Thus today my own pattern is more individual than it was ten years ago, and that might change again if I move to another parish. The same is true of the priest's own spiritual nourishment, their continuing education and development, and (if he or she has one) the priest's family's involvement in the parish. We all change, all the time, and the situations we find ourselves in change. So sometimes our discipleship and our spirituality are nourished by individuals, sometimes by private reading, sometimes by groups in the parish, and sometimes by groups elsewhere. The same is true of other parts of our lives. There have been times when my theological and philosophical interests have been developed within the parish, sometimes in an area setting, sometimes in a wider sphere, and sometimes on a purely individual level. Similarly with my interests in social policy and in the management of religious organizations, and my musical interests. Other clergy will have other interests. What matters is that every priest maintains a variety of interests and activities, for the relationship that a priest has to manage between faith, task, home, family and stipend changes constantly, and the links might break, and honesty might require moving on, which is only possible if transferable skills have been kept and a variety of interests maintained – so, in the end, honesty is only possible if we maintain a variety of skills and interests.

In Michael Ramsey's words, the priest 'displays, enables and involves' the life of the Church, focusing in his or her own life the whole of the parish's activity, being involved (to some extent at least) in all of it, expressing the ethos of the parish, enabling people to participate and to offer their gifts, and enabling the community to relate to the Church and the Church to the community. Particularly important is the development of leadership, *genuine* leadership – which doesn't mean delegation. Thus in Westcombe Park, where there was a small group of teenagers too old for our Children's Church (which has its own excellent leadership), and the Church Council believed that 'something must be done', an appeal was made for leaders for a new group, and help was bought in for a period from Greenwich Youth for Christ. People whom nobody would have expected responded to the appeal, and there is now a growing young people's group, 'Rock Solid'. Here, the priest's task is to listen, to encourage, to enable communication to occur, to seek out partnerships.

At the heart of the leadership of the parish are the churchwardens. I have tried not to be dogmatic in this chapter, but here I shall be: the churchwardens are elected by the people of the parish as the people's representatives, and the priest's task is to work with them. Some incumbents involve themselves one way or another in the selection of churchwardens; but for the incumbent to be involved in their choice means that they might not be the representatives they ought to be, so they will not be the leaders they need to be, and they will not provide the necessary communication between clergy and people: for while the priest *is* a member of the congregation, he or she is also the congregation's and the community's pastor, so a healthy relationship between the people and the priest must be developed: and this is best served by communication between the priest and two churchwardens who are as independent as possible from the priest. This relationship is especially important where particular members of the congregation are involved. I hope that our former sacristan won't mind me writing about her, but she's now dead so I can't ask her. She drank, which is why one of the churchwardens had to keep the communion wine at home. She often smelled, her flat was a pigsty, and she could sometimes be insulting and worse, particularly on the phone. So why was she still the sacristan? And why did she still sometimes lead the intercessions? Because we – the Churchwardens and myself – knew that this was all that was holding her together. Yes, we did think of taking these tasks from her, but I am glad we didn't; and it was the support of incumbent and churchwardens for one another over this issue which enabled us to keep her, to give her a place where she was needed, and to give her a place where she could contribute.

In many parishes, other leadership will emerge. Here in East Greenwich people have been encouraged to become Readers, and there is a Southwark Pastoral Auxiliary. We now have an Ordained Local Minister in training. All these vocations started with discussion at the Church Council as to what leadership was required – and it is the priest's task to encourage such debate, and, when suggestions are made, to follow them up. If necessary, and because the priest too is a member of the congregation, he or she might make specific suggestions – but with the greatest of care, and after the deepest possible listening.

When new mission activities occur, the same process is needed: consultation, listening, wide participation, and still more listening; and here in East Greenwich we are seeing this process on a broader canvas as we plan the Church's work on the Greenwich Peninsula. We participated in the ecumenical chaplaincy team at the Millennium Dome during 2000, our curate Michael Johnson and myself being members of the team. We are joining a similar process, driven partly by the development company, partly by the Borough Council, and partly by the faith communities, to provide a multi-faith chaplaincy service to the builders, employees, residents and visitors of a large and unique new development. Whilst initiative is required (and because I am still chaplain to the Dome and also chaplain to the food refinery on the peninsula it was clear that I should take a certain amount of initiative), it is vital that such projects should be as participative as possible, so there is a steering group appointed by a meeting which was as representative as possible of the Borough's faith communities, and consultation goes on in a variety of ways with the Borough's churches and with its Multifaith Forum.

Because every parish is different all I have been able to do here is suggest an overall method rather than be prescriptive: and that method is listening, participating, and more listening. Yes, there have been times when I have had to act unilaterally and with speed, but those times have been very rare and the events have always been discussed with churchwardens as soon as possible afterwards and, if a policy issue was involved, with the Church Council. And sometimes things haven't been done in quite the usual order, as when I baptized a child neither of whose parents were baptized – but the gospel is first of all a gospel of God's grace and then it is an invitation to discipleship, and, as it happens, both of those parents are now baptized and confirmed.

A prerequisite for listening is availability, and this is a matter of what the priest is and also of what the priest does. The priest must *go* to the places in the parish where people are, and in particular must *visit*. No, not for no reason; but wherever there is the slightest reason, the priest must visit. If in doubt, visit. This applies in relation to ministry to the dying, ministry to the bereaved, ministry to people in any kind of need, ministry to the rejoicing, ministry to the contentious. The priest goes into pastoral situations because he or she ought to, and also because the priest is still a person whom people might expect to want to hear about how they are approaching their deaths, about what they think of God, about what moves them, about what inspires them. The same is true of the priest's ministry to institutions: to nursing homes, schools, hospitals, industry, shops, community groups . . . The same rule applies: if in doubt, visit – and here, if you're not welcome, as in a more secular world you often won't be, stay in touch: a Christmas card will do. The conducting of funerals is dealt with elsewhere in this volume, and in a number of the chapters the priest's role is dealt with in a wider context: in relation to the parish's relationships with workplaces, regeneration, art, ecumenism, mission, evangelism, young people, and with other faiths, and in relation to the creation of an inclusive congregation. In all these contexts, listening, participation, going there, . . . these are at the heart of what the priest does, and so are at the heart of what the priest is.

In all this pastoral care the priest is a servant of the parish and its people, which is as it should be, for not only is the priest a Christian and a follower of the one who said that he came not to be served but to serve (Mark 10.45), but the priest has already been ordained deacon and will remain a deacon as long as he or she remains a priest. This is not the place to tackle the interesting issue of whether the Church of England requires a renewed permanent diaconate, but it is the place to say that the diaconal role is 'to work with [the Church's] members in caring for the poor, the needy, the sick, and all who are in trouble . . . to strengthen the faithful, search out the careless and the indifferent, and to preach the word of God',[4] and that this activity remains at the heart of what a priest is *in the parish*.

Above all, of course, both in the parish understood as a territorial reality and in the parish understood as the congregation, the priest is someone who presides at the Eucharist. Another chapter considers the parish's liturgy, but in this chapter it is surely essential to say that in the action of the Eucharist, in the taking of bread and wine, the giving thanks, the breaking of the bread, and the sharing of the bread and wine, the priest focuses the congregation's and the community's prayer and learning, their corporate life, their hopes, their sorrows – and his or her own as well, for the priest is a member of the congregation as well as its pastor. How the Church Council, churchwardens, other staff and the incumbent plan and lead the Eucharist expresses and determines the ethos and action of the parish as a whole and proclaims what the parish believes the gospel to be. In this respect, decisions about who can and who cannot participate fully at the communion are crucial, and in the two parishes of which I have been incumbent the decision has been that participation should be as wide as possible, consistently with individuals' consciences and parents' wishes in relation to their children.

Every priest has a focal event to which they look back as in some sense defining their ministry. For me, it was a series of events at New Cross, and because these events are already in the public domain in the form of an article in the *Church Times*, I shall simply repeat it here:

> It all started about two years ago [i.e. in 1989]. Already (with my encouragement and the PCC's agreement) parents were sharing their bread with their children at the communion rail: for are not children as much members of the body of Christ as the rest of us? And would Jesus have refused them?
>
> And then Charmaine, Antoinette and Justine joined the congregation of St. Catherine's: three sisters, aged 10, 8 and 4. Nobody brought them; they brought themselves and their friends. And there they were, at the communion rail, hands held out.
>
> I explained about being admitted to communion and about classes, but they weren't into classes and they weren't into waiting, they were into joining in. And in any case Justine was too young to

be admitted to communion. Sometimes a nearby adult would share their bread with the sister nearest to them, but this still left the others without; and so, after a discussion with the PCC and with the knowledge of the Bishop, I began to share the consecrated bread with them – and myself to give the consecrated bread to all the young children who came to the rail. For if the Eucharist is an effectual sign of the coming kingdom of God, a kingdom which is a gift to us, then does not the Church have an obligation to ensure that *nobody* is excluded from the communion? Young children don't 'understand' – but neither do the rest of us; and they too are Christian pilgrims, the kind of pilgrims whom Jesus gathered to teach his adult disciples what a member of the Kingdom of God is like. The asking was qualification enough, as it was for those whom Jesus healed.

It was on Sunday 17 December 1989 that I first gave Charmaine, Antoinette and Justine pieces of bread as I passed along the communion rail. On Friday 22 December 1989, Charmaine, Antoinette and Justine died in a fire at their home. A heavy grief affected the whole parish and congregation; at every Christmas service the same news had to be given; and their funeral just after Christmas was the most emotionally charged event in which I have participated: the grief audible and visible, the thankfulness tangible – for their very different personalities had enriched us all; and all but a few of the 300 present milled around the open coffins to say goodbye.

Those events are now over a year ago [the article was published on 3 May 1991], but they have left their mark: on the children's mother Yvette, on their grandmother Evelyn, on their family and friends, on the parish, on their school and nursery, on the congregation – and on me.

I would have found it difficult to forgive myself if they had died before I enabled them to participate in the Eucharist, if I had not allowed them to share in the one bread which constitutes us as the one body of Christ. As it is, they participated with the rest of us in the banquet which foreshadows that kingdom beyond words in which they now participate.[5]

The Church *is* the Body of Christ, so if we listen to the Church (and by 'Church' in the Church of England we mean the parish: its congregation and its community), then we hear the voice of God; so listening to God and listening to the parish are not separate activities. And by enabling the parish to participate in the proclamation and the living out of the gospel, the priest enables the Church to be the body of Christ which it is. There can few greater privileges.

Further reading

Cocksworth, Christopher and Rosalind Brown, *Being a Priest Today: Exploring Priestly Identity*, Canterbury Press, Norwich, 2002.
Greenwood, Robin, *Transforming Priesthood: A New Theology of Mission and Ministry*, SPCK, London, 2002.
Ramsey, Michael, *The Christian Priest Today*, SPCK, London, 1972.

Notes

1 Ramsey, Michael, *The Christian Priest Today*, SPCK, London, 1972, pp. 7–10.

2 The Ordinal, 1980, revised in 2000 (The Archbishops' Council of the Church of England, 2000). Unfortunately, the revision did not include the introduction of inclusive language.

3 The Greek *metanoeō* in Plato's time meant to change one's mind or purpose. By New Testament times the word had the more religious meaning which we normally translate 'to repent'.

4 The Ordinal, 1980. On the 'root' of a priest's life being a theological understanding of God as being for others, see Cocksworth, Christopher and Rosalind Brown, *Being a Priest Today: Exploring Priestly Identity*, Canterbury Press, Norwich, 2002.

5 *Church Times*, 3 May 1991. We are grateful to the editor of the *Church Times* for permission to reprint this article here.

15. Being of Use

A Bishop to the Parishes

COLIN BUCHANAN

A bishop who writes of his understanding of his task when he is still in post gives hostages to fortune indeed – but I am delighted to be able to contribute this chapter. I hope to grapple with realities in so doing. I write with a bursting sense of admiration and joy at the gifts, experience and reflection which the parish contributors have brought to this book. If I had been naming a team (which in fact was not my task), I would probably have gone for much the same mix; but I would have done so with a real sense that in the Woolwich Area others could offer another whole team with contributions of equal value and interest.

Although there are duties for the bishop set out in the ordinal,[1] in fact the task of any individual bishop is likely to be unique to him (or her). In my own life I have worked fairly closely with eight different diocesan bishops in four different dioceses in the last 20 years, and I have fulfilled three very different roles as a bishop myself in the last three of these. The whole stipendiary episcopate of the Church of England has turned over in that time, and I have known many of those both past and present. In addition I have travelled in around 15 provinces of the Anglican Communion, often staying with bishops and talking over their jobs – indeed their mission.[2] So this sense that there is no identikit single model is well based in experience. I have inevitably wrestled with my own calling, and, equally, have asked myself how far I am simply a functionary who is the prisoner of an iron-jacketed system, and how far I am free to initiate, to shuffle priorities, to make bold experiments, and even to try to inflict some nearly developed vision of my own on parishes which may not actually be asking for it.

The issue is further complicated (if one is disposed to let it be) by the Church of England's sense that there is somewhere a revealed doctrine of the episcopate, which, if it is not quite overt in scripture, certainly ought to be. Much of this is wrapped up in received tradition, though the received tradition has been first shaped by monarchical ideas of government, tempered by the physical impossibility of bishops before 1850 actually circulating within their large dioceses; then it has been reshaped both by a very 'high' tractarian doctrine of episcopacy (which conventionally included a great readiness to ignore any wishes or directions of one's own particular bishop), and also by enormous social and ecclesiastical changes post-1850 which have greatly affected the shape of a bishop's life. It has been refashioned again in the twentieth century by further sociological and political changes, by a slow erosion of extreme Anglo-Catholicism (though the episcopal sub-culture of that has run on), by the coming of synodical government, and by a totally new world of church finances since 1970. However, part of the broadly received wisdom has been that, in an episcopal church, in the last analysis you get decisions from God-chartered individuals – actual people whom you sometimes meet – and not simply from clumsy committees or slow-moving bureaucrats. This kind of contrast has been greatly overstated, but, because it has highlighted the bishop as an individual, it has thereby in principle canonized the individuality of individual bishops. So, it seems, episcopal idiosyncrasies are not merely pardonable, but are somehow a true expression of an authentic episcopate. While I cheerfully hang on to this quasi-doctrine as a defence of my own peculiarities ('this is how I am, and if they don't like it they will have to lump it'), it does also give me problems. The doctrine has both encouraged all bishops at times to take by themselves decisions that should have been subject to much wider consultation, and has also empowered genuinely insecure or simply poor-quality bishops to rely upon their own judgement far more than they ever should have done. I do not insist that a 'high' doctrine of episcopacy must inevitably lead to a 'high' doctrine of one's own judgements; nor do I insist that those with a 'high' doctrine of episcopacy are inevitably distracted from a realistic assessment of their own sinfulness on the one hand, and their own abilities on the other. But I do sometimes suspect a link of some sort – and I would be relieved to think that my own sins and shortcomings are simply native to Colin Buchanan as part of the entail of Adam, and are not exaggerated by my misunderstanding the nature of my office, or by my believing that I hold a peculiarly sunny spot in the favours of God.

I now put that baggage behind me, and come to the parishes. Yes, a bishop is there 'for' his parishes, and perhaps an Area bishop most pointedly so of all. Yet that has to be qualified, for the parishes of his diocese cannot be the sole concern, the immediate single target, of all that a bishop does. The received conventional expositions of a bishop's calling include that he is there to represent the 'wider church' to the parishes of his diocese, and to represent the particular diocese to the 'wider church'. He is also not simply standing behind his parishes to encourage and resource them in their mission to the communities in which they are set; for he is himself to be a frontiersman of mission, paving the way for others, tackling the principalities and powers (and political parties and borough officers) direct, using the media, and challenging the philosophical atmosphere and the unbelieving culture of his context. A bishop is, from the earliest times, not only a missionary, but also a theologian.[3] He has to be resourced himself if he is resource others.

But when the bishop has determined how much he is there directly for and with his parishes, there are yet further complications to vary the service he gives. In part it depends upon his back-up;[4] in part it depends upon the size of his diocese (and indeed whether he is a diocesan, a suffragan, or an Area bishop); and in part it depends upon the trouble or lack of it which does or does not divert his energies. One misbehaving cleric may swallow up whole weeks of a bishop's time;[5] a thousand hassles may arise about buildings, about ecumenical structures, housing curates, press misrepresentation, or complaints about – or from – undertakers. Archdeacons will field much of this, but it is within the purview of a bishop. One winter I had virtually no vacancies and no appointments to make. Another winter I had parish after parish with a vacancy to fill, entailing many overlapping meetings, interviews and institutions all happening, not quite at once, but in an echelon formation.

How then is a bishop to be bishop to his parishes? And here one bumps up against another world of difficulties – for bishops move in fields of other people's expectations. In days when bishops did not travel, parish clergy remained undisturbed. When bishops started to travel, they were still princes of the land, and were received as royalty.[6] As their numbers have multiplied, so they have been expected to be seriously of use. This is in principle a reversion to Early Church expectations; it is in principle much to be welcomed; but it also means that there are criteria of usefulness set up in the parishes, criteria that may be subjective, elusive, chimerical, and unknown to the bishop himself, and yet criteria by which he may be deemed a dead loss. If that occurs, he is not trusted to deliver, not usually given the benefit of any doubt, and consequentially does not even enjoy the respect of the parishes. Nor can such a situation be pre-empted by a bishop accepting what a colleague of mine (in my theological college days) called a milch-cow syndrome. A bishop neither can nor should be (and nor should he try to be) an omnipresent, omnicompetent provider for the clergy and parishes of his diocese, any more than the incumbent should be for the individual parishioners. Anglican clergy and parishes are not autonomous, but they do have large responsibility for their own spiritual health. If they accept that principle, then a bishop may genuinely be of use.

There is a whole series of chartered points of engagement between a bishop and his parishes:

Appointments

These are the most far-reaching places of impact on parishes. These are where my competence or incompetence will be measurable many years after I have gone. These are also the major point at which a bishop – certainly an Area bishop – holds actual powers. I recall at each vacancy that a parish may take ten years for the right leader to build up, and it may take but one night for a wrong one to destroy. Appointments are where a bishop holds the most responsible trustee-ship on behalf of his parishes.[7]

Institutions

Institutions (services in church to mark the beginning of a priest's ministry in a parish) are a highly enjoyable way of following one's part in the appointments process, and entering into the high expecta-tions of both parish and appointee. I have always endeavoured to have an hour or more with the incoming incumbent a day or two before the event; and seeing life as she or he is seeing – combined with the earlier experience of working through the description of the parish for the advertising during the vacancy – ought to shape my sermon at the institution. It ought to be a giving of a charter to *this* cleric in *this* place at *this* point in history, in other words, a word from God which is well earthed in the realities of the parish. If I think I have got this somewhere near right, I may venture to send the text of my sermon to the incumbent concerned afterwards, as a charter for revisiting.[8]

Ordaining and licensing of assistant clergy

'Matching' assistant clergy to training incumbents was a major part of my life in the twenty-one years I was on the staff of a theological college, so it continues a fascinating responsibility today. The parish is the training context, and it has to offer scope for the development of an individual's ministry; yet the individual must also be growing as a team player, and beyond all the objective assessments and job descriptions there has to be some 'chemistry' which bonds the experienced and the newly ordained (who is sometimes the older of the two to complicate matters, and who often brings much lay experi-ence). It is well down the line – perhaps after three to four years for a stipendiary – before we start to say 'Where is she or he *needed*?' For the first three years we are still engaged with the prior question 'How can the trainee get the training he or she needs?'

Baptism and confirmation

The Anglican Churches – alone on the earth's surface among the episcopal churches – restrict the administration of confirmation to bishops. In theory this both gives the candidates some awareness of belonging to a 'wider' church and gives the bishop an occasion to monitor and note the progress in any particular parish. It also gives the bishop some limited opportunities to coach the parishes. The following features of such coaching are worth putting on record:

1 A bishop can urge admission to communion for the unconfirmed and a raising of the normal minimum age for confirmation to something near to adulthood;
2 A bishop can recommend adult 'catechumenate' practice, whereby lay Christians take responsibility for new candidates, walking with them through their preparation, praying for them, presenting them at confirmation, reflecting with them after it, and seeing them set their feet upon sure paths of discipleship;
3 A bishop can look for opportunities to engage with candidates during preparation – even to the point of running residential weekends away (which I have not done, but perhaps should have);
4 A bishop has some serious part in planning and using the rite, including preaching, and taking responsibility for the shape and content of the event;
5 A bishop can look for live testimony (as mentioned in the rubrics) within the actual service;[9]
6 A bishop can attempt to follow up the confirmation – by letter, by reunion or special conference, by fastening responsibility upon clergy to know where their candidates of three years, two years or one year ago have now reached in mature discipleship;
7 A bishop can urge the newly confirmed to reintroduce themselves to him when they next meet. By my third year this was happening on revisits to parishes. By my fifth it occasionally involved encounters on trains or in shops. It gives a marvellous, if fleeting, chance for a bishop simply to ask the individuals where they have reached in their pilgrimage.

The larger evangelical parishes are frequently baptizing teenagers and adults. They tend nowadays to treat confirmation as unnecessary in such cases (and theologically they are right). But the bishop misses out. He can either urge that a case for confirmation remains, or can request to be invited to conduct baptisms himself, and possibly can even get baptisms and confirmations together. There are, of course, a few (rubrically correct) parishes where submersion is practised and the bishop must be ready to get more than his forearms wet.

But a bishop cannot well insist parishes find candidates, and some appear not ever to do so.

Special events

Bishops are constantly asked to special events – anniversaries, patronal festivals, opening of new buildings, civic services, commissioning of personnel. These usually represent growth, progress and achievement and are an opportunity for both thanking God and congratulating his servants. Because these come a bishop's way at regular intervals, he has got some wisdom, or at least experience, to offer. A bishop may well be more imaginative than the parish shows signs of being, and if so he can help them greatly. I have found that parishes are receptive to ideas if the right moment is found to feed them in. And the participation of the bishop in such planning then reinforces the sense that he is not just an outsider from the moon, but is an insider with a real stake in the parish's life.

Parish visitations (and ministerial reviews)

In my seven years as Bishop of Woolwich, for six of them I was doing six two-day parish visitations per annum, plus around 30 annual ministerial reviews. The reviews brought each licensed clergyman or clergywoman into my study for an hour or more – each one having an annual review, but one in four with me. The two days were an engagement at some depth not only with Sunday worship but also with institutions, training courses, visits to people confined to their homes, church schools, civic authorities, and a host of others. The new pattern is (in my case) around 23 one-day parish visitations in a year; and ministerial reviews conducted within those parishes at the time of the visitation. This means each parish is revisited by the bishop once every four years – and there is a real satisfaction in coming to the ministerial review well warmed to the tasks in the context of the actual sphere of operation of each licensed cleric who is to be reviewed that day. The parish has filled in a substantial questionnaire before the bishop visits; and the bishop writes a report on the basis of what he has seen and discovered. I think the parishes detect in this pattern a real desire on the bishop's part to engage with their life, to see it close to, and to recommend real steps forward which he has helped them to discern. My only problem is that they come thick and fast – I had a week recently when I did three such one-day visitations in four days, a programme that makes the writing up a demanding process indeed.

Deanery or larger events

If the parish context is the one that offers most opportunity for close personal relationships and one-to-one conversations (whether about God or quotas), the larger events enable a bishop to make a different contribution to the parishes. This is where that far-famed (and sometimes perhaps over-stated) claim that he is the focus of unity comes into play. He is gathering together and seeing together those who might otherwise miss each other. Whether it is a Synod, a rally, a breakfast,[10] or, say, a multi-parish confirmation, then he relates to the individual parishes somewhat more superficially than in the activities previously considered in this list – but he is favouring and instilling a more organic understanding of each parish's part in the church catholic.

When I asked the Woolwich clergy (in a letter sent before my installation) what they would welcome in their bishop's ministry, I received quite a cumulative response which said they wanted to see me much around the Area, rather than my sitting at home and summoning them – let alone being away and not even at home. That response (which is near to my own predilections) has marked my efforts to be bishop to the parishes of the Area. Caring for the clergy (that is, caring for their ability to be what they need to be for the mission of the Church) has to have very high priority, and there is a professionalism required here, with one professional exercising responsible oversight and care of another professional. But that cannot be boxed up as though bishops would never engage with laity, and some of the headings above illustrate this.

In addition to the above, much of trusting relationships arises through quite casual contacts – that is, at the institution of an incumbent in one parish, the bunfight gives opportunity to check on progress in another. The telephone, post, FAX and e-mail can all be used proactively, to show an interest, to filter out a problem, to exhibit an imaginative entering into others' situations – particularly if there is a suspicion of unexpected need – and to appreciate progress, good events, favourable reports about the parish, or even a good argument.[11] All in all the clergy must sense a bishop's longing to support, assist, resource, and challenge.

But virtually all I have said can be done, and often is done, with others setting the agenda. Being the victim of such agendas is an easy trap into which to fall. A bishop's life is busy, and wrestling to get one's head and energies above the routine requires determination; and one's own tiredness, insecurity, cynicism, disappointing experience, male menopause, swamping of administration, or impaired personal spirituality, let alone dismal desmonds among near colleagues, and even a doubting of the whole institution – quite apart from pressures on one's private life or on members of one's family – can sap the energy and buoyancy needed to have room for initiatives, to want to spearhead mission, to have a vision and to share it. The alternative – one which can happen to any ordained person – is that the diary, the routine, the demands of meetings and people fill each day, and, although one can finish each day with a sense that all the hours have been filled (and one can even feel near to being fulfilled in simply meeting demands), yet objectively that is a reactive and part-stultified ministry.

This book is specific to the Woolwich Episcopal Area; so the Area bishop must respond with ways he has striven to be above the routine requirements, and to be doing some spearheading. How can a bishop be proactive towards his parishes? Here are some specific ways in which I have attempted to rise above the routine agendas.

Teaching breakfasts

From the start – indeed from previous episcopal experience – I have suffered from the oddity of not having opportunity to teach and apply the Christian faith. Yes, I am a very occasional Sunday preacher in most of the parishes. Yes, I preach at confirmations. Yes, I am asked to do an occasional address to a deanery synod or a post-ordination training group or suchlike. Yet these are fairly minimal ways of teaching. One great paradox in the whole business of being a bishop is that the ordination rite charges you with being a teacher, preserver, and hander-on of the faith, and the diocese you go to loads you with administration and pastoral care and barely thinks to use you as a teacher.

My own first remedy was to take some soundings and go into the Area with my own 'Saturday breakfast teaching' events. The idea was to find a time that clashed with little in the way of parish timetables, but enabled non-stipendiary ministers and readers and others to come to the event, but still get home straight after breakfast and have the day with the family. So once a quarter over a full seven years I have advertised a totally open breakfast teaching hour, usually laying on the same topic two Saturdays running in the two separate archdeaconries. Twice a year I have expounded the scripture, twice a year tackled a contemporary theme in church or national life.[12]

Advertising forthcoming breakfasts has of itself led me into sending quarterly letters to all licensed clergy of my Area, and to readers, Southwark Pastoral Auxiliaries,[13] and ordinands. These letters only mention the breakfasts in passing, as there is always plenty of other material to pass on. In the last three years, these communications have moved across almost entirely to e-mail. I do not know how much they are read, though the come-back indicates that some recipients at least take trouble to take them aboard. The breakfasts themselves bring

total numbers varying between 20 and 70 – but it is an important
feature that they are entirely open, that anyone can come and argue,
and also that I am available without appointment afterwards to
anyone who wants to find me casually.

Further to the teaching role

I have grumbled about not being taken seriously as a teacher of the
faith. I have in fact been used a bit on our diocesan Ordained Local
Ministry Scheme, and have revelled in that. By dropping big hints I
have been let in a little on the evening diocesan certificate course in
my own Area. I have promoted conferences (and some fascinating
'colloquia') with my Liturgical Committee hat on. And I have
continued writing – and shamelessly promoting the stuff I write. I
occasionally get on to radio or TV (mostly as a token disestablish-
mentarian, as it is apparently instinctive to the Anglican Church
leaders generally to be establishment-lovers). I have discovered that
people in my Area like to think they have heard me on national radio,
and it helps their sense of belongingness – though, obviously, I am
greatly outgunned by my diocesan, Bishop Tom.[14] More rarely, I get a
letter or an article into the church or secular press. But would that
bishops were seen as first and foremost the men of God's word, and of
God's word for today. It is a real joy when a parish asks me to come for
teaching purposes.

My 2001–3 'Mission Round'

I now report on the special project that was conceived in 2001 and
completed in 2003. I had had a number of other projects leading up to
the year 2000 – including the millennium itself (the Dome being in the
Woolwich Area), and the late-stage battles I fought over the texts of
Common Worship, along with the provision of appropriate coaching
and explanatory materials to accompany those new texts. I then had a
short spell in hospital at the beginning of 2001, and by the time I was
back at work that Spring I found I was inwardly impatient at how
little I was able (as it seemed) to stimulate the Church in its mission. I
wrestled with half-formed ideas of interviewing all the clergy about
their strategies for mission. I consulted the Woolwich Area Council,
and got a mixed response. But one rural dean breathed to me that I
must think wider than the clergy. So it was in Autumn 2001 that I
allocated each rural dean a week somewhere between Advent Sunday
2001 and Palm Sunday 2002, and asked them to arrange for me to
meet within that week the clergy and lay leaders of each parish in
turn. I was briefing the parishes that I was coming simply to ask

questions, to learn how they understood the mission that God had given them.[15]

In the weeks of the mission round I found myself out every evening from Monday to Thursday, and sometimes three times on Saturdays and twice on Sundays over and above ordinary Sunday commitments. In total I completed 72 such visits.[16] They proved very stimulating. On each visit I asked the leaders how they understood 'mission', and then questioned them further as to how far they were pursuing their mission, *understood in their own terms*. This led the discussion in all sorts of different directions, and, although I had some standard issues I wished to raise (newcomers? baptism enquiries? funerals? community involvement?), these usually came naturally within the course that their own trains of thought were taking. I came home from each with pages of hand-written notes, which I then transcribed to my laptop, and found myself with 40,000 words on the machine by the time it finished.

I then wrote and published a report in book form on general trends, a report which hardly named a single parish, but picked up and highlighted common ways of approach when they were shared by, say, 15 or 20 parishes. The report was entitled *Mission in South East London: The Practice and Calling of the Church of England*. Copies went out to every parish, and invitations went to all PCC members (somewhere in excess of 1,000 people) to come to four open meetings which I convened to take the message further and handle questions and suggestions. The main thrust of these (to which over 400 people came) was that we are trying to talk of Jesus Christ as 'good news' and to see the whole Church as engaged in God's mission. But the report showed that the concept of 'mission', as put together from all the parishes, was much wider than evangelism, and was tilted quite strongly towards community involvement.[17]

In the year following I endeavoured to follow up the report, and in the meantime at various points the position in the diocese moved on. So in 2003 I wrote *Follow Up for 2003 to Mission in South East London*.[18] I had a whole series of new events and initiatives of the intervening fifteen months to report, including the basic data for the three boroughs from the Index of Multiple Deprivation of 2000 and the global totals and distribution of the various ethnicities and religions (including those of no belief) from the census of 2001.[19] It was, however, our church statistics which I was finding significant, for the great majority of our congregations were growing! The adult attendance at church on the key Autumn Sundays went up from 6,478 in 1998 to 7,187 in 2002, a sustained average increase of just over 2.5 per cent per annum. To be passing on a statistic like this at the core of a report on mission is obviously encouraging, as it suggested that we were able to set aside the press inventions about our being in terminal decline.

While our base was very low a few years back, we are steadily climbing from it.

Standing with parishes in respect of Borough plans

I have acknowledged above the sense I have of being insufficiently involved in the communities of my Area. Some of what I have done has been on a supra-parochial canvas, and is not wholly relevant here. But at intervals I have been able to lend some weight, or even spearhead a protest, in relation to planning authorities and the particular local implications of small-scale plans or even large-scale regeneration. Clearly the involvement of the local Anglican bishop on behalf of locals who are being overborne by the authorities has, if it is reasonably well-briefed and sensitive, a twofold effect: it both heartens the locals and gives pause to the councillors or their officials. The best instance of this is where I have tried to take a committed stance alongside Church Army Captain Nick Russell in the leadership he has given to the Ferrier Estate Residents' Action Group in Kidbrooke in the Borough of Greenwich in relation to the projected demolition and re-creation of the estate. The Church of England has been experienced there as a forceful local player on behalf of ill-resourced local residents, and I have been privileged to be called in, briefed, and trusted at points to assist.

There is no one brief for being a bishop, though my successor may have more of a detailed job description than I have. I have just been sent an outline of this sort, listing the desired features of a suffragan to be appointed in another diocese. It makes me quail. I came to Woolwich by an odd route, and at an advanced age.[20] So I continue to count it an unexpected and very privileged opening I received, to exercise an episcopate in this amazing Area of tight geography, extraordinary multi-ethnicity and multi-nationality, high deprivation, and, among other matters to grasp one's interest, a Church of England learning, grasping, struggling, and in measure succeeding at how to be a significant part of God's mission to the three-quarters of a million people of South-East London. I am much humbled at such a calling.

Notes

1 One of the happy ironies of my own life is that I helped draft the present (i.e, the ASB) ordinal, and I am, I believe, the first person ever ordained in the Church of England by the use of a rite which he had himself shared in compiling, that is, when I became a bishop. The irony is, of course, that I had not expected this to happen, or I might have tried to ask a little less of the bishop than the text actually does.

2 This has been a particular privilege in Africa, not least in being twinned currently with the diocese of Manicaland in Eastern Zimbabwe. Bishop Sebastian Bakare has become a good friend, and I pay tribute to him as one who has publicly and consistently withstood Mugabe despite every unfair pressure upon him.

3 In the Early Church, he was, it seems, *the* theologian. The word of God was deposited in him and with him to feed the faithful, proclaim the gospel, and hand on the truth to other generations in a quite unique way. All that has been changed, not only by fourth-century perceptions that even bishops might get it wrong, but much more by the coming of the printing press.

4 I am uniquely helped as an Area bishop in the diocese of Southwark by having two archdeaconries, that is, by having two archdeacons. I believe this to be unparalleled in area Schemes in England. And I have had magnificent colleagues. I have also for six years had a very fine secretary-cum-personal assistant (and she has had her own ministry to and for the parishes); there has been a fine Area Mission Team in place; and for four years I also gave half a discretionary post to a kind of chaplain, Christine Bainbridge.

5 I have been wonderfully free of this in my Woolwich post.

6 The problem is that visits by royalty are highly prized, and the red carpet is rolled out, and all feel greatly honoured by the great one who has come – BUT the visitor is symbolic rather than functional, cosmetic rather than useful. So it has often been with the episcopate also. And so some people – and possibly some bishops – would have it still.

7 But does not a bishop have responsibility also for the 'career path' of those whom he ordains? Has he not responsibility for finding them their next post? Ought he not at intervals to be putting a guiding hand on a shoulder and saying 'I think that God is guiding you to become vicar of St Nathanael's'? Many stipendiary clergy want to trust their bishop to do just that for them: but it is, at root, not really compatible with advertising vacancies, running competitive interviews, and seeking from within the whole nation (and sometimes outside it) the best possible appointee for this particular 'cure'. If the good of the parish comes first in the trusteeship, there may be clergy who have to learn the hard way that they are not appointable. Curiously, the much-opposed patronage trusts and private patrons are usually driven by the same concern – they are there to find the best possible person for the parish. The difference is that, unlike a bishop, they do not have to live close to their mistakes thereafter.

8 As a liturgist, I have worked on institution services in four dioceses. The main point I would make here is the desirability of the preacher being the one who chooses the readings from scripture – not now driven by a lectionary, let alone by a single standard set reading (as our ordinations tend to have), but by a specific seeking of scripture which will address this incumbent and this parish best at this juncture. What the recipient of my written sermon does with it after the event has, of course, usually lain beyond my ken.

9 This can take different forms, and it has been a joy for me to see different forms take root in parishes which initially said 'That's not our tradition'. At its simplest, testimony is a candidate responding privately to my question 'Why then are you being confirmed this day?' and sometimes 'What has God been doing in your life?' A regular pattern now is a duplicated set of testimonies (say, 20–100 words each) bound into the service booklet. Less frequent, but often very moving, is a spoken word by the candidates individually to the congregation.

10 See below on 'Teaching breakfasts'.

11 Perhaps I could hang another side-thought on this word 'argument'. As a theological college lecturer, I was unable to get away with anything without being challenged, and the result was plenty of argument, and therefore plenty of sifting what was a good argument and what was not. I think there is a deep notion in many Anglicans that they should not argue with bishops – if you disagree with your bishop, you smile secretively, tiptoe away, and complain to someone else. I have attempted to argue about theology, practice and policies on a level playing-field, and to deliver those with whom I disagree into arguing vigorously eyeball to eyeball instead of tiptoing away.

12 The 'themes' I have attempted to draw from the contemporary scene. Thus in December 2001 I did some homework (which I might not otherwise have done) on 'The Just War' theory. But it can go badly wrong – in early May 2003 I advertised my next breakfasts at the end of June on 'Women in the Episcopate', but by the time we got there the world was only interested in gay relationships (and some named persons). Often General Synod's agenda has prompted me. I have viewed nothing as off-limits – in other words a 'generalist' bishop ought to find access to enough resourcing to be able to give an hour's intelligent start to Christian people's consideration of any theme to which they come cold. No doubt my own selective interests have figured in the list, but in principle I have been ready to try to equip myself in any relevant area.

13 Southwark Pastoral Auxiliaries – officially selected, trained and appointed by the diocese, exercising a chartered lay ministry in many parishes.

14 I report this without any concern here as to whether I am right or wrong in what I say – the response by the local hearers is one of being in on the act, and I expect I could repeat the idiosyncrasies of my famous predecessor of four decades ago, and the response would be similar. So perhaps this is not exactly a 'teaching' role, more an 'appearing' one.

15 I found I had to emphasize that I was coming to learn, as at least one incumbent who was not abashed by the threatened presence of the area bishop wrote to me to tell me that I had no reason to think I had anything to teach them from my ivory tower about their task on the ground. I replied, I hope gracefully, saying I was coming simply to learn – and they allowed me in.

16 There are 92 benefices in my episcopal Area, but a few were vacant (and were thus describing themselves down a different route), a few

which were under pastoral reorganization met me as two parishes together, in a couple I had done a two-day visitation just before Advent 2001, and in one parish and one alone I was not-very-politely declined.

17 The report itself started from the Lambeth Conference fivefold 'marks of mission' which include both compassion for the needy and engagement with structures of government and society.

18 Both *Mission in South East London* and the *Follow Up* to it are still in print and obtainable for £2 each postfree from Southwark Diocesan Office, Trinity House, 4 Chapel Court, Borough High Street, London SE1 1HW.

19 Lest other parts of the country misunderstand the nature of these three London boroughs and see them simply as typical parts of an affluent South East of England, I should point out that, of the 87 wards in the three boroughs, 29 of them – exactly a third – fall into the most needy 10 per cent of all the wards in England. And an enormous number fall into the next 10 per cent also. To use old-fashioned terminology – the Woolwich Area is one large Urban Priority Area. I put the coloured map of Southwark diocese which makes this point on the front cover of my *Follow Up* report.

20 David Sheppard, who was appointed Bishop of Woolwich 34 years prior to my writing this, is just four years older than I am. His successor, Michael Marshall, who came in 28 years ago, is two years younger than I am. It is likely I shall have fallen off the end of the plank at the age of 70 within weeks of publication of this volume.

16. Essentially Reflective

Listening to the Parish Community and Rethinking Faith in God

JEFFREY HESKINS

Introduction

Some time ago I found myself standing outside a church reading its notice board. At the end of the list of services for Holy Week and Easter was the message 'You are welcome at any of our services.' It was, no doubt, a well-intended message of welcome, but it spoke volumes about how the church community saw itself, or might be seen by others, in that particular wider community. I left wondering who the 'you' was (being offered the invitation) and what they thought of the 'we' that owned the services on offer.

It is the dichotomy of Anglican life that we purport to run a parish system and yet, so often, when we talk about the 'parish' we really think no further than the congregation gathering for Sunday worship. Yet those of us who exercise a full-time paid ministry within a parish structure inevitably chance across numbers of parishioners who do not line up week by week at Sunday worship. Opportunities for this kind of encounter have already been described as essential if the Church is seriously to reconsider what it means to engage in the areas of mission and evangelism (see chapters 10 and 13). There are often also opportunities for pastoral care, which can address the dilemma which Alyson Peberdy describes in Chapter 3, namely that such care is often seen as merely reactive in nature rather than initiating.

This chapter puts the view that reactive pastoral care can lead to initiating other dimensions of pastoral care by simply considering it from different points of view, all of which demands a commitment to finding effective reflective processes in ministry. It describes a particular pastoral encounter in which two parishioners, not members of any congregation, are met and share insights that challenge the way we think about faith in God. The encounter happens to be, in this instance, one that centres on the preparation for a funeral, but this is not a chapter on thinking about funerals. It is about reflective practice and the principles explored are relevant to any number of pastoral scenarios. My purpose in writing is to offer the hypothesis that it is only when we take time to reflect on what we do in this way that the Church grows through listening to the insights of parishioners. I recommend a simple method for doing this and claim that reflective practice is not merely a luxury for the 'full-time' minister to indulge in when there is enough time, but is an essential practice for everyone.

Essentially reflective

Reflective practice seems to be something of a buzz phrase in the world of practical theology and ministerial training. In a series of meetings with a variety of students training for ordained ministry on regional schemes and theological colleges, I asked what they did on their respective courses to become reflective practitioners in ministry. They were all familiar with the phrase, all of them understood the value of reflective practice, and they all said that they were encouraged to be reflective. I then asked them how they set about doing the task of being reflective. One remembered a lecture on the liberation theology cycle that encouraged base communities to reflect on practice. One described a checklist of things they had to do. Several on the same course said that they were all encouraged to keep 'reflection' journals throughout the course, but the journals were private, were never seen by anyone else, and the keeping of them was voluntary. No one relayed any account of time set aside for open and active analysis of experience. A similar pattern seems to occur in post-ordination training. Newly ordained clergy in one diocese struggled to begin an active reflective exercise on pastoral practice when their Director of Post-Ordination Training introduced it to their training programme. They eventually decided that, as an exercise it was simply the way they thought about what they did. In another, one newly ordained priest reported back to her vicar that everyone else on her course had been stunned when she announced that she spent time with him working at being a reflective practitioner. In my own diocese I have a wad of papers to fill out if I want to be considered to train a newly ordained curate. It asks me some of the oddest things, like whether my Church Council members have a sense of vocation to being a training parish, but nowhere does it ask what the policy is on reflective practice as part of a training programme for the newly ordained. If ostensibly we value the idea of reflective practice, then it is clearly the case that finding the time to do it is a problem, or we don't know what the purpose of the exercise is, or we simply don't know how to get started.

The world of scholarship offers some starting points, but often what it advocates is complex and defined by its context. So, for example, in an extremely good article called 'Practical Theology as a Theological Form',[1] Emmanuel Lartey offers a method for establishing a process of reflection. However, the context is the university and an academic course he is planning for students. It is difficult to translate this material for use in the parish. Others, like Stephen Pattison, recognize this dilemma. In 'Some Straw for the Bricks: A Basic Introduction to Theological Reflection',[2] he offers a simple methodology for reflective practice. He describes a three-way conversation in which the person taking part engages their ideas and feelings with the contemporary situation under scrutiny and the perceptions provided by the Christian tradition. With some adaptation this seems to be a simple enough formula to be workable in the parish context I inhabit and from which this chapter emerges. Because the reflection has now become a written exercise rather than a solely spoken one, I have created the rather artificial divisions of dynamic and theological analysis. Through these divisions I hope to illustrate that reflective practice is rather more than a checklist of tasks or simply how we think about what we do with the view to doing it better. It is also about discerning who we think we are, how others perceive us, and how all of that impacts on the images of God that might emerge. In this particular example it serves to challenge how we might remain open to a rethink of faith in God because of the pastoral encounter.

The parish context

The benefice of Charlton consists of two Church of England parishes situated south of the River Thames between the visible affluence of Greenwich with its tourist attractions (Old Royal Naval College, Maritime Museum, meridian line, Royal Observatory) and some of the starkest social deprivation in Woolwich. Together the two parishes are a geographical area in which slightly more than 20,000 people live. It is a place of contrasts, racially mixed, predominantly working-class and with a strong bias to the Labour Party in its politics. It has an ageing population. The residential care homes are generally full and the mortality rate fairly high, particularly during the winter months. Faith groups are various. There are a significant number of Muslims and Sikhs, each with places of worship. Black-led Pentecostal churches are numerous, but (with one notable exception) small. The number of church-going Anglicans makes up less than 1 per cent of the parish population suggesting an attitude of ambivalence at best towards organized religion. However, because of the mortality rate and the need to prepare funeral services, there are numerous pastoral opportunities for a Church prepared to serve a community wider than its own membership. Observing death in the urban context can tell us a lot about life in it and about how people choose to live in that context. Life here is fast and impersonal. It often seems entirely secularized, practical, economically driven and devoid of measured thought. It is a process that sees any encounter with organized religion almost as an afterthought, if thought of at all. It is because of this that I consider engagement with life in this context one of the most fertile pastoral encounters for theological reflection.

A typical funeral arrangement will see the minister involved at quite an advanced stage in the proceedings. The next of kin are granted a death certificate, which they take to a funeral director. The director makes the arrangements for the funeral to take place, usually at the nearest crematorium. The funeral parlour then notifies the local minister as to the time and venue for the service. The minister then makes contact with the family and meets them to discuss the service. There is an 'allowance' of half an hour per service at the crematorium chapel. Services in church are, of course, available but tend not to be openly encouraged. The reason sometimes cited for this is that of not wanting to burden the families with needless expense. Word from funeral company employees is that higher levels of management press company employees to fit in as many funerals as possible. A church funeral will take almost twice as long to manage. Time is money.

In this situation the Christian minister trying to make sense of death in an increasingly secular context forces a re-think of religious identity and of how we think and talk about God, if we are prepared to take the time to do it. In this particular example, using the tools of reflective practice, the minister finds a dimension to ministry in the parish community which reveals some of the ways people implicitly think about God, though they rarely articulate those ideas, and discovers how this knowledge can be used in the pastoral encounter.

What follows is a conversation between two Christian clergy, trying to reflect on two funeral services conducted in the same week. It is a summarized transcript. Where necessary, names have been altered.

The conversation

Jim   So tell me, how did the two funerals go this week?

Ann   They were different but interesting. I got a call from the undertakers and went to see the widow of Leonard. As I walked in the door she handed me a piece of paper and said, 'I know what you priests like; you like the list of the names of all the family and I've done all this before. So, here we are; that's my name, those are my children's names and their partner's names. What else do you need?' I then found it quite difficult to get going. We then went through being offered a cup of tea and those things. It was all a bit brisk and stiff upper-lip and there was an underlying feeling that she wanted to get me out the door as soon as I had got there. The only thing she seemed concerned about was that I wouldn't preach a sermon and that I wouldn't go on too long, but please could I say something about him being 'upstairs'.

Jim What do you think she meant by that?

Ann Well, clearly she was uncomfortable with any God language, but was quite happy for me to sentimentalize the hereafter. When her daughter had died X number of years ago she wrote this little poem to put on the tombstone which runs along the lines of: 'If memories were lanes and treasures stairways, the stairway to heaven would be rich in you.' What she wanted me to say was that Leonard had joined the daughter on the stairway. Another daughter had managed to console the grandson with a photograph of the deceased daughter and dogs and cats and said they were all upstairs (and she actually pointed at the ceiling.) So, he just needed to think of granddad upstairs with the dogs and the late daughter.

Jim How did you feel?

Ann Stuck. They just kept telling me what a cheerful sort of person he was. I didn't quite know how to make sense of someone whose only contribution to life was that he was a bit of a joker. The whole thing seemed very superficial.

Jim Did you think there was any kind of religious faith there?

Ann I didn't think so. That seemed clear at the funeral itself. They all arrived in solemn black, had no eye contact with me, or the coffin, and afterwards just walked straight past me. They had spent vast amounts of money on floral displays, but seemed incapable of saying anything in the eulogy, anything of depth or significance about him to each other or to God. I felt drained by it all, but also cross and frustrated. Cross because I felt like I was some masked voice brought in to be an authority that they didn't really believe in, but need to pronounce on him being 'upstairs'. Frustrated that I was seen as some sort of technician. They had no relationship with me, didn't want one and didn't want one with God, or anything I was representing. They just wanted it done 'properly', whatever they meant by that.

Jim That was their word?

Ann That was their word. I felt frustrated by my own inability to deal with this kind of secularism, which was doggedly determined not to use anything that might well be a resource in terms of grief.

Jim So, how did it compare with the next one?

Ann It was different. I made a decision to introduce God whether it was a comfortable question or not. It would make some sense of my own role and what I was trying to do there and what they were asking me to do. Because I think that underlying the idea that 'we want it done properly' is the notion that somehow the priest is being asked to provide something, but it is difficult to know what if they won't allow you the language.

Jim Good. How did the theory work out?

Ann I got a phone call again from the undertakers and went to see a similar family – working-class, same area. Owen was a man who was clearly uncomfortable with clergy. We got into the same thing of how nice his wife was and so on and so eventually I decided to ask the faith question. It transpired that she had actually been brought up as a Presbyterian and had quite a strong faith. Though he claimed no faith of his own, he clearly knew the language of her faith. He said she liked the psalms (which were the old sort of prayers) and she liked hymns because they spoke to her of a God that she could understand. He was uncomfortable with all that, but it gave me the opportunity to make sense of the situation and his response was very different afterwards. He asked me for my prayers when I left and invited me to come and see him again.

Jim Right, so there was a real change in the course of that one. It seems to be marked by the introduction of the formal religious language?

Ann Yes, I think so, but also because he was quite willing to be real with me about his own struggles and about God. I felt like I was doing a pastoral office.

Reflecting on the dynamic analysis

What the reflective exercise does in the first instance is to raise to consciousness the questions relating to the dynamics of the encounter. Who do I think I am in this? Who do they think I am? What do we really think that we are doing when we talk about preparing a funeral service? This is the first aspect of reflective analysis. Both interviews went reasonably well albeit the first had a difficult start. In the first encounter the minister resists the temptation to scorn the idea of the dead going 'upstairs' in an attempt to remain on side with the family and find a different way of relating to them. The situation is difficult. The minister is an outsider and all the things that she stands for are outside the everyday life of this family. There is no sense of community participating in this; only a family doing its thing and struggling to face the finality of death with no adequate language of faith.

Just a generation ago, in this part of London, this would have been almost unheard of. My mother, who was brought up on the other side of the river Thames just before World War Two, was able to give account of numerous East-end funerals. They were a reflection of the area. The community gathered and expressed its grief in very practical gestures. Someone would make a street collection to buy flowers for the funeral or offset some of the costs. The body would be brought into the house where it would lie in state for friends and neighbours to visit. The priest and undertaker would lead the funeral procession and the mourners would meet afterwards in the pub where they would have food and drink laid on. The community turnout was to give the deceased a 'right good send-off'.

The erosion of all such forms of participation in a society marching to a tune of individualism reveals the nakedness of a class culture when trying to deal with death. This is not a new phenomenon. With the repeal of the Chantries in 1547 came the abolition of the concept of Purgatory – which was the intention of this Act of Parliament. What it also did was to destroy all the little groups and communities who had banded together to see that each member had a proper funeral and at the same time ensure that the group members participated in the preparation of the funeral. [3]

So, the wider local community is absent and the minister seems isolated by a family apparently unable to talk about death in any meaningful way. The symbols and ritual that would have rescued a pre-war Cockney-style funeral are absent from the sanitized local crematorium and its half-an-hour slot to say farewell to the lifetime of the deceased. Even the friendly manager of my local cemetery cannot understand why I choose to walk in procession to the grave rather than go in his car or take the short-cut. All that is left is the dressing in black and the vast floral displays. Robbed of all other ways of dealing with death, they 'said it with flowers', as one later remarked.

The dynamic reflection at this point suggests that the pastoral encounter seems to have been a failure. Feeling cold-shouldered and unappreciated, the minister reflecting on the encounter falls silent. It is at this point that she starts to see herself in a new way, and one that offers a ray of hope. Our thinking becomes three-way. Thus far we have dialogued with each other and the situation, but what do our Christian traditions have to say? We go back to the beginning. Leonard is 'upstairs' with his daughter and the cats and dogs. Southwark Diocese has just celebrated 40 years since the publication of Bishop John Robinson's *Honest to God*.[4] In it the then Bishop of Woolwich begins by telling the reader that it is no longer good enough to be thinking about God as the old man in the sky (in other words, 'upstairs'). The irony is not lost on us. Here we are in the Woolwich Episcopal Area 40 years on, with a family that can only think of an afterlife in this way. So, Robinson or no Robinson, this has to be our starting point with them.

While it may be difficult to see the 'upstairs' language as serious Christian imagery, it might be construed as an attempt at religious metaphor. Certainly it is not entirely out of keeping with the triple-tier world-view of ancient Judaism or with some of the gospel and other New Testament images. Luke gives a picture in Acts 1.9 where the visual image, read literally, has Jesus transported on a cloud upwards and out of sight. The writer to the Thessalonians (1 Thess. 4.17) uses the same imagery. This is a recommended text for funeral services. Heaven is engrained upon the human soul as 'going up'. Leonard's widow wants to give this perception of an afterlife 'upstairs' some authority. She does not have this authority herself, but sees it in the minister. The minister counts as God's representative, even if she is unable to articulate a formal faith for herself. So, will the minister say these things for her? The minister exercises caution, uncertain as to whether she is being manipulated or if this is a cry for help from one who is genuinely lost for the right kind of words. What she does next is critical. She does not scorn the idea of 'upstairs', but instead stays with the encounter although it is confusing and uncomfortable, and in the reflection finds that she begins to listen in a different way. In the infantile images there is an attempt to say something of faith.

The minister notes that she has become a listener in an encounter where words have been inadequate. She has to listen for the things that the widow cannot say. Perhaps it is in the way that we listen that we begin to reshape our God language. She concludes that it is the God of listening that has emerged, and this is what she takes from this first encounter as being of paramount value. There are echoes of Bonhoeffer in this insight as found in his classic work *Life Together*:[5]

> The first service that one owes to others in the fellowship consists in listening to them. It is God's love for us that he not only gives us his Word, but also lends us his ear. Christians, especially ministers, so often think that they must contribute something when they are in the company of others. They forget that listening can be a greater service than speaking. We should listen with the ears of God that we might speak the word of God.

But listening in this way is difficult because, as the clinical psychologists tell us (and as many of those involved in this kind of listening also know), it puts us in touch with suffering and pain and with our own sense of mortality.[6] It is never an easy thing to do, but this kind of listening has given this particular reflective process a positive way of expressing the experience. It was this God of the listening encounter that came to life in thinking about the second funeral.

This was helped partly because there was less 'denial' in the encounter. Owen was clearly uncomfortable in the company of clergy and professed no formal faith of his own. He would probably not have volunteered any information about his late wife's religious faith had the question not been posed. In this case the minister's decision to pose it made the difference. The images of God that were evoked in that encounter were not removed from the context that held Owen's grief. Owen struggles with his grief because he lives in a culture that demands that grief is something that you have to 'get over', like an obstacle in an obstacle course. What we need to see is that grief is not something that happens to us. It is part of who we are. If we can see it that way then it might cease to paralyse us and instead serve to provide us with insights as to what we really think we mean when we talk about the resurrection.

What happens to the apostles between Good Friday and Pentecost is that they come to realise that the death of a loved person is a growing point. Those insights are no different for any human being if we look at it this way. If images of God are to be found at all then they will be found in the human story. The listening God is not to be found outside ourselves, but within us, and God is revealed in the telling of the human story even (and especially) when it is as grief-wracked as this story is. Owen comes to see something of that in telling his wife's story. It is painful for him to do that. His wife believed in a God found in the records of human experience (like the psalms and some hymns) and, whilst he is uncomfortable with that, he honours her way of thinking about it. Though he does not identify God in the experience of his grief, there is a sense in which recounting her story in the company of the representative of God (a God in whom he doesn't believe) effects a kind of spiritual journey. When the Chantries Act killed off Purgatory it also killed off all the practical benefits of the lay fraternities who prepared the funerals of the day. The most notable loss was the sense of being 'accompanied' towards, during and after death by the prayers and support of the community. Members walked with criminals on their way to execution or gave Christian burial to the abandoned or destitute. In the painful loneliness of his grieving, Owen allows the minister to accompany him in his story. As he does so, he begins to change. The minister is more comfortable to have around. He thanks her for the visit and even asks for her prayers. This is quite a move in a short space of time.

What we seem to be noticing here is that faith in God can begin with some kind of display of faith in the minister. After an uncertain start, Owen allows the minister to stand for him when he cannot stand by himself. She will conduct his wife's funeral and will say the things that he, Owen, would like to say but cannot. He may purport not to believe in God, but he has made an important act of faith. He trusts her to conduct the funeral service and thereby enables a positive image of Christian ministry to emerge from within the parish community, the listening God and the serving Church.

This part of the reflection now draws to a close. The shaky start has led to some unexpected pastoral images and positive insights about who we think we are and how others see us in the pastoral encounter. For some this alone justifies the process of reflective practice. But as it stands, it is only a little more than a work consultancy exercise. However improved the practice, we need to examine the encounter for any theological insights.

Reflecting on the theological analysis

A few years ago there was a flurry of correspondence in the church press between the then Bishop of Edinburgh, Richard Holloway, and a freelance journalist called Anne Atkins.[7] Mrs Atkins had appeared on Granada Sky's talk channel to attack clergy who expressed doubts, describing them as self-confessed 'atheists', and asking how they could square such a position with their consciences while in the pay of the Church.[8] Bishop Holloway countered with the view that Anne Atkins had confused faith with certainty. The reality of faith was that it had to co-exist with doubt and so certainty was the opposite of faith. If this is so then it is a helpful insight when looking for models of faith and for theological images as they reveal themselves in the kind of context in which our pastoral encounter has occurred.

The London urban context is one that is dominated by secularization and there are some Christian caucus groups that deal with this through an attitude of what they call counter-culture. In other words, the existing culture is one that is to be resisted because it is one that erodes the boundaries of the religious systems in which they choose to live. Unless it is resisted, the core of their faith is perceived as compromised or 'watered down'. Personally, I think that this is a mistake, as can be seen from the experience under analysis here. Even in a context of overwhelming secularization, there seems to be an understanding of faith which struggles to find a language outside the 'given' language of Church and other religious institutions. Time and again I meet adult children preparing a funeral for their last remaining parent who will invite me to 'say something about them being together again'. This is not an informed Christian hope, but it is an important statement about wanting to believe in life beyond death and is perhaps a starting point for rethinking faith in God. New life of some kind is a human hope whether expressed in formal Christian terms of the resurrection or not. It exists at a deep level of consciousness no matter how illogical it might seem. We should not be surprised or offended by this.

Something similar occurred in the earliest Christian communities. In writing to the Church in Corinth Paul makes a passing reference to the practice of baptism on behalf of the dead (1 Cor. 15.29). Whether the practice was appropriate or not, Paul passes no judgement on the matter. Whatever was happening in Corinth, he may have perceived the practice as an act of love for the dead and as a statement of faith in God. The mystical community of the Johannine church has Jesus speak in metaphors of an afterlife in God's company as being a place of many rooms which he, Jesus, will prepare for his followers (John 14.1–6). John 14.1–6 is a prescribed reading for a funeral service and one which we readily expect countless numbers of mourners to key into. My experience of their response to it from the glazed look on their faces at the crematorium is that it contains a language which belongs to another context. It is somebody else's expression. So, while living within the Christian tradition, I think that there might be more integrity to a metaphor like this than there is in the idea that death is about popping upstairs with the cats and dogs, the 'upstairs' image has to be my starting point.

It is a common practice of scholarship to gain new insights into old texts by deploying what is called a 'hermeneutic'. As I understand it, this hermeneutic is a tool rather like a catalyst in a chemistry experiment. It doesn't actually become anything in the findings themselves, but it does enable the process to happen, and without it the process cannot happen. So, for example, fresh insights gained by feminist scholars about familiar texts of scripture have occurred through borrowing a liberation theology hermeneutic; the 'hermeneutic of suspicion'. This hermeneutic, when applied to traditional scripture texts written by men only in a male dominated social and economic context, allows the role and contribution of women in the early Christian movement to emerge with a new significance.[9] This in turn offers a new way of looking at how an old text might have been understood then. It can then effect a new contemporary changing of attitude and practice. At least, that is the theory. Good examples of this can be found in what are now regarded as feminist classics like Elisabeth Schüssler Fiorenza's *In Memory of Her*.[10] In this book she begins by scrutinizing the account of the anointing at Bethany in the Gospel of Mark. The unnamed woman whose story will always be told 'in memory of her', through the deployment of this hermeneutic, emerges from the typecast tradition of the little woman, probably of ill repute, into a story of a woman of stature within a radical prophetic tradition. From being an unnamed nobody, this hermeneutic allows her to be seen as a divine instrument in the revolutionary story of the Passion.

In the pastoral context we are reflecting on here, it will be helpful to devise a similar 'pastoral hermeneutic' to look for theological images in the encounter. So, in this instance, rather than use the hermeneutic of suspicion, let us for argument's sake create one that we might call 'optimistic hope'. This hermeneutic can act as the reverse of the hermeneutic of suspicion by enabling me to look at the situation and reflect with an attitude that gives the subject of the experience the benefit of any doubt in what they are trying to communicate to me.

The first encounter seemed to see God much as the minister: an embarrassing addendum occasionally let across the threshold but not allowed to stay too long. In his book *God of Surprises*[11] Gerard W. Hughes, the Jesuit writer, argues that the Church has largely done that with the figure of Jesus. The reality of whatever Jesus might mean for everyday people, even in spiritual terms, has become so impossible to live with that either we shut it out, create God in our own image, or place God under church-arrest. Ostensibly, the images of God conveyed in the first encounter were not dissimilar to the welcome the minister felt during the visit and the funeral itself. God was distant and abstract. God was given a useful list of names. God was told what God ought to be doing because the family had done all this before and such things could be expected of God because God was unchanging. God is transcendental in this first encounter, most likely a 'he' living beyond the sky where he gathers all these people up a stairway to himself. God is depicted in personal terms, but is a rather sanitized figure. Bishop Robinson would not have been amused by this figure!

Even if we use our hermeneutic of optimistic hope, this is a fairly depressing picture of God. It is hampered in the first instance because there is some dishonesty in speaking of the deceased who was a laugh a minute and never upset anybody. It is very important for this family not to see God in any kind of judgement mode: so God's envoy should not be given any evidence that might mark down Leonard's chances of getting up the staircase. The problem seems to be that, unlike the 'many rooms' of the Johannine afterlife with God, the staircase image is not being used as a metaphor. The family cannot cope with anything quite that sophisticated. Reality and fantasy have become blurred. However, they have an image of heaven that has some biblical precedence (should they be remotely concerned with such a justification). Jacob's ladder and the images of angels are used in Old and New Testament scriptures (Gen. 28.10–19 and John 1.50–51).

Leonard's widow is anxious for the man who made them all laugh, but if we read this situation with our interpretative tool of optimistic hope, though her faith is immature, it is one that gives her hope for a merciful God and thus the certainty of a life beyond the grave. She can only deal with that in present-life images – dogs and cats and being 'family'.

In contrast to this rather archaic and infantilizing God, the language

of faith in the second pastoral encounter emerges from three important areas. First, it emerges from Owen's personal struggle to make
sense of death and the way it seems to victimize the vulnerable.
Second, it emerges from telling the human story. This in terms of his
wife is a story he is proud to tell though there are things in it he really
cannot make sense of. Third, it is through the reality of suffering, for
suffering has been a feature of his own life in the fight against cancer
and that of his wife who finally died after chronic illness. He continually stresses no formal faith of his own, but acknowledges, when
pressed, that his wife did have a personal faith, which she had long
ceased to practise in church. While it was a faith he could not subscribe to, she obviously articulated it in terms that he could meet
respectfully. Thus while he would say that he had no faith in God and
he places God out of the picture, when challenged on the matter he
was able to speak about suffering and admit that his denial of God
was 'feeling-based'. This made room for God to come into the picture
again through human experience and in particular through the
religious experience articulated by his wife.

Owen struggled on two fronts. One was with an archaic personal
God who was all-powerful and yet seemed to do nothing about
suffering. He didn't feel so good about this God and his feelings led
him to a rejection. The other was a remarkably sophisticated understanding that if the human experience of the psalmists and some
hymn writers was to be believed, then the only sense he could make
of any of it was that God was somewhere in the suffering. The God of
Owen's experience (rather than his feelings) was the only one he
could live with.

Rethinking faith through a lens of optimistic hope leaves God, for
Owen, as a kind of travelling companion to be found in his relationships. God emerges through the honesty of an imperfect world, but
one in which God wants to be intimately involved. God's representative in the shape of the minister proved to be an agreeable companion
for what could have been a difficult encounter. It also reminded him
that his wife had journeyed through life with him through thick and
thin. Perhaps the God of the journey was there too. If he learned anything from the minister in this encounter, it must surely have been
that there are some people around who will companion us in difficult
times. If that is to be translated into God imagery, it must lead to the
conclusion that God is no fair-weather friend. This is an image worth
preserving.

Concluding thoughts

Not all funerals are like the two described. Part of this exercise has been to show that the uniqueness of the experience is created to a great degree by the unique nature of the parish system. One of the obvious benefits of such a system, if we are prepared to make use of it, is that the diversity that exists across a parish community can be of benefit to the worshipping congregation within it and the Christian ministers who serve it. Such benefit became evident here in the way two parishioners, who take no part in weekly parish worship, were able to challenge the parish clergy into a re-think of faith and how faith in God is perceived.

Opportunities like this are not unique to one particular parish because of its unique context. They exist everywhere within the diversity of the parish system. However, as stated at the outset, this has not been a chapter about funeral-taking, but one on how the discovery of an appropriate means of reflecting on pastoral experience can enhance our thinking across the entire community. So the reflective process, far from being a time-consuming act of navel-gazing, becomes a vital part of Christian pastoral ministry on at least two fronts. In the first instance, it allows for the possibility of personal growth and change as ministers become more aware of who they are in the pastoral encounter. In the second instance it allows for the possibility of discovering God through the encounter and of reshaping our thinking about God in new ways. As a practical means of gaining theological insights and self awareness, the creation of time for reflection is essential for any Christian engaged in a pastoral ministry.

Further reading

Pattison, Stephen and James Woodward (eds.), *The Blackwell Reader in Pastoral and Practical Theology*, Blackwell, Oxford, 2000
Heskins, Jeffrey, *Unheard Voices*, Darton, Longman & Todd, London, 2001

Notes

1 Lartey, Emmanuel, 'Practical Theology as a Theological Form', in Pattison, Stephen and James Woodward (eds.), *The Blackwell Reader in Pastoral and Practical Theology*, Blackwell, Oxford, 2000, pp. 128–34.

2 Pattison, Stephen, 'Some Straw for the Bricks: A Basic Introduction to Theological Reflection', *Contact*, Vol. 99, 1989, pp. 2–9, and in Pattison and Woodward (eds.), *Reader*.

3 Murphy, Anne, 'Christian experience from the shadow side of history', in *The Way*, April 1993.

4 Robinson, John, *Honest to God*, SCM Press, London, 1963.

5 Bonhoeffer, Dietrich, *Life Together*, SCM Press, London, 1954, pp. 75–6.

6 Lake, Frank, *Clinical Theology*, Darton, Longman & Todd, London, 1966, p. 4, quoting Frida von Reichmann.

7 *Church Times*, London, December 1996.

8 Granada Sky's talk TV channel, December 1996.

9 See Schüssler Fiorenza, Elisabeth, 'Missionaries, Apostles, Co-workers: Romans 16 and the Reconstruction of Women's Early Christian History', in Loades, Ann (ed.), *Feminist Theology: A Reader*, SPCK, London, 1989.

10 Schüssler Fiorenza, Elisabeth, *In Memory of Her*, SCM Press, London, 1991.

11 Hughes, Gerard W., *God of Surprises*, Darton, Longman & Todd, London, 1985.

Conclusion

I pray that you may have the power to comprehend, with all the saints, what is the breadth and length and height and depth, and to know the love of Christ that surpasses knowledge, so that you may be filled with all the fullness of God. (Eph. 3.18, 19)

The love of Christ might surpass knowledge, but it can still be known, and our contention is that it is known in and through the parish: through this patch of ground, its built environment, its community, its community's members, its congregation, its congregation's members, its parish church, and its clergy. Our readers will have to judge whether we have made that case. Only if we have made *that* case will we have made a case for the parish.

A book like this is necessarily episodic. It is about particular places at particular times, and it is by particular people with particular perspectives, so there is a sense in which it can be nothing but a collection of individual essays. But we believe that we have also written a book, and that the common thread is a way of being the Church which God has blessed and will, we believe, continue to bless. We are well aware of the importance and depth of secularizing processes in our society, we are aware of the importance of ecumenism and of dialogue between different faiths, and we are aware of our sister church, the Roman Catholic Church, which to some extent shares with the Church of England and with Anglicanism more widely a parochial structure; but as we have written this book we have come to believe more strongly that the Anglican parish is an important response to secularization and that it is a significant gift which Anglicanism has to offer to ecumenism and to inter-faith dialogue and to the world at large.

We have written a modest book: there is no triumphalism here. The world and the Church are in a period of considerable change, the parish is changing, and some of the contributions to this book suggest how it might need to change; but we offer no blueprint. We believe that one of the virtues of the parish is its sheer locality, for theologically this enables it to be an expression of a God incarnate in a particular person and in a sense incarnate still, and sociologically it enables it to adapt as its environment changes and thus to continue to proclaim the Christian gospel in a diverse and changing world.

Whether or not we see a progressive disestablishment of the Church of England, the Church is now in a marketplace of religions. In this situation it will surely be essential for the Church of England to retain its distinctiveness. We have come to believe that an important element in that distinctiveness is the parish: the territory, the community, the congregation, the building, the priest. The Church of England is not just its parishes, but they are surely its heart, and without them it would not be the same Church. The parish is therefore a sacred trust. This does not mean that it should be preserved from change: rather the opposite, for in a changing world the parish will only survive if it changes constantly. But it does mean that as the world and the Church change we shall constantly ask whether the parish is still with us. If we find we can't answer that question in the affirmative, then we might have dropped the gift and we shall need to find it and renew it.

It might well be an accident of history that the parish has evolved, but it has evolved, it is still very much alive, and we are privileged to be part of it. We commend its appreciation to our readers.

Now to him who by the power at work within us is able to accomplish abundantly far more than all we can ask or imagine, to him be glory in the church and in Christ Jesus to all generations, for ever and ever. Amen. (Eph. 3.20–21)

Glossary

This glossary is a 'jargon-buster', and is included to enable the reader to understand the book. The explanations of the terms listed are not intended to be tight legal definitions and should not be taken as such.

Admission to communion	In the Diocese of Southwark, and in various other dioceses, parishes have permission to admit children to communion before they are confirmed. In the Diocese of Southwark children are admitted to communion if they are over seven years of age and have attended a course of preparation.
All Souls Day	The 2 November, the day following All Saints Day. Many parishes hold services to remember and/or pray for the dead, and people recently bereaved are often invited.
Alpha Course	A course of study for enquirers published by Holy Trinity, Brompton. The course consists of a series of evenings on which participants share a meal, listen to a talk, and hold a discussion. There is also a weekend about the Holy Spirit.
Anglican	The Anglican Communion is all those dioceses (in the Church of England and world-wide) that are in communion with the Archbishop of Canterbury: in practice, all those whose bishops attend the Lambeth Conference once every ten years. There is no such thing as the Anglican Church, though the term is sometimes used of the federation of dioceses in communion with the Archbishop of Canterbury, or of the federation of dioceses that constitute the Church of England.
Anglicanism	A set of practices and ideas that characterize the Anglican Communion or more specifically of the Church of England.

Anglo-Catholic	A rather loose term to describe those parts of the Church of England closest in liturgy and in other ways to the way the Roman Catholic Church used to be.
Annual Parochial Church Meeting (APCM)	A meeting held in each parish during April to elect churchwardens, to elect Parochial Church Council members, to elect deanery synod members (once every three years), to hear reports, and conduct other necessary business. Anyone on the electoral roll can vote.
Archbishops' Council	The executive body of the Church of England. It is made up of the Archbishops of Canterbury and of York, of people elected by General Synod, and by a number of co-opted members. The various departments (such as Ministry Division, which regulates and pays for training for the ordained ministry) report to the Archbishops' Council, which in turn reports to General Synod. The Council holds the Church of England's central budget.
Archdeacon	A bishop's assistant, with legal and other functions of their own but which can be delegated. To be appointed an archdeacon someone must be a priest and must have been in holy orders for at least six years. In practice the archdeacon can be a pastoral figure in the diocese.
Baptism	The initiation rite for a Christian. It can be carried out at any age, and when a child is baptized godparents speak for them.
Beating the bounds	On Rogation Sunday (the fifth Sunday after Easter: now called the sixth Sunday of Easter), the day on which people blessed the fields and prayed for good crops, there is an ancient tradition of a procession emerging from the parish church and walking the parish boundaries. As many urban parish boundaries are railway lines, roads or (in the case of many parishes mentioned in this book) the middle of the River Thames, the spirit rather than the letter of the tradition might be followed.
Benefice	A parish or parishes of which a priest is incumbent.
Bishop	Someone ordained by other bishops to the first order of the Church's threefold ministry of bishop, priest and deacon. The bishop's role is outlined in the ordinal. And see Chapter 15.

Canons	'Canon' has two meanings: a) the title of a cathedral dignitary, either residentiary (i.e. receiving a stipend to work on the cathedral staff) or honorary (i.e. receiving a stipend for some other post but having the right to sit in a cathedral stall). b) a rule governing the Church. The canons are revised by General Synod and agreed by Parliament.
Chancellor	The legal officer of a diocese. He decides whether to issue faculties for changes to church buildings and for other purposes.
Chaplain	Someone fulfilling a pastoral role in an institution, usually a hospital, factory, university, etc. The chaplain might or might not be a member of the clergy.
Chapter	A regular meeting of the clergy of a deanery which they are expected, but not obliged, to attend.
Church	With a lower-case initial letter it means a congregation of Christians or the building within which they meet. With a capital initial letter it means the entire universal body of Christian believers and all of its local manifestations. The word can also have a capital letter if it is part of a denomination's title, as in 'Methodist Church'. In many contexts in this book the word will start with a capital letter because it is short for 'Church of England'. The word also has a sociological meaning: see below on 'denomination'.
Church House, Westminster	The home of General Synod, of the Archbishops' Council, and of the divisions (for training, education, etc.) responsible to it.
Church of England	A federation of dioceses in England which have bishops in communion with the Archbishop of Canterbury, and, since dioceses are federations of parishes with umbrella organizations to serve them, the Church of England is a federation of parishes and of umbrella organizations.
Church representation rules	Rules established by General Synod to govern elections, meetings, etc. of Parochial Church Councils and other parts of the synodical system.
Churches Together	Many areas have 'Churches Together' groups. These might or might not be formally constituted. There is usually a regular meeting of representatives of churches in the area, and joint projects might be

	planned. There is a national 'Churches Together in England', and there is also a 'Churches Together in Britain and Ireland'.
Churchwarden	An ancient elected office. Each parish has two churchwardens elected annually. The churchwardens have a number of powers, such as the ability to veto the appointment of an incumbent (except when the living is 'suspended', when the bishop appoints a Priest in Charge rather than licensing an incumbent); and they have a number of responsibilities, such as the annual completion of articles of enquiry sent by the archdeacon.
Clergy	A collective noun for bishops, priests and deacons. Whether the clergy remain lay people is an interesting question. A priest remains a deacon, and a bishop remains a priest and a deacon, so it might be thought that they all remain lay people. But the Church's synodical structure separates people into bishops, other clergy, and laity.
Common Worship	The name of the collection of alternative services authorized for use in the Church of England in 2000.
Confirmation	The bishop lays his hands on the candidate's head and prays for the Holy Spirit to 'confirm' them. Historically this action was part of a single baptismal rite. Normally only people who are confirmed (or are ready to be confirmed) receive communion. But now members of other denominations are also welcome to receive communion; and see above on 'admission to communion'.
Congregation	Any gathering of Christians for the purpose of worship.
Conventional district	An area within one or more parishes under the care of a minister. When such a district is established the parishes within which it lies lose most of their functions in relation to the district. Conventional districts are established where new housing and other developments occur and it is not initially clear how parish boundaries should be reorganized.
Curacy	An assistant priest's post. An assistant priest in a parish can be either stipendiary or non-stipendiary. The term often applies to an ordained minister's first and training post where the curate is under the

	supervision of a training incumbent. For the first year the curate is a deacon and thereafter a priest.
Curate	Someone undertaking a curacy.
Cure of souls	The care of the people of the parish. At an institution this becomes the responsibility of the new incumbent.
Daily office	Morning and evening prayer said daily. The clergy are meant to say the daily office. Some do, as do some of the laity.
Deacon	Someone ordained by the bishop to the second order of the Church's threefold ministry of bishop, priest and deacon. The deacon's role is outlined in the ordinal. See Chapter 14. The deacon cannot preside at the Eucharist or be incumbent of a parish.
Deanery	An area, sometimes coterminous with a natural community or communities but not always, usually comprising a dozen or so parishes. Every deanery has a Deanery Synod (chaired by the lay chair and the rural dean) and a clergy chapter (chaired by the rural dean).
Deanery Synod	The governing body of a deanery.
Denomination	A federation of congregations, usually with an umbrella organization or organizations to fulfil functions best carried out centrally, such as the payment of clergy. The word also has a separate but connected meaning in the social sciences, where it means a category of religious organization between the categories of 'sect' and 'church'. The denomination has more open boundaries than a sect, but boundaries less open than for a church (with 'church' here defined in terms of characteristics such as open boundaries and diverse belief-systems, i.e., not as defined above).
Diocesan Synod	The governing body of a diocese. There are three houses: bishops, clergy (but not bishops), and laity. A vote by houses can be requested. The synod sets diocesan policy and the budget of the diocese. All bishops in the diocese are members, and there are elections for the house of clergy (amongst all clergy) and for the house of laity (the electors being deanery synod members).

Diocese	A federation of parishes with an umbrella organization to carry out those functions best dealt with centrally, such as the payment of clergy.
Diocese of Southwark	The parishes of South London and of parts of Kent and Surrey.
District	In a parish with more than one church building districts can be established. The Parochial Church Council can delegate to District Church Councils certain decisions relating to particular buildings, the congregation which meets in it, and the Church's mission in the community in which the building is situated.
District Church Council	The governing body of a district. The Parochial Church Council of the parish in which the district lies decides which decisions to delegate to the District Church Council.
Ecumenical Borough Deans	In London Boroughs, and elsewhere, each denomination appoints a borough dean to represent the denomination to the local authority and other parts of civil society. The borough deans meet, and often act together.
Ecumenism	The relating of different denominations to each other at local, regional or national level.
Electoral roll	A list of all those who fill in a form to say they want to be on the roll. Anyone who lives in the parish or who worships regularly in the parish church can be on the roll. It is the nearest thing the Church of England's got to a membership list. In order to fill in the form you have to declare yourself to be a member of the Church of England or of a church in communion with it.
Eschatology	The last things: i.e., those events that parts of the Bible describe as preceding the final coming of God's Kingdom: see 1 Thessalonians 4 and Mark 13. The themes of death, judgement, heaven and hell are also sometimes described as 'eschatological'.
Eucharist	A fourfold action of taking bread and wine, giving thanks over them, breaking the bread, and sharing the bread and wine. The word's meaning generally extends to the whole event, including hymns, readings, prayers, the peace, etc.

Faculty	A document giving a parish permission to alter the parish church or to undertake a particular activity within it.
Faith community	Any body of people who are adherents of a religion.
Free Church	This term normally designates any denomination apart from the Church of England and the Roman Catholic Church, e.g., the Methodist Church. (There are many non-affiliated congregations which can be regarded as free churches in their own right.)
Freehold	A priest who is inducted as rector or vicar (or team rector) holds the freehold of the benefice. This is a useful legal fiction. It means that the incumbent owns the parish church and the parsonage house but can't do anything with them except look after them. A priest who holds the freehold can stay in post until he or she is 70 years old.
General Synod	The national governing body of the Church of England. There are three houses: bishops, clergy (but not bishops), and laity. A measure has to pass in all three houses if a vote by houses is requested. The synod sets national policy and the budget of the Church's central departments. All diocesan bishops are members, and there are elections for the house of clergy (amongst all clergy) and for the house of laity (the electors being deanery synod members).
Hermeneutic	A method for interpreting a text, and in this case the Bible. There are many different hermeneutics. A 'hermeneutic of suspicion' is a means of interpreting the Bible which starts out from suspecting the motives of its writers in order to enable the situation in which the text was written to speak to us as well as the text itself.
Holy Communion	See Eucharist.
Holy Orders	Someone is in holy orders if they are a deacon, a priest, or a bishop.
Holy Spirit	The third person of the Trinity. For this and other theological terms readers should consult a good theological dictionary.

House of Bishops	The term can either mean all the bishops who sit in a particular synod, or just the diocesan bishops.
House of clergy	The members of clergy elected to a synod, apart from the bishops, who have a house of their own.
House of laity	The members of the laity elected to a synod. Clergy cannot be members of the house of laity even if they might still be members of the laity.
Incumbent	The priest who holds the freehold of the benefice.
Induction	A brief event, following an institution, at which the archdeacon inducts the priest into the freehold of the parish.
Industrial chaplain	A chaplain in an industrial institution, though in practice many industrial chaplains undertake a variety of activities in connection with the Christian faith's relationship to the economy.
Industrial mission	The activity of relating the Christian faith to the world of work and to the economy. An industrial mission is an institution set up for this purpose.
Institution	The event, conducted by the bishop, which marks the beginning of a new incumbent's ministry in the parish. At the heart of the event is the bishop's sharing of the cure of souls with the new incumbent.
Intercessions	Prayers requesting God to do things.
Inter-faith	A description of worship or other activity in which institutions and/or members of different faiths are involved. Because inter-faith activity such as joint worship might distress members of individual faith communities, such activity tends to be small-scale and for individuals committed to inter-faith work.
Johannine	'Of John' – the term describes the text of the Fourth Gospel and of the three letters under John's name, the distinctive theology expressed by those books, and the community for which the books were written.
Laity	Anyone other than bishops, priests and deacons. Whether bishops, priests and deacons remain laity after their ordination is an interesting question.
Lambeth Conference	A conference convened once every ten years to which the Archbishop of Canterbury invites every bishop whom he believes to be in communion with him.

Lay Reader	An old name for a Reader.
Lay person	A member of the laity.
Liberation theology	A theology that uses the themes of Israel's escape from Egypt and Jesus' resurrection, amongst others, to give hope for the coming of the Kingdom of God here in our world today as well as in the future.
Licence	A document giving a deacon, priest or reader permission to fulfil their ministry in a particular parish or parishes.
Local Ecumenical Partnership	A formally constituted relationship between churches (buildings and/or congregations) of different denominations. Provision is often made for joint worship within certain limits.
Lord's Supper	See Eucharist.
Mass	See Eucharist.
Measure	Legislation passed by General Synod and approved by Parliament.
Minister	A rather loose term to refer to anyone undertaking a liturgical or pastoral function. The minister can be a bishop, a priest, a deacon, a reader, a Southwark Pastoral Auxiliary, or a lay person.
Multi-faith	A description of activity in which institutions and/or members of different faiths are involved. Unlike 'inter-faith', joint activities which might distress members of the faith communities involved are avoided.
Muslim	An adherent of Islam, the religion founded on the Quran and of which Mohammed is the final prophet.
Non-stipendiary minister	A deacon or priest who does not receive a stipend. Most non-stipendiary clergy are curates and are usually designated 'hon. Curate'.
Occasional offices	Services held according to need rather than in relation to a particular day. So marriages, funerals and baptisms are 'occasional offices'.
Ordained Local Minister	A minister ordained deacon and then priest following a diocesan training course. The licence usually restricts the minister's role to a particular parish or parishes.

Parish	See the beginning of Chapter 1 and the history in Chapter 4. The parish is a patch of land with its community and institutions, with a congregation or congregations, with a priest or priests, and with a building or buildings for worship. See the different chapters of this book for discussion of various aspects of the life of a parish.
Parish Communion	See Eucharist.
Parochial Church Council (PCC)	The governing body of a parish. The churchwardens and the incumbent are ex officio members. Members are elected from the electoral roll at the Annual Parochial Church Meeting. The Council takes all decisions relating to the life of the parish except for a few reserved to the incumbent (mainly in relation to the conduct of worship).
Passion	Jesus' suffering and death.
Passion play	A play about the last week of Jesus' life, usually performed during the week before Easter.
Pastoral	Anything to do with the care of the parish's people, or with the parish's organization or boundaries, or with the structures within which clergy operate. For 'pastoral office' see 'occasional office'. For 'pastoral measure' see 'pastoral' and 'measure'.
Pentecostal	A description of congregations or federations in which speaking in tongues and the other spiritual gifts mentioned by Paul in 1 Corinthians 12 and 14 are central to prayer and worship.
Pew rent	Members of the congregation used to have to rent their pew. There were sometimes benches at the back for people who couldn't afford to do so. Parishes now have to find other means to raise money.
Post-modern	'Post-modernism' has no definition other than 'after what's modern'. The word was originally an architectural term, and in this sense it describes the architectural period after the 'modern' period. We know what 'modern' buildings look like: they tend to be functional, cubic office-blocks. 'Post-modern' buildings have no particular style of their own but rather employ a variety of styles. The Sainsbury's wing at the National Gallery is a typical post-modern building.

In literary and philosophical circles the term has come to mean something similar. There have been various 'metanarratives', i.e., ways of understanding the whole of reality. Plato's theory of Forms (ideas of good, justice, etc. existing in a world of their own and in which the things we experience merely participate somehow) is a typical case. During the modern period the metanarrative was a scientific one, and everything, including religion, was expected to conform to it (and religion often justified itself in scientific terms). In the post-modern period there is no longer a metanarrative. (It was the French philosopher Lyotard who announced the death of the metanarrative.) There are simply lots of different narratives, with nothing to suggest that any one of them is the right one, or that any one of them is the one against which others should be judged. There is simply diversity. Some theologians are rather enjoying this situation, as it means that they can propound any manner of theological statement without having to justify it anywhere. Some of us think that language-games still need to connect with each other if we are all to live in the same universe, and that justification of science by religion and of religion by science are still necessary tasks.

Priest	Someone ordained by the bishop to the second order of the Church's threefold ministry of bishop, priest and deacon. The priest's functions are outlined in the ordinal. See Chapter 14.
Reader	Someone trained in preaching and in leading worship (but not the Eucharist) and licensed by the bishop to fulfil these functions in a parish or parishes.
Rector	One of the two designations of an incumbent of a parish. The other is 'vicar'. Historically the vicar stood in for a rector.
Regeneration	See the beginning of Chapter 12. Whilst the word might once have had a religious meaning, it now refers to the improvement of the social fabric and the built environment of communities – which of course is a religious meaning.
Registrar	The diocese's solicitor who deals with leases, elections to General Synod, and other legal matters.
Requiem Mass	A Mass to remember and pray for the dead.

Roman Catholic Church	A federation of parishes and dioceses in communion with the Bishop of Rome.
Rural Dean	A priest appointed by the bishop to convene the clergy chapter and chair the Deanery Synod. There is some debate as to whether the rural dean is the bishop's representative to the deanery or the deanery's representative to the bishop. He or she is usually in practice a bit of both.
Sacrament	An outward and visible sign of an inward spiritual reality. The Church of England recognizes two sacraments: baptism and the Eucharist. Other Churches recognize rather more.
Service of the word	A service of readings, prayers and hymns. The first part of a service of holy communion is a service of the word.
Seven last words	According to the different Gospels, Jesus spoke seven sentences from the cross.
Simultaneous Eucharist	A Eucharist conducted together by different denominations, usually the Roman Catholic Church and the Church of England. The Roman Catholic rite is used, the two priests use separate altars, and people normally receive communion from the priest of their own denomination. Simultaneous Eucharists are rare and are in danger of extinction.
Southwark Pastoral Auxiliary	Someone trained in pastoral work and authorized by the bishop to serve in a parish or parishes in the Diocese of Southwark.
Stipend	What parochial clergy are paid. It is not a salary as there is no contract of employment. The payment is intended to enable the priest and their family to live without anxiety and thus to be of service to the parish.
Synod	A gathering of elected and ex officio members for deliberation and decision-making. The Church of England has synods at the parish level (Parochial Church Council), the deanery level (Deanery Synod), the diocesan level (Diocesan Synod), and the national level (General Synod).
Synodical	Anything to do with synods.

Team ministry	A team of clergy, comprising a team rector and team vicar(s), serving a parish or parishes. The team rector is the incumbent, and the team vicar(s) are not. They are all told that they are of incumbent status.
Team rector	Every team ministry has a team rector who is expected to fulfil a co-ordinating role. The team rector holds the freehold of the benefice for a limited period, usually for seven years. The team rector is not a rector.
Team Vicar	Every team ministry has one or more team vicars. A team vicar is of 'incumbent status', as is the team rector. The team vicar is not a vicar but can be designated vicar of a particular parish or district.
Thames Gateway	A great deal of empty land ripe for development on both sides of the Thames estuary along with existing communities adjacent to it. In South London the Thames Gateway includes Thamesmead, Woolwich, the north end of Charlton and the Greenwich Peninsula.
Vicar	One of the two designations of an incumbent of a parish. The other is 'rector'. Historically the vicar stood in for a rector. A team vicar or a team rector can also be designated vicar of a parish or a district even though neither is a vicar or a rector.
Word and sacrament	The two main aspects of a priest's liturgical role: preaching God's word and presiding at the sacraments of baptism and Eucharist.